Uncover 2 Combo

Ben Goldstein • Ceri Jones
with Kathryn O'Dell

Student's Book

CAMBRIDGE
UNIVERSITY PRESS

University Printing House, Cambridge CB2 8BS, United Kingdom

One Liberty Plaza, 20th Floor, New York, NY 10006, USA

477 Williamstown Road, Port Melbourne, VIC 3207, Australia

314–321, 3rd Floor, Plot 3, Splendor Forum, Jasola District Centre, New Delhi – 110025, India

103 Penang Road, #05-06/07, Visioncrest Commercial, Singapore 238467

Cambridge University Press is part of the University of Cambridge.

It furthers the University's mission by disseminating knowledge in the pursuit of education, learning and research at the highest international levels of excellence.

www.cambridge.org
Information on this title: www.cambridge.org/9781316643655

© Cambridge University Press 2017

This publication is in copyright. Subject to statutory exception and to the provisions of relevant collective licensing agreements, no reproduction of any part may take place without the written permission of Cambridge University Press.

First Published 2017

20 19 18 17 16 15 14 13 12 11 10

Printed in Poland by Opolgraf

A catalog record for this publication is available from the British Library.

ISBN 978-1-107-49320-9 Student's Book 2
ISBN 978-1-107-49323-0 Student's Book with Online Workbook and Online Practice 2
ISBN 978-1-107-49331-5 Teacher's Book 2
ISBN 978-1-107-49328-5 Workbook with Online Practice 2
ISBN 978-1-107-49338-4 Presentation Plus Disc 2
ISBN 978-1-107-49333-9 Class Audio CDs 2
ISBN 978-1-107-49335-3 DVD 2

Additional resources for this publication at www.cambridge.org/uncover

The publishers have no responsibility for the persistence or accuracy of URLs for external or third-party Internet websites referred to in this publication, and do not guarantee that any content on such websites is, or will remain, accurate or appropriate. Information regarding prices, travel timetables and other factual information given in this work is correct at the time of first printing but Cambridge University Press does not guarantee the accuracy of such information thereafter.

Art direction, book design, layout services, and photo research: QBS Learning
Audio production: John Marshall Media

Acknowledgments

Many teachers, coordinators, and educators shared their opinions, their ideas, and their experience to help create *Uncover*. The authors and publisher would like to thank the following people and their schools for their help in shaping the series.

In Mexico:
María Nieves Maldonado Ortiz (Colegio Enrique Rébsamen); Héctor Guzmán Pineda (Liceo Europeo); Alfredo Salas López (Campus Universitario Siglo XXI); Rosalba Millán Martínez (IIPAC [Instituto Torres Quintero A.C.]); Alejandra Rubí Reyes Badillo (ISAS [Instituto San Angel del Sur]); José Enrique Gutiérrez Escalante (Centro Escolar Zama); Gabriela Juárez Hernández (Instituto de Estudios Básicos Amado Nervo); Patricia Morelos Alonso (Instituto Cultural Ingles, S.C.); Martha Patricia Arzate Fernández, (Colegio Valladolid); Teresa González, Eva Marina Sánchez Vega (Colegio Salesiano); María Dolores León Ramírez de Arellano, (Liceo Emperadores Aztecas); Esperanza Medina Cruz (Centro Educativo Francisco Larroyo); Nubia Nelly Martínez García (Salesiano Domingo Savio); Diana Gabriela González Benítez (Colegio Ghandi); Juan Carlos Luna Olmedo (Centro Escolar Zama); Dulce María Pascual Granados (Esc. Juan Palomo Martínez); Roberto González, Fernanda Audirac (Real Life English Center); Rocio Licea (Escuela Fundación Mier y Pesado); Diana Pombo (Great Union Institute); Jacobo Cortés Vázquez (Instituto María P. de Alvarado); Michael John Pryor (Colegio Salesiano Anáhuac Chapalita)

In Brazil:
Renata Condi de Souza (Colégio Rio Branco); Sônia Maria Bernal Leites (Colégio Rio Branco); Élcio Souza (Centro Universitário Anhaguera de São Paulo); Patricia Helena Nero (Private teacher); Célia Elisa Alves de Magalhães (Colégio Cruzeiro-Jacarepaguá); Lilia Beatriz Freitas Gussem (Escola Parque-Gávea); Sandra Maki Kuchiki (Easy Way Idiomas); Lucia Maria Abrão Pereira Lima (Colégio Santa Cruz-São Paulo); Deborah de Castro Ferroz de Lima Pinto (Mundinho Segmento); Clara Vianna Prado (Private teacher); Ligia Maria Fernandes Diniz (Escola Internacional de Alphaville); Penha Aparecida Gaspar Rodrigues (Colégio Salesiano Santa Teresinha); Silvia Castelan (Colégio Santa Catarina de Sena); Marcelo D'Elia (The Kids Club Guarulhos); Malyina Kazue Ono Leal (Colégio Bandeirantes); Nelma de Mattos Santana Alves (Private teacher); Mariana Martins Machado (Britannia Cultural); Lilian Bluvol Vaisman (Curso Oxford); Marcelle Belfort Duarte (Cultura Inglesa-Duque de Caxias); Paulo Dantas (Britannia International English); Anauã Carmo Vilhena (York Language Institute); Michele Amorim Estellita (Lemec – Lassance Modern English Course); Aida Setton (Colégio Uirapuru); Maria Lucia Zaorob (CEL-LEP); Marisa Veiga Lobato (Interlíngua Idiomas); Maria Virgínia Lebrón (Independent consultant); Maria Luiza Carmo (Colégio Guilherme Dumont Villares/CEL-LEP); Lucia Lima (Independent consultant); Malyina Kazue Ono Leal (Colégio Bandeirantes); Debora Schisler (Seven Idiomas); Helena Nagano (Cultura Inglesa); Alessandra de Campos (Alumni); Maria Lúcia Sciamarelli (Colégio Divina Providência); Catarina Kruppa (Cultura Inglesa); Roberto Costa (Freelance teacher/consultant); Patricia McKay Aronis (CEL-LEP); Claudia Beatriz Cavalieri (By the World Idiomas); Sérgio Lima (Vermont English School); Rita Miranda (IBI – [Instituto Batista de Idiomas]); Maria de Fátima Galery (Britain English School); Marlene Almeida (Teacher Trainer Consultant); Flávia Samarane (Colégio Logosófico); Maria Tereza Vianna (Greenwich Schools); Daniele Brauer (Cultura Inglesa/AMS Idiomas); Allessandra Cierno (Colégio Santa Dorotira); Helga Silva Nelken (Greenwich Schools/Colégio Edna Roriz); Regina Marta Bazzoni (Britain English School); Adriano Reis (Greenwich Schools); Vanessa Silva Freire de Andrade (Private teacher); Nilvane Guimarães (Colégio Santo Agostinho)

In Ecuador:
Santiago Proaño (Independent teacher trainer); Tania Abad (UDLA [Universidad de Las Americas]); Rosario Llerena (Colegio Isaac Newton); Paúl Viteri (Colegio Andino); Diego Maldonado (Central University); Verónica Vera (Colegio Tomás Moro); Mónica Sarauz (Colegio San Gabriel); Carolina Flores (Colegio APCH); Boris Cadena, Vinicio Reyes (Colegio Benalcázar); Deigo Ponce (Colegio Gonzaga); Byron Freire (Colegio Nuestra Señora del Rosario)

The authors and publisher would also like to thank the following contributors, script writers, and collaborators for their inspired work in creating *Uncover*:
Anna Whitcher, Janet Gokay, Kathryn O'Dell, Lynne Robertson, and Dana Henricks

Unit	Vocabulary	Grammar	Listening	Conversation (Useful language)
1 Traditions pp. 2–11	- Categories - Clothes and objects	- Simple present review with *be* and *have* - *whose* and possessives Grammar reference p. 106	- Whose shoes are they?	- Keeping a conversation going
2 What's Playing? pp. 12–21	- Types of movies - Types of TV shows	- Simple present review - Adverbs of frequency - Verb + infinitive or *-ing* form (gerund) Grammar reference p. 107	- Deciding what to watch	- Asking for and giving opinions
3 Spending Habits pp. 22–31	- Places to shop - Money verbs	- Present continuous review - Simple present vs. present continuous - Quantifiers Grammar reference p. 108	- Shopping habits	- Making requests when shopping
4 Our Heroes pp. 32–41	- Cool jobs - Adjectives of personality	- Simple past statements review and *ago* - Simple past questions review and *ago* Grammar reference p. 109	- Interview with a teenage hero	- Asking for and giving clarification
5 It's a Mystery! pp. 42–51	- Action verbs - Adverbs of manner	- Past continuous - Adverbs of time - Simple past vs. past continuous - *when* and *while* Grammar reference p. 110	- I saw something strange last night.	- Telling and reacting to a story

Units 1–5 Review Game pp. 52–53

Writing	Reading	Video	Accuracy and fluency	Speaking outcomes
A description of a family tradition	*At Home in Two Worlds* Reading to write: *Our Summer Tradition* Culture: *Colorful Hands and Heads*	*Carpets of Dagestan* *What's your favorite place in town?* *A Very Indian Wedding*	*whose* vs. *who's* Pronouncing the possessive of names ending in -s	I can . . . identify and talk about modern and traditional things talk about modern and traditional things in my life ask and answer questions about possessions keep a conversation going talk about sports, weddings, and other traditions
A movie review	*Cinema's Best Villains* Reading to write: *My All-Time Favorite Movie* Culture: *Hooray for Bollywood!*	*A Life on Broadway* *What types of TV shows do you like watching?* *Mumbai: From Computers to Film* *Who's Real?* (CLIL Project p. 116)	Infinitive or -*ing* form (gerund) vs. base form after some verbs Irregular spellings of third person simple present form The /ʃ/ sound	I can . . . identify different types of movies talk about my movie-watching habits talk about different types of TV shows, preferences, and TV habits ask for and give opinions compare Hollywood movies with other movies
A product review	*A Day at the Mall in Dubai* Reading to write: *Product Reviews* Culture: *Adopt an Animal*	*Unusual Fun* *How do you spend your money?* *Zero: Past and Present*	*enough* and *not enough* Irregular spellings of the -*ing* form syllable stress in compound nouns	I can . . . identify places to shop talk about the things I do every day and the things I'm doing now ask and answer questions about spending and saving money make requests when shopping talk about using money to help people or animals
A description of a person you admire	*Young and Talented!* Reading to write: *My Hero* Culture: *The Island of Champions*	*Wildlife Hero* *Who is your role model and why?* *The Chilean Mine Rescue* *Amelia Earhart: Famous Flyer* (CLIL Project p. 117)	Irregular verbs in the simple past Spelling rules for the simple past Short and long *i* sounds	I can . . . identify some cool jobs share facts about someone's life ask and answer questions about being brave ask for and give clarification talk about famous athletes from my country
A narrative about an interesting or unusual event	*Whodunit?* Reading to write: *An Urban Legend* Culture: *The World's Number One Detective*	*Mysteries in the Mountains* *What's an unusual or interesting thing that happened to you recently?* *The Case of the Missing Woman* *An Underwater Mystery* (CLIL Project p. 118)	The simple past for an event that interrupts an event in progress Spelling rules for forming adverbs Pronouncing *was*	I can . . . tell a story with action verbs talk about what I was doing in the past talk about past events and describe how I do things tell an interesting or unusual story understand information and talk about fictional characters

Unit	Vocabulary	Grammar	Listening	Conversation (Useful language)
6 Home, Sweet Home pp. 54–63	■ Furniture and other household items ■ Household appliances	■ Comparative and superlative adjectives and adverbs ■ *should (not), (not) have to, must (not)* Grammar reference p. 111	■ A clothing emergency	■ Asking for and offering help
7 Visions of the Future pp. 64–73	■ Computers and communication ■ Technology verbs	■ *will* and *won't* for predictions ■ Adverbs of possibility ■ First conditional with *will (not), may (not)*, and *might (not)* Grammar reference p. 112	■ They're always coming out with something new.	■ Asking for and giving instructions
8 The Choices We Make pp. 74–83	■ Life events ■ Containers and materials	■ *be going to* and *will* ■ Present continuous and simple present for future Grammar reference p. 113	■ An eco-project	■ Agreeing and disagreeing
9 Watch Out! pp. 84–93	■ Accident and injury verbs ■ Parts of the body	■ Present perfect statements with regular and irregular verbs ■ Present perfect questions ■ Present perfect vs. simple past Grammar reference p. 114	■ I'm accident-prone.	■ Reacting to good and bad news
10 Have Fun! pp. 94–103	■ Free-time activities ■ Adjectives of feeling	■ Indefinite pronouns ■ *too* and *enough* Grammar reference p. 115	■ I'll never forget . . .	■ Making and responding to suggestions

Units 6–10 Review Game pp. 104–105

Writing	Reading	Video	Accuracy and fluency	Speaking outcomes
■ An email about your house	■ *A Home in the Jungle* ■ Reading to write: *My House* ■ Culture: *Life on the Water*	■ *A Cool Life* ■ *Which do you prefer – houses or apartments?* ■ *Moving House*	■ Using *must* for obligation ■ Pronouncing the letters *er* and *or*	I can . . . ■ identify rooms in a house and household items ■ compare two or more rooms ■ identify and talk about household appliances ■ ask for and offer help ■ talk about the kind of house I'd like to live in
■ An opinion paragraph	■ *Computers: A Big Past, A Small Future* ■ Reading to write: *How do you think people will listen to music in the future?* ■ Culture: *Television Grows Up . . . and Down!*	■ *A Pizza Robot* ■ *How important is your cell phone?* ■ *Music Sharing* ■ *The Secret of the Pyramids* (CLIL Project p. 119)	■ First conditional vs. simple present ■ Different sounds for the letters *ou* ■ Using commas with *if* clauses	■ talk about computers and technology ■ make predictions about the future ■ talk about how to use technology ■ ask for and give instructions ■ talk about how I watch TV today and in the future
■ An application letter	■ *Life in the Outback* ■ Reading to write: *Farah's Application Letter* ■ Culture: *A Summer in Alaska*	■ *A School at Home* ■ *What are you going to do when you leave school?* ■ *Time for an Adventure!*	■ Present continuous for future arrangements ■ The vowel sound of *will* and *we'll* ■ Using *think*, *probably*, and *maybe* with *will*	I can . . . ■ identify and talk about life events ■ discuss future plans and predictions ■ talk about future plans and scheduled events ■ agree and disagree with someone ■ talk about places I'd like to volunteer
■ An email to refuse an invitation	■ *It's Hard Being a Teen!* ■ Reading to write: *Your Invitation* ■ Culture: *Beware of the Amazon!*	■ *Danger in Our Food* ■ *Have you ever had an accident?* ■ *A Deadly Job*	■ The present perfect with *never* ■ Forming past participles ■ The sound of *have* in Wh- questions ■ Using accident and injury words as both nouns and verbs	I can . . . ■ talk about accidents and injuries ■ talk about things I have and haven't done ■ ask, answer, and give details about things I've done ■ react to good and bad news ■ talk about dangerous animals
■ An invitation	■ *Jodi's Blog* ■ Reading to write: *Your Invitation* ■ Culture: *April Fool's!*	■ *A New York City Food Tour* ■ *How do you celebrate your birthday?* ■ *Punkin Chunkin!* ■ *An Ancient Answer* (CLIL Project p. 120)	■ Indefinite pronouns with *any-* in negative sentences ■ The sound of the letters *gh*	I can . . . ■ talk about free-time activities ■ talk about weekend plans ■ describe feelings and situations with *too* and *enough* ■ make and respond to suggestions ■ talk about April Fool's Day and jokes

1 Traditions

Discovery EDUCATION
BE CURIOUS

- Carpets of Dagestan
- What's your favorite place in town?
- A Very Indian Wedding

1. Where are the women?

2. What are they like? How are they different from other people in the photo?

3. Do you ever wear traditional clothes? When?

UNIT CONTENTS

Vocabulary Categories; clothes and objects
Grammar Simple present review with *be* and *have*; *whose* and possessives
Listening Whose shoes are they?

Vocabulary: Categories

1. Label the sets of traditional and modern pictures with the correct words.

art   clothing   food   ✓music   places   sports

1. _____music_____   2. _____

3. _____   4. _____

5. _____   6. _____

> **NOTICE IT**
> Another word for **clothing** is **clothes**. Clothing is usually used for the general category. Clothes is usually used for specific items.
> There are two **clothing** stores in the mall.
> I need some new **clothes**.

2. Listen, check, and repeat.

3. Do the pictures in Exercise 1 show modern or traditional things? Check (✓) the correct answers.

Photo	a	b	c	d	e	f	g	h	i	j	k	l
Traditional	✓											
Modern		✓										

Speaking: Likes and dislikes

4. **YOUR TURN** Work with a partner. Do you like traditional or modern things for the categories in Exercise 1? Can you name any traditional and modern things for each category?

> I like modern music. Hip-hop is modern. I don't like traditional music. Jazz is traditional.

> I like traditional and modern sports. Sumo wrestling is traditional. Basketball is modern.

Reading At Home in Two Worlds; Our Summer Tradition; Colorful Hands and Heads
Conversation Keeping a conversation going
Writing A description of a family tradition

Unit 1 | 3

OLD and NEW

At Home in Two Worlds

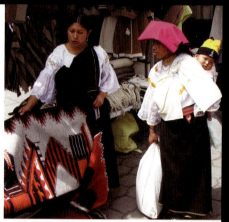

Meet Maria! She is 14, and she lives in Otavalo, Ecuador. She has a traditional and a modern life. She lives in a modern house with her family. Maria has a brother. He's 17. She also has a sister. She's 12. Maria and her family make traditional art, and they sell it at a big market in Otavalo. They sell their art online, too. Maria's brother and father are also musicians, and they play traditional music. Maria likes traditional music, but she also listens to modern rock music at home.

Maria doesn't have modern clothes. She wears traditional clothes and jewelry. She eats traditional food with her family. She has meat with corn, potatoes, or beans. After school, she sometimes eats in modern restaurants with her friends. Maria speaks Quechua, an ancient Incan language, with her parents. She speaks Spanish with her brother, sister, and friends. She and her sister also have English classes at school. Maria likes her traditional and modern life!

DID YOU KNOW...?
The market in Otavalo has clothing, art, and food. It's popular with people from Ecuador and from around the world.

Reading: An article about life in Otavalo, Ecuador

1. **Look at the photos. Is the family modern or traditional?**

2. **Read and listen to the article. Who is in Maria's family? What do they do?**

3. **Read the article again. Check (✓) the things that are true for Maria. Sometimes both answers are possible.**

   1. ☐ lives in a traditional house   ☐ lives in a modern house
   2. ☐ has a younger sister   ☐ has an older sister
   3. ☐ has one brother   ☐ has two brothers
   4. ☐ listens to traditional music   ☐ listens to modern music
   5. ☐ wears traditional clothes   ☐ wears modern clothes
   6. ☐ eats traditional food   ☐ eats modern food

4. **YOUR TURN** **Work with a partner. How are you like Maria? How are you different?**

   > Maria is 14, and I'm . . .

Grammar: Simple present review with *be* and *have*

5. Complete the chart.

Use the simple present of be to identify people and give locations and dates.
Use the simple present of have to talk about possessions, characteristics, and relationships.

be	have
Wh- questions and answers	
Where **are** you? **I'm** in Otavalo. **I'm** _____ in Quito.	When **do** you _____ art class? I **have** art at 10:00. I **don't have** art at 9:00.
How old _____ she? **She's** 14. She **isn't** 17.	What **does** she **have** for dinner? She _____ meat. She **doesn't have** fish.
Who **are** they? They _____ Maria's parents. They **aren't** her grandparents.	What **do** they **have**? They **have** a computer. They _____ a desk.
Yes/No questions and answers	
_____ you in Otavalo? Yes, I **am**. / No, **I'm not**.	**Do** you **have** art at 10:00? Yes, I _____. / No, I **don't**.
Is she 14? Yes, she _____. / No, she **isn't**.	_____ she **have** meat for dinner? Yes, she **does**. / No, she **doesn't**.
Are they Maria's parents? Yes, they **are**. / No, they _____.	**Do** they **have** a computer? Yes, they **do**. / No, they _____.

> Check your answers: Grammar reference, p. 106

6. Match the questions with the answers.

1. Is your brother tall? _c_
2. Are they from Ecuador? ___
3. Where are you? ___
4. How many sisters do you have? ___
5. Does Jake have a truck? ___

a. I have three.
b. I'm in my English class.
c. No, he's not.
d. No, he doesn't.
e. Yes, they are.

7. Complete the conversations with the correct form of *be* or *have*.

1. **A:** When _____ your music class?
   B: It _____ on Monday.
2. **A:** _____ Kate and Dennis _____ a truck?
   B: Yes, they _____. They _____ two trucks.
3. **A:** _____ your parents home?
   B: No, they _____. They _____ at work right now.
4. **A:** _____ your house small?
   B: No, it _____. It _____ big.

Speaking: My life

8. Work with a partner. Tell your partner about something modern and something traditional in your life.

> I have a traditional house. It's very old. My clothes are modern. They . . .

Find out about carpet makers in Russia. What is life like in Dagestan? (Workbook, p. 72)

1.1 CARPETS OF DAGESTAN

MY Things

Listening: Whose shoes are they?

1. Do your parents or grandparents have things from the past? What do they have?

2. Listen to Wendy and Josh talk about old things in their grandparents' house. Check (✓) the people the things belong to.

   ☐ father ☐ grandfather ☐ great-grandfather
   ☐ mother ☐ grandmother ☐ great-grandmother

3. Listen again. Circle the adjectives that describe the things Wendy and Josh find. There is more than one answer for each item.

   1. First object: **big / small / heavy / colorful / slow**
   2. Second object: **new / old / cool / old-fashioned**
   3. Third object: **white / black / big / small**

Vocabulary: Clothes and objects

4. Match the words with the correct pictures. Then listen and check your answers.

   1. _e_ a computer   6. ___ a photograph / a photo
   2. ___ a dress   7. ___ a telephone / a phone
   3. ___ a hat   8. ___ a television / a TV
   4. ___ a jacket   9. ___ a watch
   5. ___ a pen   10. ___ shoes

YOUR TURN Work with a partner. What are the items in Exercise 4 like today?

TVs are big today, and they have flat screens. TV shows are in color.

6 | Unit 1

Grammar: *whose* and possessives

6. Complete the chart.

Use whose to ask about possession. *Use a name/noun + 's, a possessive adjective, or a possessive pronoun to show possession.*		
Whose	_____ computer is it? / **Whose** is it? **Whose** shoes are they? / **Whose** are they?	
Possessive 's or s'	It's Dad**'s** computer. They're our grandmother____ shoes. That's our grandparent**s'** house.	
Possessive adjectives	It's **his** computer. They're **her** shoes. That's **their** house.	my your _____ her its our _____
Possessive pronouns	It's **his**. They're **hers**. That's **theirs**.	mine yours his _____ its ours _____

> Check your answers: Grammar reference, p. 106

7. Write questions and answers for the information in the chart. Use possessive 's and s' for the answers.

	Doug	Sofia	my cousins
1. hat		✓	
2. TV			✓
3. pens	✓		

1. *Whose hat is it? It's Sofia's hat.*
2. _____
3. _____

Get it RIGHT!
Do not confuse *whose* with *who's*:
who's = *who is*.
Whose phone is this?
NOT: ~~Who's phone is this?~~

8. Rewrite the sentences two ways. Use possessive adjectives and possessive pronouns.

1. It's my sisters' soccer ball.   *It's their soccer ball. It's theirs.*
2. They're Jack's paintings.   _____
3. It's my aunt's jacket.   _____

Speaking: Whose is it?

9. YOUR TURN Work with a small group. Each person puts two small items in a bag. The others don't look. Take out an item and have the others guess whose it is. Take turns.

Say it RIGHT!
If a name ends in -s, add 's after the final -s. You can also just use an apostrophe (') after the final -s. Both are correct, and they are pronounced the same way. For example, *Lucas's* and *Lucas'* both sound like *Lucases*. Listen to the sentences.
  Lucas has hats. = They're Lucas's hats. / They're Lucas' hats.
Pay attention to the way you pronounce your classmates' names with the possessive in Exercise 9.

> Workbook, pp. 4–5

REAL TALK 1.2 WHAT'S YOUR FAVORITE PLACE IN TOWN?

New TRADITIONS

Conversation: A cool tradition

1. **REAL TALK** Watch or listen to the teenagers. Check (✓) their favorite places.

   ☐ a bedroom   ☐ a gym   ☐ a restaurant   ☐ an ice cream shop
   ☐ a computer lab ☐ a library ☐ a stadium   ☐ a movie theater
   ☐ a park   ☐ a mall   ☐ a supermarket

2. **YOUR TURN** What's *your* favorite place in town? Tell your partner.

3. Listen to Tom telling Eva about a family tradition. Complete the conversation.

   USEFUL LANGUAGE: Keeping a conversation going
   Tell me about it.   That's interesting.   Really?   Then what?

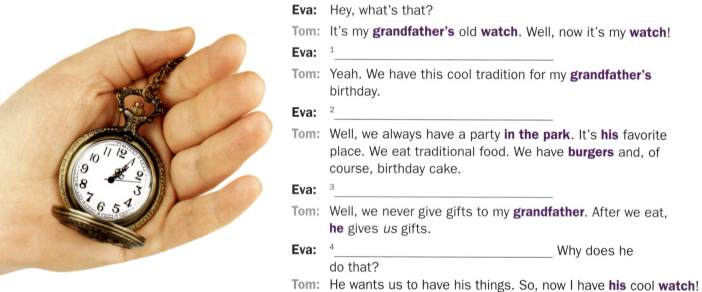

Eva: Hey, what's that?
Tom: It's my **grandfather's** old **watch**. Well, now it's my **watch**!
Eva: ¹_____
Tom: Yeah. We have this cool tradition for my **grandfather's** birthday.
Eva: ²_____
Tom: Well, we always have a party **in the park**. It's **his** favorite place. We eat traditional food. We have **burgers** and, of course, birthday cake.
Eva: ³_____
Tom: Well, we never give gifts to my **grandfather**. After we eat, **he** gives *us* gifts.
Eva: ⁴_____ Why does he do that?
Tom: He wants us to have his things. So, now I have **his** cool **watch**!

4. Practice the conversation with a partner.

5. **YOUR TURN** Repeat the conversation in Exercise 3, but change the words in purple. Use the information in the chart for one conversation and your own ideas for another.

		My ideas
Person	aunt	
Item	scarf	
Place	in a restaurant	
Food	tacos	

8 | Unit 1

Our Summer Tradition

by Carla Lucero

I have a big Italian family, and we have an unusual tradition. On the last day of school, we always have dinner at an Italian restaurant. We celebrate the start of summer! There are always a lot of people at the restaurant — my parents, my grandparents, my brother, my sister, my cousins, and me!

We have traditional Italian food. There are many great dishes on the menu, like minestrone soup and pasta. We also have dessert. There is traditional Italian music at the restaurant, too. After dinner, we go to my grandparents' house and watch an Italian movie. Then we look at family photos. It's really fun.

Reading to write: A family tradition

6. Look at the photo. Where are the people? Who do you think they are? Read the article to check.

> ### Focus on CONTENT
> When you write about a tradition, include this information:
> - what
> - why
> - when
> - who
> - where

7. Read Carla's article again. Find examples for the categories in the Focus on Content box.

> ### Focus on LANGUAGE
> **there is / there are**
> Use **there is / there are** to give information about what, when, where, why, and who in a description of something, such as a family tradition.
> - **There is** a big table in the restaurant.
> - **There are** many musicians at our summer picnic.

8. Find examples of *There is / There are* in Carla's article.

9. Complete the sentence with *There is* or *There are*.

   1. _____ a lot of modern art at the museum.
   2. _____ three birthdays in my family in June.
   3. _____ many books in our house.
   4. _____ a singer in the restaurant.
   5. _____ a lot of people at the wedding.
   6. _____ a good show on TV.

 Writing: My family tradition

PLAN
Choose a tradition in your family. Make a word web with the topics from the Focus on Content box.

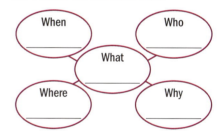

WRITE
Now write about the tradition. Use your notes to help you. Write at least 60 words.

CHECK
Check your writing. Can you answer "yes" to these questions?

- Is information for each category from the Focus on Content box in your article?
- Do you use *there is* and *there are* correctly?

COLORFUL HANDS AND HEADS

What color is your hair? In many cultures, people change their hair color for some traditions. Face and body painting is a tradition in many places, too. These traditions are new and old!

The Romanian soccer team at the World Cup

Citrus College fans at a soccer game

_____

Some sports teams color their hair with their team colors. For example, a high school swim team has blue hair for a swimming event. A professional soccer team has yellow hair for the World Cup. Sports fans often paint their faces with school colors, too. At many sports events, there are people in school colors from head to toe!

A wedding in, India

_____

In some traditional weddings in India, the bride has designs on her hands with henna, a special paint. During the wedding, the groom colors the middle of the bride's hair red. It is a symbol of marriage.

A teenager in the Omo Valley

_____

It is hot and sunny in the Omo Valley in Africa. Mursi and Surma people paint their faces, heads, and bodies with clay from the earth. It protects them from the sun. It is a tradition, and it is also art. They have white, yellow, red, and gray designs on their faces and bodies. They have colorful clay in their hair, too, and sometimes they make and wear interesting hats.

New or old, hair coloring and face painting are interesting traditions!

Culture: Hair coloring and face painting traditions

1. Look at the photos. Where are the people? What colors do you see?

2. Read the article. Complete the text with the headings. Then listen and check your answers.

   Tradition and Art   A New Sports Tradition
   An Old Wedding Tradition

3. Read the article again. Are the sentences true (*T*) or false (*F*)?

   1. A bride in India has paint on her hands. ___

   2. A bride in India has blue paint in her hair. ___

   3. It is cold in the Omo Valley. ___

   4. Sports players never have colored hair. ___

4. **YOUR TURN** Work with a partner. Ask and answer the question.
   What are some sports and wedding traditions from your culture?

DID YOU KNOW…?

Face painting and body painting are thousands of years old. There are natural colors in things from the earth, like plants and clay. People use these for paint.

Find out about a traditional Indian wedding. What are some of the traditions? (Workbook, p. 73)

1.3 A VERY INDIAN WEDDING

UNIT 1 REVIEW

Vocabulary

1. Label the photos with the correct categories.

art	food	places
clothing	music	sports

1. _____

2. _____

3. _____

4. _____

5. _____

6. _____

2. Complete the sentences with the correct words.

computer	hat	photo	TV
jacket	phone	shoes	watch

1. I have a _____ on my head.
2. I use my _____ to do my homework.
3. There are a lot of good shows on _____.
4. Lori is on the _____. Do you want to talk to her?
5. It's cold! I have on a _____ over my shirt.
6. See this _____ of my mother? It's from 1980!
7. Sam and Ann left their _____ by the door.
8. I don't have a _____, so I check the time on my phone.

Grammar

3. Circle the correct words.

   Vicky: Hey, Paolo! ¹**Is / Are / Do / Does** you have an art class this year?
   Paolo: Yes, I ²**am / am not / do / don't**. I ³**am / is / has / have** two art classes.
   Vicky: ⁴**Is / Are / Do / Does** Mrs. Meyers one of your teachers?
   Paolo: No, she ⁵**is / isn't / does / doesn't**. Why?
   Vicky: Oh, she ⁶**is / isn't / does / doesn't** my aunt. She ⁷**is / are / has / have** three art classes this year.
   Paolo: I see. My art teachers ⁸**is / are / has / have** Mr. Klein and Ms. Rodriguez.

4. Match the sentences with the same meaning.

   1. It's my volleyball. ___   a. It's mine.
   2. It's Sandra's dress. ___   b. It's yours.
   3. It's Ted's pen. ___   c. It's his.
   4. It's your sandwich. ___   d. It's hers.

Useful language

5. Circle the correct answers.

   1. **A:** We have an unusual tradition in my family.
      B: Tell me ____ it.
      a. on   b. in   c. about

   2. **A:** We always have a big dinner for my birthday.
      B: ____? Me, too.
      a. When   b. Really   c. Then

   3. **A:** Why is your face green?
      B: Oh, it's for the soccer game.
      A: That's ____. Is green your school color?
      a. always   b. never   c. interesting

   4. **A:** We always have a picnic at the park on Saturdays.
      B: Then ____?
      a. what   b. why   c. where
      A: We usually play games.

PROGRESS CHECK: Now I can . . .

☐ identify and talk about modern and traditional things.
☐ talk about modern and traditional things in my life.
☐ ask and answer questions about possessions.
☐ keep a conversation going.
☐ write about a family tradition.
☐ talk about sports, weddings, and other traditions.

2 WHAT'S Playing?

Discovery EDUCATION

BE CURIOUS

A Life on Broadway

What types of TV shows do you like watching?

Mumbai: From Computers to Film

Who's Real?

1. What are the people watching?

2. How do you think they feel about it?

3. Do you like to do this activity?

UNIT CONTENTS
Vocabulary Types of movies; types of TV shows
Grammar Simple present review; adverbs of frequency; verb + infinitive or *-ing* form (gerund)
Listening Deciding what to watch

Vocabulary: Types of movies

1. Match the phrases (a–i) with the correct movie posters.

a. an action movie   ✓ d. a drama   g. a martial arts movie
b. an animated movie   e. a fantasy movie   h. a musical
c. a comedy   f. a horror movie   i. a romance movie

1. _d_
2. ___
3. ___
4. ___
5. ___
6. ___
7. ___
8. ___
9. ___

 2. Listen, check, and repeat.

3. Write the types of movies.

1. A lot of things happen quickly in this type of movie. _action movie_
2. The music in this type of film is great, and the actors are very good singers. _____
3. People say these movies are for children, but adults watch them, too. _____
4. This type of movie usually has events that couldn't happen in real life and great special effects. _____
5. The story and characters in these movies are very funny. They make you laugh! _____

Speaking: More movies

4. YOUR TURN Work with a partner. Name a movie for each type of movie.

> *Bend It Like Beckham* is a drama.

> *Twilight* is a drama, too. And it's also a romance movie.

5. What are some of your favorite movies? What types of movies are they?

> One of my favorite movies is *The Hunger Games*. It's a fantasy and an action movie. I also like . . .

 Say it RIGHT!

The letters *sh*, *ci*, and *ti* can make the /ʃ/ sound. Listen to the sentence.
She liked the spe**ci**al effects in the ac**ti**on movie.

Listen to the words in Exercise 1 again. Which other word makes the /ʃ/ sound? What letters make the sound?

 Workbook, p. 8

Reading Cinema's Best Villains; My All-Time Favorite Movie; Hooray for Bollywood!
Conversation Asking for and giving opinions
Writing A movie review

Let's Go to the Movies!

Welcome to my blog about movies.

I sometimes go to the movies three times a week! How often do you go to the movies?

My favorite types of films are horror, action, and fantasy movies. What types of movies do you like?

I also love the "bad guys" in movies. Here are my top three villains.

Cinema's Best Villains
by Erica Thompson

Cruella De Vil
Movie: *101 Dalmatians* Actor: Betty Lou Gerson (voice) Famous phrase: "You beasts!" I don't like this movie very much, but Cruella is a great villain. She loves puppies and especially Dalmatians – because she wants to wear them!

Darth Vader
Movie: *Star Wars V: The Empire Strikes Back* Actor: David Prowse Famous phrase: "You don't know the power of the dark side!" This is my favorite movie, and Darth Vader is the perfect villain because he never shows his face. He also speaks with a strange voice.

The Penguin
Movie: *Batman Returns* Actor: Danny DeVito Famous phrase: "Nyuk, nyuk, nyuk." The Penguin is a villain in some of the Batman movies, TV shows, and comic books. His real name is Oswold Cobblepot. Sometimes he's funny, and sometimes he's scary, but he's always dangerous. I like him best in *Batman Returns*.

Who is your favorite movie villain?

Reading: A blog about movie villains

1. Look at the photos of the three movie characters. What types of movies do you think they are from?

2. Read and listen to the blog post. Which of the movies that Erica writes about does she like?

3. Read the blog post again. Answer the questions.
   1. What types of movies does Erica like?
      _____
   2. Why does Cruella De Vil like puppies?
      _____
   3. Why does Erica think Darth Vader is a perfect villain?
      _____
   4. What is the Penguin's real name?
      _____
   5. Which movie doesn't Erica like? Which one is her favorite?
      _____

4. **YOUR TURN** Work with a partner. Do you agree with Erica's best villains? Who are your top three favorite movie villains? Why?

> One of my favorite villains is . . . because . . .

DID YOU KNOW...?
David Prowse was Darth Vader, but he didn't talk in the movie. Another actor, James Earl Jones, was Darth Vader's voice.

Grammar: Simple present review

5. Complete the chart.

Use the simple present to talk about routines, habits, and facts.

Wh- questions	Affirmative answers	Negative answers
What movies _____ you _____?	I **like** horror movies.	I **don't like** musicals.
How often **does** Erica **go** to the movies?	She _____ to the movies three times a week.	She _____ to the movies on Sundays.
Yes/No questions	**Short answers**	
Do you **like** horror movies?	Yes, I _____.	No, I **don't**.
_____ Erica _____ to the movies?	Yes, she **does**.	No, she _____.
Contractions do not = _____	does not = _____	

> Check your answers: Grammar reference, p. 107

6. Circle the correct words. Then answer the questions with information about you.

1. (**Do**) / **Does** you (**go**) / **goes** to the movies on the weekends?
   What types of movies (**do**) / **does** you (**see**) / **sees**?
   Yes, I do. I see action movies and comedies.

2. **What** / **Where** types of movies **do** / **does** your friends **like** / **likes**?
   Do / **Does** you **like** / **likes** the same types of movies?
   _____

3. **How** / **When** late **do** / **does** the movie theaters **stay** / **stays** open in your city?
   _____

> Spell it **RIGHT!**
>
> | I/you/we/they | he/she/it |
> |---|---|
> | go | go**es** |
> | study | stud**ies** |
> | teach | teach**es** |

7. Rewrite the sentences. Put the adverbs of frequency in the correct places.

1. Jamie watches movies with his friends. (usually)
   Jamie usually watches movies with his friends.

2. Amy buys popcorn at the movies. (always)
   _____

3. Carol reads movie reviews online. (sometimes)
   _____

4. I'm at the movie theater early. (often)
   _____

Adverbs of frequency

always   usually   often   sometimes   never

Adverbs of frequency usually come after the verb *be*, but before other verbs.
   I'm **never** late. They **never** learn.
Usually and *sometimes* may come before the subject.
   Sam **usually** goes to the movies three times a week.
   Usually, Sam goes to the movies three times a week.

Speaking: Movie-watching habits

8. YOUR TURN Work with a partner. Ask and answer questions about where and how often you watch movies.

> Where do you watch movies?

> I usually watch movies at the movie theater.

> I never watch movies at home.

> **BE CURIOUS** Find out about a musical on Broadway. Who is involved in *Annie*? (Workbook, p. 74)

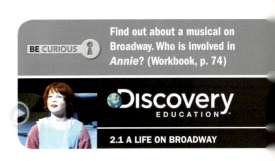

2.1 A LIFE ON BROADWAY

> Workbook, p. 9

Unit 2 | 15

WHAT'S ON?

Listening: Deciding what to watch

1. Who do you watch TV with? What shows do you watch together?

2. Listen to Joanna and Alex decide what to watch on TV. What shows do they want to watch? Write *J* (Joanna), *A* (Alex), or *B* (both).

   1. *Big Brother* ___   2. *Elementary* ___   3. *The Big Bang Theory* ___

3. Listen again. Are the statements true (*T*) or false (*F*)?

   1. Sheldon and Leonard are scientists on a TV show. ___
   2. Penny is Joanna's neighbor. ___
   3. Alex saw *Big Brother* in the past. ___
   4. Joanna likes animated shows. ___
   5. Alex and Joanna both like dramas. ___

Vocabulary: Types of TV shows

4. Label the pictures with the correct words. Then listen and check your answers.

a cartoon	a game show	a soap opera
a crime series	a reality TV show	a talk show
✓ a documentary	a sitcom	the news

1. _a documentary_

2. _____

3. _____

4. _____

5. _____

6. _____

7. _____

8. _____

9. _____

5. **YOUR TURN** Work with a partner. Talk about how often you watch each type of TV show.

   > I never watch documentaries. I often watch crime series.

DID YOU KNOW…?
Sitcom is short for *situation comedy*.

16 | Unit 2

Grammar: Verb + infinitive or -ing form (gerund)

6. Complete the chart.

Verb + infinitive	Verb + -ing form (gerund)
They **want to watch** a drama.	Sheldon **dislikes try**_____ new things.
He **needs** _____ **see** who gets voted off *Big Brother*.	Leonard **enjoys trying** different things.

Verb + infinitive or -ing form (gerund)
I **like to read** comic books. I **like reading** comic books.
They **love to read** comic books. They **love** _____ comic books.
She **hates to watch** reality TV shows. She **hates watching** reality TV shows.
He **prefers** _____ the news online. He **prefers getting** the news online.

> Check your answers: Grammar reference, p. 107

7. Complete the questions and answers with the *-ing* form (gerund) or infinitive of the verbs. Sometimes more than one answer is possible.

1. **A:** Do you want ____to get____ (get) this big screen TV?
   B: No. I hate _____ (pay) full price. Let's see if one is on sale.
2. **A:** I like _____ (watch) movies online.
   B: Not me. I prefer _____ (go) to a movie theater.
3. **A:** Ugh! I need _____ (wash) the dishes before we watch TV.
   B: Do you dislike _____ (do) them? I can help you.
4. **A:** Does your sister like _____ (work) for a TV studio?
   B: Yes. She loves _____ (think) of new ideas for TV shows.

8. YOUR TURN Use the words and your own ideas to write sentences that are true for you.

1. my parents / like / watch / . . . *My parents like watching talk shows.*
2. my friends / enjoy / read / . . . _____
3. I / need / get / . . . _____
4. I / want / see / . . . _____

Get it RIGHT!

Use the infinitive or -ing form (gerund) of a verb, not the base form, after some verbs.
I **want to write** a TV show. NOT: I ~~want write~~ a TV show.
She **loves to watch** TV at night.
OR She **loves watching** TV at night.
NOT She ~~loves watch~~ TV at night.

Speaking: TV-watching habits

9. YOUR TURN Read the sentences and check (✓) "Yes" or "No" in the "You" column.

	You Yes	You No	Your partner Yes	Your partner No
I love watching sitcoms.				
I hate to watch documentaries.				
I want to watch less TV.				
I enjoy watching TV shows online.				

10. Work with a partner. Ask and answer questions about the information in Exercise 9. Check (✓) "Yes" or "No" in the "Your partner" column.

> Do you like watching sitcoms?

> No, I don't. I hate to watch sitcoms.

Workbook, pp. 10–11

Unit 2 | 17

REAL TALK 2.2 WHAT TYPES OF TV SHOWS DO YOU LIKE WATCHING?

TV and Movie FAVORITES

Conversation: It's really funny!

1. **REAL TALK** Watch or listen to the teenagers. Check the shows they mention.

   ☐ animated movies ☐ documentaries ☐ horror movies ☐ soap operas
   ☐ cartoons ☐ dramas ☐ musicals ☐ sports news
   ☐ comedies ☐ game shows ☐ reality TV shows ☐ talk shows

2. **YOUR TURN** What types of TV shows do *you* like watching? Tell your partner.

3. Listen to Jay and Tina talking about TV shows. Complete the conversation.

   USEFUL LANGUAGE: Asking for and giving opinions
   How do you feel about | What do you think about | I think | In my opinion

   Jay: Do you watch a lot of TV, Tina?
   Tina: Yes, I do.
   Jay: What do you like to watch?
   Tina: I really like **sitcoms**.
   Jay: ¹_____ *Modern Family*?
   Tina: That's my favorite show! It's really **funny**!
   Jay: I like it, too. ²_____ **reality TV shows**?
   Tina: ³_____ they're **boring**. I never watch them. What about you?
   Jay: They're OK. I sometimes watch them, but I prefer **game shows**.
   Tina: Really? Why?
   Jay: ⁴_____, they're **exciting**.
   Tina: Yeah, I guess so.

4. Practice the conversation with a partner.

5. **YOUR TURN** Work with a partner. Practice the conversation in Exercise 3 again, but change the words in purple. Use the information in the chart for one conversation and your own ideas for another.

		My ideas
Type of 1st TV show	crime series	
Name of 1st TV show	*CSI*	
Description of 1st TV show	cool	
Type of 2nd TV show	soap operas	
Description of 2nd TV show	terrible	
Type of 3rd TV show	documentaries	
Description of 3rd TV show	interesting	

18 | Unit 2

| Home | Review | Article | Videos | | Login | Register |

My All-Time Favorite Movie
by Sofia Ramos

My favorite movie is *Twilight*, the first film in the Twilight Saga series. It stars Kristen Stewart as Bella and Robert Pattinson as Edward. The director is Catherine Hardwicke.

The movie is about Bella, a teenage girl in modern times. She moves to Forks, a small town in Washington. She meets Edward, a smart and good-looking classmate. She discovers he is a vampire, but she falls in love with him anyway. Another vampire wants to hurt Bella, so Edward tries to protect her.

I like this movie because the acting is really good. The music and camerawork make it dark and mysterious. I love watching fantasy movies, and this movie combines fantasy and romance.

Reading to write: A movie review

6. Look at the photo in Sofia's movie review. What type of movie do you think it is? Read the review to check.

> ### Focus on CONTENT
> When you write a movie review, include this information:
> - the main characters and actors
> - the time and place
> - the director
> - the type of movie
> - a short description of the story
> - why you like it or don't like it

7. Read Sofia's review again. What information from the Focus on Content box does she include in each paragraph?

> ### Focus on LANGUAGE
> **Connectors *so* and *because***
> Use **so** when one event is the result of another event:
> - *Edward is smart and good-looking, **so** Bella falls in love with him.*
>
> Use **because** to explain the reason something happens.
> - *I like action movies **because** they are exciting.*

8. Find an example of *so* and an example of *because* in Sofia's review.

9. Complete the sentences with *so* or *because*.

1. Harry Potter has special powers, _____ he goes to the Hogwarts School for wizards.
2. Peter Parker becomes Spider-Man _____ a spider bites him.
3. In *Toy Story*, Woody and Buzz get lost, _____ they try to find their way home.
4. At the beginning of *The Lion King*, Simba is sad _____ his father dies.

Writing: Your movie review

PLAN
Choose your favorite movie or a movie you saw recently. Include the information in the Focus on Content box and take notes in a chart like the one below.

The main characters and actors	
The director	
The type of movie	
The time and place	
A short description of the story	
Why you like it or don't like it	

WRITE
Now, write your movie review. Use your notes to help you. Write at least 60 words.

CHECK
Check your writing. Can you answer "yes" to these questions?

- Is information from the Focus on Content box in your review?
- Do you use *so* and *because* to show how events connect?

Workbook, pp. 12–13

HOORAY for BOLLYWOOD!

Forget Hollywood! Bollywood is number one in the world of cinema! Bollywood is the name of the Hindi film industry in India. Its home is in Mumbai. Mumbai's name was Bombay in the past, so Bollywood gets its name from *Bombay* and *Hollywood*. Bollywood makes about 1,000 movies every year. That's about two times more than Hollywood. More people watch Bollywood movies, too – over three billion people watch them! About 14 million Indians go to the movies every day.

Bollywood movies are different from Hollywood movies. They are very long and usually last about three or four hours. Many of them are musicals. The movie *Indra Sabha* has the record for the most songs. It has 71 songs in it.

Music and dancing are very important in Bollywood movies. They often contain typical Indian music and traditional Indian dance styles, like Kathak and Bharata Natyam. The dancing helps tell the story in the movie. Bollywood movies also contain modern dance forms, like hip-hop and jazz. The films often include romance, comedy, action, and adventure in their stories.

These movies aren't only popular in India. People around the world love watching them! The movies are usually in Hindi, but there are often subtitles in other languages, like Bengali, Arabic, and English.

Culture: Bollywood movies

1. Look at the photos. What types of movies do think they are?

2. Read and listen to the article. Check the best description of Bollywood movies.

   ☐ Traditional Indian movies in several languages
   ☐ Hindi movies, often with singing and dancing
   ☐ Hollywood movies made into Indian movies

3. Read the article again. Are the sentences *T* (true) or *F* (false)? Correct the false sentences.

   1. Bollywood is a combination of the words *Bengali* and *Hollywood*. ___
   2. More people go to see Bollywood movies than Hollywood movies. ___
   3. A lot of Bollywood movies are musicals. ___
   4. *Indra Sabha* has the record for the longest movie. ___
   5. Kathak is a type of traditional Indian music. ___
   6. Bollywood movies are popular in many countries. ___

4. **YOUR TURN** Work with a partner. Ask and answer the questions.

   1. Do you want to see a Bollywood movie? Why or why not?
   2. Do you watch Hollywood movies? How often?
   3. Do you prefer to watch Hollywood movies or movies from other countries? What is better about the movies you prefer?

DID YOU KNOW…?
There is often an intermission during Bollywood movies because they are so long. Moviegoers take a short break and often buy snacks during the intermission.

BE CURIOUS Find out about the city of Mumbai. What is it like? (Workbook, p. 75)

Discovery EDUCATION
2.3 MUMBAI: FROM COMPUTERS TO FILM

UNIT 2 REVIEW

Vocabulary

1. **Put the letters in the correct order to make words for different types of movies.**

   1. aonercm _____
   2. meydoc _____
   3. nafstya _____
   4. roorhr _____

2. **Match the types of TV shows to their descriptions.**

   1. a talk show ___
   2. a game show ___
   3. the news ___
   4. a soap opera ___
   5. a crime series ___

a	Police officer Jules Kiln finds new clues to an old mystery on *The Scene*.
b	Today on *Green Street*, Sam is unhappy with Gina. Tara tells Mick her secret.
c	Tom Buckley speaks to the children of famous musicians on *Tell Me Today*.
d	Sarah Carver gives today's top events and weather at 8:00 p.m.
e	Watch three people try to win $25,000 on *Make It Big*.

Grammar

3. **Complete the sentences with the simple present forms of the verbs.**

do	not like	watch	go

   1. We usually _____ TV in the evening. Our favorite shows are sitcoms.
   2. Casey always _____ to the movies on the weekends.
   3. When _____ you usually _____ your homework?
   4. Vicky _____ soap operas. She thinks they're boring.

4. **Circle the correct answers. Sometimes both answers are correct.**

   1. Greg loves **to watch** / **watching** sitcoms at night.
   2. Sandra and Kelly want **to see** / **seeing** that new animated movie.
   3. I need **to leave** / **leaving** the theater right after the movie.
   4. Liv dislikes **to have** / **having** the TV on when she does her homework.

Useful language

5. **Circle the correct answers.**

   Jan: Hey, Doug. How do you [1]**think** / **feel** / **tell** about reality TV shows?

   Doug: In my [2]**thought** / **opinion** / **decision**, they're terrible.

   Jan: Really? I like them.

   Doug: Not me. I [3]**agree** / **dislike** / **think** they're boring.

   Jan: Well, I'm going to be on a reality TV show! How do you [4]**think** / **feel** / **tell** about that?

   Doug: Oh, uh, well . . . that's cool, I guess.

PROGRESS CHECK: Now I can . . .

- ☐ identify different types of movies.
- ☐ talk about my movie-watching habits.
- ☐ talk about different types of TV shows, preferences, and TV habits.
- ☐ ask for and give opinions.
- ☐ write a movie review.
- ☐ compare Hollywood movies with other movies.

CLIL PROJECT
2.4 Who's Real?, p. 116

▶ **REVIEW UNITS 1–2, Workbook, pp. 14–15**

Unit 2 | 21

3 Spending Habits

BE CURIOUS

Unusual Fun

How do you spend your money?

Zero: Past and Present

1. What do you think the people have in their bags?

2. Do you like to shop alone or with friends? Why?

3. How often do you go shopping? What do you usually buy?

UNIT CONTENTS

Vocabulary Places to shop; money verbs
Grammar Present continuous review; simple present vs. present continuous; quantifiers
Listening Shopping habits

22 | Unit 3

Vocabulary: Places to shop

1. Complete the key in the map with the correct numbers.

_7_ bank and ATM
___ bookstore
___ clothing store
___ department store
___ electronics store
___ food court
___ jewelry store
___ music store
___ pharmacy
___ shoe store
___ sporting goods store

2. Listen, check, and repeat.

3. What things are there in each place in Exercise 1?

> There are jeans, T-shirts, and jackets in a clothing store.

> A clothing store also has hats, dresses, and . . .

NOTICE IT
ATM stands for *automated teller machine*. A *teller* is a person in a bank whose job is to receive money from or give money to customers.

Speaking: Your favorite stores

4. **YOUR TURN** Work with a partner. What are your three favorite stores? Why?

> One of my favorite stores is a department store. There are many different things for sale there. Another favorite store is . . .

5. Now work with the class. Make a list of everyone's favorite stores. Which stores are the top three favorites?

Workbook, p. 16

Say it RIGHT!
In one-word compound nouns, the first syllable is stressed. In compound nouns with two or more words, the first syllable of the first word is usually stressed. Listen and repeat the words.

• **book**store   **jew**elry store   **spor**ting goods store

Listen and circle the stressed syllable in each compound noun.
food court   music store
clothing store   shoe store

Reading A Day at the Mall in Dubai; Product Reviews; Adopt an Animal
Conversation Making requests when shopping
Writing A product review

STORES and MORE

A Day at the Mall in DUBAI

I'm Lucas. I'm from Mexico, but I live in Dubai now because my parents work here. I'm writing about my life in my new city.

Today, I'm at the Dubai Mall with my family. It has about 1,200 stores, including five department stores, two music stores, more than 25 electronics stores, and about 50 shoe stores!

Are we shopping? No, we're not! There are a lot of other things to do at this mall. My dad and my sister are watching the fish in the Aquarium and Underwater Zoo right now. There are more than 33,000 fish – even sharks! My mom and I are skating on the Olympic-size Dubai Ice Rink. It's hot in Dubai, but it's cold at the ice rink! Later, I want to go to the mall's theme park, the Sega Republic. It has 170 games and many rides.

Outside of the mall is the Dancing Fountain. The water goes up 150 meters! At night, the water changes color because the fountain has lights with 25 different colors.

I hope we stay here all day and night!

Reading: An article about a mall in Dubai

1. Look at the photos. What do you see?

2. Read and listen to the article. Match the photos (a–d) with the places (1–4).

   1. The Aquarium and Underwater Zoo ___
   2. The Dubai Ice Rink ___
   3. Stores in the mall ___
   4. The Dancing Fountain ___

3. Read the article again. Complete the sentences with the correct numbers.

   1. The mall has about _____ stores.
   2. There are about _____ shoe stores in the mall.
   3. The aquarium has over _____ fish.
   4. There are _____ games at the theme park.
   5. The water in the fountain goes up _____ meters.
   6. There are _____ different colors in the fountain lights.

4. **YOUR TURN** Work with a partner. What would you do at the Dubai Mall? Why?

   > I'd go to the ice rink. I like to ice-skate!

DID YOU KNOW...?
The Dubai Mall is one of the biggest malls in the world. More than 50 million people visit it every year.

24 | Unit 3

Grammar: Present continuous review; simple present vs. present continuous

5. Complete the chart.

Use the present continuous to talk about activities that are happening now.

Wh- questions	Affirmative answers	Negative answers
What **are** you **doing**?	I _____ **writing** a book.	I'm **not writing** about my job.
What **is** he _____?	He**'s skating**.	He's _____ **running**.
What _____ they **doing**?	They**'re watch**___ TV.	They _____ **skating**.
Yes/No questions	**Short answers**	
_____ you **writing** about Dubai?	Yes, I _____.	No, I'm _____.
_____ he **skating**?	Yes, he _____.	No, he **isn't**.
Are we **shopping**?	Yes, we **are**.	No, we _____.

Remember: Use the simple present for facts, habits, and routines.
At night, the water **changes** color. = routine
Look! The water **is changing** color. = activity happening now

▸ Check your answers: Grammar reference, p. 108

6. Complete the sentences with the present continuous forms of the verbs.
1. Cassandra _____ (write) a blog about her life in the city.
2. What _____ you _____ (buy) at the electronics store?
3. I _____ (wait) in line at the pharmacy.
4. We _____ (not shop) at the mall today.
5. Marta _____ (not get) money at the ATM now.

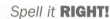

Spell it **RIGHT!**
The **-ing** form:
For verbs ending in **-e**, remove the **e**, and then add **-ing**: wri**te** ➔ wri**ting**.
For verbs ending with one vowel and one consonant, double the final consonant: sho**p** ➔ sho**pping**.

7. Complete the conversation with the simple present or the present continuous forms of the verbs.

Abe: Hi, Lori. What ¹_**are**_ you _**doing**_ (do)?
Lori: I ²_____ (shop) with my parents. We ³_____ (look) for a new school bag and clothes at a department store.
Abe: Just in time! School starts on Monday.
Lori: I know. We ⁴_____ (do) the same thing every year. We always ⁵_____ (shop) the weekend before school starts.
Abe: I ⁶_____ (not do) that! I ⁷_____ (buy) my things for school online during the summer.
Lori: That's a good idea! So, what ⁸_____ you _____ (do) right now?
Abe: I ⁹_____ (watch) a movie on TV.
Lori: Lucky you!

Speaking: At the mall

8. YOUR TURN Work with a partner. You are at a mall in different stores. Think of at least five questions you can ask each other on the phone. Use the simple present and present continuous.

> Where are you? What are you doing? Why . . . ?

9. Create a conversation with your partner.

> Where are you? What are you doing?

> I'm in the shoe store. I'm looking for new sneakers. I want ...

BE CURIOUS — Find out about places in Dubai. What are some things people do in Dubai? (Workbook, p. 76)

Discovery EDUCATION
3.1 UNUSUAL FUN

▸ Workbook, p. 17

Unit 3 | 25

Spending and SAVING

Listening: Shopping habits

1. Do you usually shop at stores or online? Why?

2. Listen to a reporter talk to teens about shopping and money. What do Josh and Megan have in their shopping bags?

3. Listen again. Circle the correct answers.
   1. Josh wants **a new video game** / **a T-shirt**.
   2. Josh usually buys clothes **at a mall** / **online**.
   3. It's **Megan's** / **Josh's** birthday.
   4. Megan has a **necklace** / **soccer ball** for herself.
   5. Megan wants a new **job** / **phone**.

Vocabulary: Money verbs

4. Look at the pictures. Complete the sentences with the simple present forms of the verbs. Then listen and check your answers.

   ✓ borrow   earn   save   withdraw
   deposit   lend   spend

   Jordan's friend is selling a bike. It costs $200. Jordan wants to buy the bike, but he only has $50. He ¹_____borrows_____ money from his aunt. His aunt ²_____ him $50. He ³_____ the money in his bank account. He gets a part-time job at a pizza place in the food court, and he ⁴_____ $100 a week. He ⁵_____ some of that money on movies and video games. He ⁶_____ $25 a week for a month and puts it in the bank. Finally, he ⁷_____ $200 from the bank, and he buys his friend's bike!

5. **YOUR TURN** Work with a partner. Ask and answer the questions.
   1. Do you earn money? How do you earn it?
   2. Do you usually save money or spend money? What do you spend money on?
   3. Do you ever borrow money? Who lends you money?
   4. Do you ever lend money? Who borrows money from you?
   5. Where do you or your parents deposit and withdraw money?

Grammar: Quantifiers

6. Complete the chart.

Use quantifiers to show the amount of something.

With countable plural nouns	With uncountable nouns
How **many** T-shirts do you have?	How **much** money do you have?
I have **some** / _____ / **enough** T-shirts.	I have _____ / **a lot of** / **enough** money.
I don't have **many** / _____ / **a lot of** / **enough** T-shirts.	I don't have **much** / **any** / **a lot of** / _____ money.
Are there **many** / **any** / _____ / **enough** T-shirts in your dresser?	Is there _____ / **any** / **a lot of** / **enough** money in your bank account?
Yes, there are. / No, there aren't.	Yes, there is. / No, there isn't.

Get it RIGHT!

enough = as many as needed
not enough = less than what is needed
Enough goes before nouns and after adjectives:
*I don't have **enough** money to buy a phone.*
*I'm not **old enough** to get a job.*

> Check your answers: Grammar reference, p. 108

7. Circle the correct words.

1. Cynthia has **much** / **a lot of** money.
2. I save **some** / **any** money every month.
3. Are there **much** / **any** department stores in that mall?
4. How **much** / **many** time do you spend at the mall?
5. I'm not old **some** / **enough** to drive a car.
6. There aren't **a lot of** / **much** cars for sale here.

8. Complete the conversation with the correct words.

a lot of   enough   how much   ✓ any   some

Eddie: Oh, no! The bus is coming, and I don't have ¹___any___ money. Can I borrow ²_____ money from you?
Maya: Well, I don't have ³_____ money. I only have $5. ⁴_____ is a ticket?
Eddie: It's $2.50.
Maya: Oh, OK. I have ⁵_____ money, so I can lend you $2.50. No problem.
Eddie: Thanks!

Speaking: A money quiz

9. YOUR TURN Read the questions and use the words to write answers that are true for you. Then add one more question to the list. Write the answers.

a lot of   some   enough   not enough   not any

1. How much money do you save a month? _____
2. How many times do you go shopping each month? _____
3. How much do you spend on clothes each month? _____
4. _____

10. Work with a partner. Ask and answer the questions from Exercise 9.

How much money do you save a month?

I don't save any money. How much money do you save?

I save a lot of money.

> Workbook, pp. 18–19

REAL TALK 3.2 HOW DO YOU SPEND YOUR MONEY?

What We BUY

Conversation: Shopping time

1. **REAL TALK** Watch or listen to the teenagers. Check the things they spend money on.

   ☐ a video game ☐ comic books ☐ plans with friends
   ☐ birthday gifts for friends ☐ food ☐ shoes
   ☐ bus tickets ☐ jewelry ☐ sporting goods
   ☐ clothes ☐ music ☐ things for a cell phone

2. **YOUR TURN** How do *you* spend *your* money? Tell your partner.

3. Listen to Lisa talking with a store clerk. Complete the conversation.

   USEFUL LANGUAGE: Making requests when shopping
   I'd like to buy   I'd prefer   I'll take it!   Can I try it on?

   Lisa: Excuse me. ¹_____ **a dress**.
   Clerk: OK. How about this **blue dress**? It's new.
   Lisa: ²_____ a different color. Does it come in **black**?
   Clerk: Yes, it does. Here it is.
   Lisa: Nice. How much is it?
   Clerk: It's **$49**.
   Lisa: ³_____
   Clerk: Of course. What size do you wear?
   Lisa: **Size 8**.
   Clerk: OK. What do you think?
   Lisa: Actually, it's not big enough. I need a larger size.
   Clerk: OK. Try **a 10**. How is it?
   Lisa: Great. ⁴_____

4. Practice the conversation with a partner.

5. **YOUR TURN** Repeat the conversation in Exercise 3, but change the words in purple. Use the information in the chart for one conversation and your own ideas for another.

		My ideas
Item	a sweater	
First color	red	
Second color	green	
Price	$35	
First size	a small	
Second size	a medium	

28 | Unit 3

A WARM JACKET!

by Wayne, October 16
★★★★☆

The K-Light Jacket is a great jacket. The jacket is at Tom's Sporting Goods Store in a lot of colors. It costs $49.99. The jacket is warm, and it's good for hikes in cooler weather. It's not warm enough for very cold weather. Buy this jacket today. Wear it on your next hike! Note: Don't buy your usual size. I usually wear a medium, but I have this jacket in a large.

A TERRIBLE TABLET!

by Victoria, December 2
★☆☆☆☆

I'm writing this review about my new TS1 tablet. J & T Electronics sells it for $309.00. Don't buy this tablet! It's terrible. I work hard to earn my money, and this tablet isn't worth it. There is one good thing – the size. It's very small. But it's also very slow, and sometimes it stops working. You can't download many apps on the tablet. Save your money! Don't spend it on this awful product.

Reading to write: Product reviews

6. Look at the reviews. Do you think the people like the products? Read the reviews to check.

> ● *Focus on* **CONTENT**
> When you write a product review, include:
> - the name of the product
> - the price
> - what you like about it
> - what you don't like about it
> - where you can buy it
> - your recommendation

7. Read Wayne's and Victoria's reviews again. Find examples for the categories in the Focus on Content box for each review.

> ● *Focus on* **LANGUAGE**
> You can use the imperative to make recommendations. Use the base form of a verb for affirmative sentences. Use *don't* with the base form of a verb in negative sentences.
> - **Buy** this TV now! **Don't buy** that TV!
> - **Get** the new Lazer cell phone today. **Don't get** the new Starz cell phone.

8. Find examples of imperatives in Wayne's and Victoria's reviews.

9. Put the words in the correct order to make sentences with the imperative. Write an affirmative and a negative sentence for each item.

at home or work / use / this cell phone

1. _____
2. _____

on this book / money / spend

3. _____
4. _____

Writing: Your product review

◯ PLAN
Choose a product you have. Write notes about it.

Name	
Where to buy it	
Price	
What you like	
What you don't like	
Recommendation	

◯ WRITE
Write a review about the product. Use your notes to help you. Write at least 60 words.

◯ CHECK
Check your writing. Can you answer "yes" to these questions?

- Is information for each category from the Focus on Content box in your review?
- Do you use the imperative correctly?

Workbook, pp. 20–21

Unit 3 | 29

Adopt an ANIMAL

Students around the world are saving their money, and then they're saving animals!

One way students save an animal is to "adopt" one. This means students give money to an organization. The organization uses the students' money to help animals. The students get a photo of the animal and information about it. For example, some students adopt tigers. They give money to an organization that helps tigers in Asia. Other students adopt whales. They look at photos of whales online, and they choose a whale to help. The whales have names! Students get a photo of the whale, and they can also see how the whale is doing online.

Mrs. Monson's students are adopting an animal in another way. They're helping a cat without a home. Now, the cat is living in their classroom! Her name is Shadow. She eats a lot of food, and she needs to see a vet. The students are having a bake sale and selling cakes and cookies. They're using the money to feed and take care of Shadow. Shadow plays when the students are working! She sleeps in the classroom, too. At the end of the year, one student gets to keep Shadow!

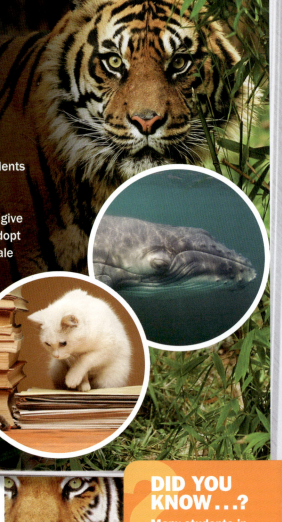

Culture: Students helping animals

1. **Look at the photos. What animals do you see? Where do they live?**

2. **Read and listen to the article. What does it mean to adopt a pet?**
   3.08

3. **Read the article again. Are the sentences T (true) or F (false)? Correct the false sentences.**
   1. An organization helps tigers in the United States. ___
   2. An organization helps whales in the ocean. ___
   3. The tigers have names. ___
   4. Students get a photo of the animal they help. ___
   5. Shadow is living at a school. ___
   6. Shadow doesn't eat enough food. ___

4. **YOUR TURN** Work with a partner. Answer the questions.
   1. Do you know anyone who earns or saves money to help people or animals? What do they do?
   2. How could you earn money to help people or animals? What people or animals would you help?

DID YOU KNOW…?

Many students in the United States have bake sales to earn money. They make food and sell it at school events. They spend the money on different things, like adopting an animal or buying sports uniforms.

BE CURIOUS Find out about the number zero. Who created it? (Workbook, p. 77)

3.3 ZERO: PAST AND PRESENT

UNIT 3 REVIEW

Vocabulary

1. **Where do you buy or get these things? Label the pictures with the correct places.**

a bank	a food court	a pharmacy
a bookstore	a music store	a sporting goods store

1. _____   2. _____

3. _____   4. _____

5. _____   6. _____

Grammar

2. **Complete the sentences with the present continuous or simple present forms.**

   1. Kyle _____ coffee at the café every morning.
   2. What _____ you usually _____ at a department store?
   3. Why _____ they always _____ money inside the bank instead of at an ATM?
   4. Peter _____ his birthday money right now.

3. **Circle the correct answers.**

   1. There aren't **much / many** shoe stores at the mall.
   2. Are there **much / many** watches at the jewelry store?
   3. I don't have **some / enough** time to go to the ATM.
   4. Do you want to eat **some / enough** food now?

Useful language

4. **Complete the conversation with the correct sentences and phrases.**

I'd like to buy	I'd prefer
I'll take them!	Can I try them on?

   Jack: Hello. ¹_____ some new pants.

   Clerk: OK. How about these blue pants?

   Jack: ²_____ brown pants.

   Clerk: OK. We have these in brown. What size do you need?

   Jack: A medium, I think.
   ³_____

   Clerk: Sure. Take a medium and a large. So, do you like them?

   Jack: Yes, the medium pants are good.
   ⁴_____

PROGRESS CHECK: Now I can . . .

- ☐ identify places to shop.
- ☐ talk about the things I do every day and the things I'm doing now.
- ☐ ask and answer questions about spending and saving money.
- ☐ make requests when shopping.
- ☐ write a product review.
- ☐ talk about using money to help people or animals.

4 Our HEROES

Discovery EDUCATION
BE CURIOUS

- Wildlife Hero
- Who is your role model and why?
- The Chilean Mine Rescue
- Amelia Earhart: Famous Flyer

1. What are the people doing?
2. How do you think the boy feels about the man?
3. Who are some people you feel this way about?

UNIT CONTENTS

Vocabulary Cool jobs; adjectives of personality
Grammar Simple past statements review and *ago*; simple past questions review and *ago*
Listening Interview with a teenage hero

32 | Unit 4

Vocabulary: Cool jobs

1. **Label the pictures with the correct jobs.**

an actor	a painter	a singer	✓ a writer
a dancer	a runner	a soccer player	
a lawyer	a scientist	a tennis player	

NOTICE IT
The word *actor* can be used for both men and women. The word *actress* is sometimes used for women.

1. _a writer_ 2. _____ 3. _____ 4. _____ 5. _____

6. _____ 7. _____ 8. _____ 9. _____ 10. _____

 2. **Listen, check, and repeat.**

3. **Write the jobs in the correct places in the chart.**

Sports	Arts and Entertainment	Academic
	a writer	

 Say it RIGHT!
The letter *i* can make the short *i* sound /ɪ/. It can also make the long *i* sound /aɪ/. Listen to the sentence. The first *i* in *scientist* is long. The second *i* is short.

/aɪ/ /ɪ/
My parents are scientists.

Listen to the jobs again. Which other words have a short *i* (/ɪ/)? Which ones have a long *i* (/aɪ/)?

Speaking: Who does that job?

4. **YOUR TURN** Work with a partner. Can you think of a person (a family member, a friend, or a famous person) for each job?

   > My uncle is a lawyer.   > My mom is a lawyer, too.

5. **Would you like these jobs? Why or why not?**

   > I'd like to be a writer. I want to write short stories.

   > I wouldn't like to be a writer. I don't like to work alone.

▶ Workbook, p. 22

Reading Young and Talented!; My Hero; The Island of Champions
Conversation Asking for and giving clarification
Writing A description of a person you admire

SUPERSTARS

Home | Contact | About Us

Young and Talented!

From sports and music to technology and film, today's stars are young and talented! These young people are at the top of their professions. Find out why!

Javier "Chicharito" Hernández was born in Guadalajara, Mexico. He started playing soccer when he was seven. At 15, he signed his first professional contract. In 2010, he moved to England to play for Manchester United. He won an award for Most Valuable Player (MVP) in 2011 when he was 23 years old. He now plays for both Manchester United and the Mexican national team.

Nick D'Aloisio was born in Australia, but he grew up in London, England. He got his first computer when he was nine, and he wrote his first app at 12. In 2013, at 17, he sold an app to Yahoo for 30 million dollars! He also got a job with the company.

Beyoncé won her first talent show when she was seven and joined her first band, Girl's Tyme, when she was eight. This band later became Destiny's Child. In 2001, she became a solo singer. She made her first solo album in 2003. She is now one of the best-paid singers in the world, and she also acts.

? DID YOU KNOW…?
Talent often runs in the family. Javier Hernández's father and grandfather were professional soccer players. Beyoncé's sister is also a singer and actress.

Reading: A web page about young stars

1. Look at the photos. Do you know these people? What are their jobs?

2. Read and listen to the article. At what age did each person take the first step to his or her future job? What was the first step?

3. Read the article again. Complete the sentences with *Nick D'Aloisio*, *Javier Hernández*, or *Beyoncé*.

   1. _____ and _____ won awards for their talents.
   2. _____ became a millionaire at age 17.
   3. _____ worked with a group and then worked alone.
   4. _____ and _____ moved to different countries.
   5. _____ got a job with a famous company.

4. **YOUR TURN** Work with a partner. Think of a famous person from your country who is alive today. What does he or she do? What is he or she famous for?

   > Diego Luna is a famous actor from Mexico City. He's famous for TV shows in Mexico and for movies in Mexico and in the United States.

Grammar: Simple past statements review and *ago*

5. Complete the chart.

Use simple past statements to describe things in the past and to talk about past events and activities. Use ago to say how far back in the past something happened or was.

	Affirmative statements	Negative statements
be	He _____ MVP in 2011. They **were** in Brazil a week **ago**.	He **wasn't** MVP in 2010. They **weren't** in Spain last week.
Regular verbs	He _____ for Mexico. I **moved** a month **ago**.	He **didn't play** for Spain. I _____ last week.
Irregular verbs	She _____ a solo album in 2003. I **got** a tablet a year _____.	She **didn't make** an album in 2001. I _____ a laptop.

> Spell it **RIGHT!**
>
> For regular verbs:
> + **-ed**: *work* → *worked*
> + **-d**: *live* → *lived*
> -**y** → **-i** + **-ed**: *try* → *tried*
> double consonant + **-ed**: *shop* → *shopped*
> For irregular verbs: See p. 121.

> Check your answers: Grammar reference, p. 109

6. Circle the correct words.

1. Gene Kelly (**was**) / **were** a famous dancer, actor, and singer.
2. I **wasn't** / **weren't** very good at singing when I **was** / **were** young.
3. You **wasn't** / **weren't** in class when the famous writer **was** / **were** there.
4. The Olympic runner **was** / **were** very tired after the race.

7. Rewrite the sentences in the simple past. Add the phrases in parentheses. The verbs in blue are irregular. Check the correct forms of those verbs on page 121.

1. John wants to be a professional tennis player. (10 years ago)

   John wanted to be a professional tennis player 10 years ago.

2. You **write** great short stories. (last year)

   _____

3. Lorena **is getting** a job as a lawyer. (last week)

   _____

4. I **sing** in a band. (in 2012)

   _____

5. The scientists don't work in the lab. (a week ago)

   _____

6. The runners are shopping for new shoes. (yesterday)

   _____

> Get it **RIGHT!**
>
> Remember that you do not add **-ed** to the end of irregular verbs in the simple past.
> She **sang** alone. NOT: She ~~singed alone.~~

Speaking: Who is it?

8. YOUR TURN Think of a famous person. Write five facts about his/her life. Use the suggestions or your own ideas.

| where he/she was born | when he/she became famous | an award he/she won |
| his/her job | how old he/she is | |

9. Work with a group. Tell your group about your famous person. Can they guess who it is?

> She was born in Mexico. She is a singer, and she started singing when she was nine years old. She also acted in soap operas. She . . .

> Is it Thalía?

> Yes, it is!

> **BE CURIOUS** Find out about a wildlife hero. What is her job? (Workbook, p. 78)
>
> **Discovery EDUCATION**
> 4.1 WILDLIFE HERO

Workbook, p. 23

Being BRAVE

Listening: Interview with a teenage hero

1. Did you see or help in an emergency in the past? What happened?

 2. Listen to Marcos talk to a news reporter. What was the emergency? What did Marcos do?

3. Listen again and circle the correct answers.
   1. Marcos was **in his house / outside** when the fire started.
   2. He saw **smoke / a strange light** in the sky.
   3. Max was **in the house / outside**.
   4. **Marcos / Max's dad** saw a ladder in the yard.
   5. Marcos **broke / opened** the window.
   6. Max climbed **down the ladder / into Marcos's arms**.

Vocabulary: Adjectives of personality

4. Match the pictures with the correct sentences. Then listen and check your answers.
   1. _a_ George is very **quiet**. He doesn't talk a lot.
   2. ___ Katy's really **funny**. She makes me laugh a lot.
   3. ___ Lou is very **serious**. He studies all the time.
   4. ___ Martina's really **brave**. She isn't scared of anything!
   5. ___ Leticia is so **cheerful**. She's so happy and always smiles.
   6. ___ Julia was **calm** during the emergency. She didn't get excited, and she called the police right away.
   7. ___ Brett is really **friendly**. He likes to meet new people.
   8. ___ Tonya is very **kind** to animals. She helped a cat get down from a tree.
   9. ___ Sometimes, Isabel is **stubborn**. She doesn't listen to her sister.

5. **YOUR TURN** Work with a partner. In what situations do the adjectives describe you?

   > I'm calm and brave in an emergency. I'm usually friendly at parties. I'm . . .

36 | Unit 4

Grammar: Simple past questions review and *ago*

6. Complete the chart.

Use simple past questions to ask about past things, events, and activities.
Use ago to ask how far back in the past something happened or was.

	Wh- questions and answers	Yes/No questions and answers
be	How **was** he an hour _____? He **was** happy. Where **were** they? They _____ at home.	_____ he happy an hour **ago**? Yes, he **was**. / No, he **wasn't**. **Were** they at home? Yes, they _____. / No, they **weren't**.
Regular verbs	How long **ago did** it **start**? It **started** an hour **ago**. Why _____ you _____ him? I **carried** him because he was hurt.	**Did** it **start** an hour **ago**? Yes, it **did**. / No, it _____. _____ you **carry** him? Yes, I _____. / No, I **didn't**.
Irregular verbs	What _____ you _____? I **saw** a fire. Where **did** they **put** the ladder? They **put** it against the house.	**Did** you **see** a fire? Yes, I _____. / No, I **didn't**. **Did** they **put** the ladder against the house? Yes, they **did**. / No, they _____.

▶ Check your answers: Grammar reference, p. 109

7. Complete the sentences with the simple past forms of the verbs.

1. When __were__ you scared in the past? Why _____ you scared? (be)
2. _____ your friends ever _____ a fire? When _____ they _____ it? (see)
3. When _____ one of your friends brave? _____ you with him or her? (be)
4. _____ you _____ a stranger in the past? Who _____ you _____? (help)

8. Work with a partner. Ask and answer the questions in Exercise 7.

> When were you scared in the past? Why were you scared?

> I was scared last night. It was dark and stormy outside.

9. Complete the conversations with the simple past forms of the verbs.

✓ go   see   talk   think

1. **A:** __Did__ you __go__ out last night?
   B: Yes, I did. I saw my cousin play tennis. She's a great tennis player.
2. **A:** Who _____ you _____ to at the party?
   B: To Sam and Patricia. They were very friendly.
3. **A:** _____ you _____ Carl in class?
   B: No, but I saw him about an hour ago. He was really cheerful.

Speaking: I was brave!

10. YOUR TURN Work with a partner. Ask and answer questions about a time you were brave. Use one of the suggestions or your own idea.

| you helped someone in danger | you did something you were afraid to do | you gave a presentation |

When were you brave? What happened? What did you do?

> When were you brave?

> I was brave last month. I went outside in the dark to find our cat.

Workbook, pp. 24–25

Unit 4 | 37

REAL TALK 4.2 WHO IS YOUR ROLE MODEL AND WHY?

People WE ADMIRE

Conversation: Everyday heroes

1. **REAL TALK** Watch or listen to the teenagers. Match the role models with the reasons.

   1. Usain Bolt ___
   2. big sister ___
   3. Anne Hathaway ___
   4. grandfather ___
   5. a school friend ___
   6. history teacher ___

   a. saved his sister from a fire
   b. helps children
   c. teaches well
   d. is the fastest runner in the world
   e. is nice, smart, and hardworking
   f. dances well

2. **YOUR TURN** Who is *your* role model and why? Tell your partner.

3. Listen to Darren and Lydia talking about heroes. Complete the conversation.

   USEFUL LANGUAGE: Asking for and giving clarification
   Are you saying that   What do you mean?   What I'm trying to say is that   I mean

   Darren: We talked about heroes in class today.
   Lydia: That's interesting.
   Darren: Yeah, but I didn't agree with most of the people in the class.
   Lydia: Really? ¹_____
   Darren: Most people chose **movie stars**. I don't think they're heroes.
   Lydia: ²_____ celebrities can't be heroes?
   Darren: Well, they can be, but maybe they shouldn't be. ³_____, **acting** isn't heroic.
   Lydia: But a lot of **movie stars** help people.
   Darren: Yes, but most celebrities help people *after* they're famous. ⁴_____ I think everyday people are more heroic.
   Lydia: Oh, I see. So, who is your hero?
   Darren: **My Aunt Karin. She started a rescue center for wild animals.**
   Lydia: Well, that is pretty heroic!

4. Practice the conversation with a partner.

5. **YOUR TURN** Repeat the conversation in Exercise 3, but change the words in **purple**. Use the information in the chart for one conversation and your own ideas for another.

		My ideas
Type of hero the class chose	pop star	
Activity	singing	
Darren's/your hero	grandfather	
Reason	He fights for peace.	

38 | Unit 4

MY HERO by Gloria Marconi

My hero is **Captain Sullenberger**. He is famous because he saved the lives of many people. In 2009, he was the pilot on a flight from **New York City**. The airplane engines stopped working. Captain Sullenberger stayed calm and landed the plane in the **Hudson River**. After 2009, he wrote two books about being brave.

I admire Captain Sullenberger due to his heroic act. I also admire him because he is serious about safety. Now he is a **safety expert**, and he gives people and companies advice about being safe. He's also kind and teaches children about aviation and safety. Since he's a good role model, he is my **hero**!

Reading to write: Gloria's hero

6. Look at the photos in Gloria's text. What job does her hero have? Why is he a hero? Read the description to check.

> ### Focus on CONTENT
> When you write about someone you admire, include this information:
> - who he/she is and his/her job
> - heroic things he/she did or does
> - his/her personality
> - why you admire him/her

7. Read Gloria's description again. What information from the Focus on Content box does she include?

> ### Focus on LANGUAGE
> **Connectors to show reasons: *because, since, due to***
> Use a subject and a verb after ***because*** and ***since***. The clause with ***because*** or ***since*** can be at the beginning or end of a sentence.
> *I admire my mother **because** <u>she works</u> very hard.*
> ***Since*** <u>my aunt helps</u> *animals, she's my role model.*
> Use a noun after ***due to***. The clause with ***due to*** can be at the beginning or end of a sentence.
> *Nelson Mandela was famous **due to** <u>his fight</u> for peace.*
> ***Due to*** <u>his fight</u> *for peace, Nelson Mandela was famous.*

8. Find examples of *because*, *since*, and *due to* in Gloria's description.

9. Circle the correct word or phrase.
1. My cousin Lou was Player of the Year **because / due to** his skills.
2. **Because / Due to** Jenny is kind, we admire her.
3. Painters Frida Kahlo and Diego Rivera were even more famous **since / due to** they were married to each other.
4. J. K. Rowling is a well-known writer **since / due to** her Harry Potter series.

Writing: Your hero

PLAN
First, choose a person you admire. It can be a famous person or someone you know. Use the categories in the Focus on Content box and take notes.

Who he/she is and his/her job	
Heroic things he/she did or does	
His/Her personality	
Why you admire him/her	

WRITE
Now, write about the person you admire. Use your notes to help you. Write at least 60 words.

CHECK
Check your writing. Can you answer "yes" to these questions?
- Is information for each category from the Focus on Content box in your description?
- Do you use connectors to show reasons correctly?

The Island of CHAMPIONS

Only about three million people live in Jamaica, a small Caribbean island, but many famous athletes are from this country. Athletics is an important part of life in Jamaica, and its athletes are national heroes. Most elementary schools have sports programs, and many high school students compete in an athletics championship, or "Champs," in Kingston every year. Many of the schoolchildren are Olympic champions of the future.

Jamaica's first Olympic heroes were Arthur Wint and Herb McKenley. They won gold and silver medals in the men's 400m race in 1948. From that moment, Jamaican athletics became a national obsession. In 1980, at the Moscow Olympics, Merlene Ottey became the first Jamaican woman to win a medal. She won bronze in the 200m race. She won eight more Olympic medals over 20 years, including two in the 2000 Sydney Olympics at age 40!

In 2008, in Beijing, a new hero won the men's 100m and 200m Olympic gold medals: Usain Bolt. In the London Olympics, in 2012, he became the first athlete to win the "double-double" when he won gold medals in both races again. Jamaican Yohan Blake won silver in both of those races. Shelly-Ann Fraser-Pryce won the gold in the women's 100m and silver in the 200m, bringing home two more medals for Team Jamaica. In fact, Jamaica dominated the medals list in the 2012 Olympics. They won 12 medals, all in track and field events. Jamaica really is the home of champions!

Culture: Athletes from Jamaica

1. **Look at the photos. Which country do you think the article is about? Do you know who the runners are?**

2. **Read and listen to the article. Circle the main idea.**
   a. Jamaican high school students are heroes.
   b. Jamaican men and women are equally good at athletics.
   c. There are many Olympic champions from Jamaica.

3. **Read the article again. Are the sentences true or false? Write T (true), F (false), or NI (no information).**
   1. Jamaica is unusual because it's small, but many athletic champions are from there. ___
   2. Arthur Wint and Herb McKenley were the only Jamaican athletes to win a medal in the 1948 Olympics. ___
   3. Merlene Ottey's first Olympic medal was gold. ___
   4. Usain Bolt won both the 100m and 200m races in Beijing and London. ___

4. **YOUR TURN** Work with a partner. Make a list of famous athletes from your country. Why do people admire them?

   > Lorena Ochoa is famous because she was one of the top female golfers in the world.

   > Yes, and people admire her because she started a golfing school for people in Mexico.

DID YOU KNOW...?
Over 30,000 people go to "Champs" to watch the athletes. Many young runners break national records at the championship.

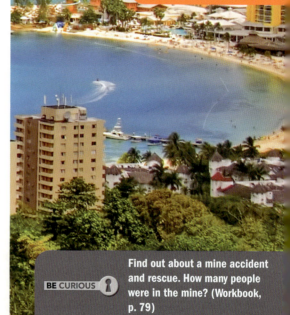

BE CURIOUS Find out about a mine accident and rescue. How many people were in the mine? (Workbook, p. 79)

Discovery EDUCATION
4.3 THE CHILEAN MINE RESCUE

UNIT 4 REVIEW

Vocabulary

1. Label the pictures with the correct jobs.

1. _____   2. _____

3. _____   4. _____

2. Complete the sentences with the correct adjectives.

| cheerful | funny | serious | kind |

1. My brother isn't good at telling jokes. He's not very _____.

2. Martin is always telling jokes. He's not very _____.

3. Jacquelyn doesn't smile or laugh very often. She's not very _____.

4. Liz and Josh help kids with their homework after school. They're very _____.

Grammar

3. Circle the correct words.

1. Where **were / did** you last weekend?

2. **Were / Did** you play sports in high school?

3. **Was / Did** Mike a fast runner as a child?

4. **Were / Did** your parents at home last night?

4. Complete the sentences with the simple past. Then rewrite the sentences with the correct time periods and *ago*.

1. I ___had___ (have) lunch at 1:00 p.m. Now it's 2:00 p.m.

   _____*I had lunch an hour ago.*_____

2. Jack _____ (start) school on Monday. Today is Thursday.

   _____

3. I _____ (call) you at 9:15 a.m. Now it's 9:20 a.m.

   _____

4. Marcos _____ (be) Most Valuable Player in March. Now it's April.

   _____

Useful language

5. Complete the conversations with the correct phrases.

| Are you saying that | I mean |
| What do you mean? | What I'm trying to say is that |

Kim: I think athletes are overpaid.

Todd: ¹_____

Kim: ²_____, they make too much money.

Luke: My brother is the fastest runner in the world!

Sara: ³_____ he runs faster than Usain Bolt?

Luke: No. ⁴_____ he runs really fast!

PROGRESS CHECK: Now I can . . .

- ☐ identify some cool jobs.
- ☐ share facts about someone's life.
- ☐ ask and answer questions about being brave.
- ☐ ask for and give clarification.
- ☐ write a description of someone I admire.
- ☐ talk about famous athletes from my country.

REVIEW UNITS 3–4, Workbook, pp. 28–29

CLIL PROJECT

4.4 Amelia Earhart: Famous Flyer, p. 117

5 It's a Mystery!

Discovery EDUCATION
BE CURIOUS

- Mysteries in the Mountains
- What's an unusual or interesting thing that happened to you recently?
- The Case of the Missing Woman
- An Underwater Mystery

1. Who do you think made these statues on Easter Island?
2. Why do you think people made them?
3. Do you know of any mysterious things or places? Where are they?

UNIT CONTENTS

Vocabulary Action verbs; adverbs of manner
Grammar Past continuous; adverbs of time; simple past vs. past continuous; *when* and *while*
Listening I saw something strange last night.

Vocabulary: Action verbs

1. Look at the pictures of a police officer's story.
   Match the sentences with the pictures.

a. I **caught** the thief after he fell.
b. I **chased** the thief down the street.
c. The thief **climbed** the wall.
d. The thief **hid** the bag.
e. The thief **fell** on the ground.
f. The thief **jumped** into someone's yard.
✓ g. The thief **stole** a bag and **ran** by my police car.
h. The thief **threw** the bag over a wall.

2. Listen, check, and repeat.

3. Work with a partner. One person is a reporter and the other is the police officer.
   Ask and answer questions for each event in the story in Exercise 1.

   > What did the thief steal?

   > He stole a bag.

   > Where did he run?

   > He ran by my . . .

Speaking: What can you . . . ?

4. **YOUR TURN** Work with a partner. Think of as many answers as you can for each question. Make a list.

   What can you . . .
   1. catch?   2. chase?   3. climb?   4. hide?   5. jump over?   6. throw?

   > catch – a thief, a basketball, a baseball, a bus, a cold . . .

5. Join another pair. Compare your lists.

▶ Workbook, p. 30

Reading Whodunit?; An Urban Legend; The World's Number One Detective
Conversation Telling and reacting to a story
Writing A narrative about an interesting or unusual event

Unit 5 | 43

Solving MYSTERIES

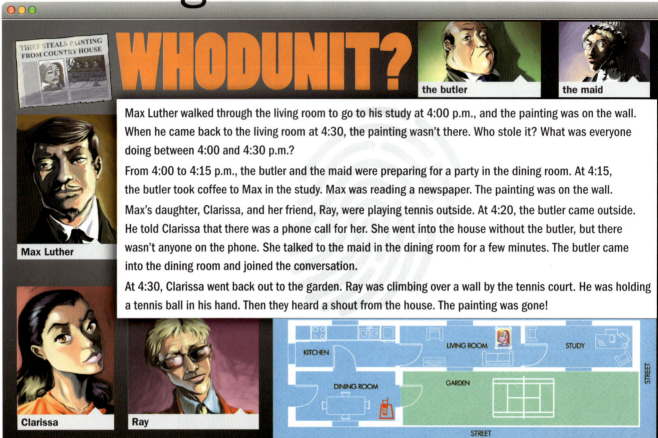

Reading: An article about a stolen painting

1. Look at the pictures. What was the crime? Where did it happen?

 2. Read and listen to the crime story. Who do you think stole the painting? How do you think it happened?

3. Read the article again and answer the questions.

   1. Where was the painting?
      _____

   2. What time did the painting disappear?
      _____

   3. Why were the butler and maid in the dining room?
      _____

   4. Why did Clarissa go into the house?
      _____

   5. What did Ray lose behind the wall?
      _____

4. Work with a partner. Who stole the painting? Explain your idea. Then check your idea on page 121.

5. **YOUR TURN** Work with a small group. Do you know any other stories about a thief (real or fictional)? What did the thief steal? Did the police catch him or her?

   > There was a famous bank robbery last year.
   > The thief stole $500,000. The police . . .

DID YOU KNOW...?

Whodunit is an informal word for *Who did it?* People use it to describe crime stories with a mystery.

Grammar: Past continuous

6. Complete the chart.

Use the past continuous to talk about activities that were in progress in the past.		
Wh- questions	**Affirmative answers**	**Negative answers**
What _____ you **doing**?	I **was talking** on the phone.	I **wasn't talking** to Max.
What **was** Max **reading**?	He **was reading** a newspaper.	He _____ **reading** a book.
What **were** they **doing**?	They _____ **playing** tennis.	They **weren't playing** soccer.
Yes/No questions	**Short answers**	
Were you **talking** to Max?	Yes, I **was**.	No, I **wasn't**.
Was Max **reading**?	Yes, he _____.	No, he **wasn't**.
_____ they **playing** tennis?	Yes, they **were**.	No, they _____.

> Check your answers: Grammar reference, p. 110

7. Complete the police report with the past continuous.

POLICE REPORT   CASE NO: 76543

Police officer: Alfred Baker   Name of witness: Jim Hanson   Crime: Stolen bike

Q: What [1] _**were**_ you _**doing**_ (do) at the time?

A: My friends and I [2] _____ (play) in the park. I [3] _____ (stand) on a hill. From there, I saw the thief steal the bike.

Q: What [4] _____ the thief _____ (wear)?

A: He [5] _____ (wear) a blue jacket and jeans.

Q: [6] _____ your friends _____ (watch) the thief?

A: No, they [7] _____. They [8] _____ (ride) their skateboards. They didn't see him.

8. Put the words in the correct order to make questions. Then answer the questions with your own information.

yesterday at 8:00 a.m. / you / what / were / doing

1. _What were you doing yesterday at 8:00 a.m.?_
2. _I was_ _____

doing / were / last Saturday at 2:00 p.m. / your friends / what

3. _____
4. _____

Adverbs of time

Use adverbs of time to say when things happened or were happening at a specific time in the past.

this morning/afternoon; yesterday
last night/Monday/weekend/week/month/year
at 2:00 p.m./4:00 p.m./10:00 p.m.

Speaking: What were you doing?

9. Work with a partner. Think of something you were doing at one of these times. Give your partner clues. Your partner guesses.

yesterday at 12:00 p.m.   last night
last Saturday afternoon   last Friday at 2:00 p.m.

— I was sitting in a stadium and watching something last Saturday afternoon.

— Were you watching a soccer game?

— Yes, I was.

Say it RIGHT!

In the word **was**, the **a** makes the short /u/ sound, and the **s** makes the /z/ sound. Listen to the sentences. *What **was** she doing yesterday afternoon? She **was** playing tennis.* Pay attention to your pronunciation of **was** in Exercise 8.

 Find out about an archeological dig in Bolivia. What did Scotty and his team find out about the bones? (Workbook, p. 80)

5.1 MYSTERIES IN THE MOUNTAINS

Unsolved MYSTERIES

Listening: I saw something strange last night.

1. Did you see or read about something you couldn't explain in the past? What was it?

2. Listen to Kati tell Todd about an unexplained event. What did she see?

3. Listen again. Who did it? Write *K* for Kati or *T* for Todd.

   1. was at home last night _____
   2. was watching TV last night _____
   3. was studying last night _____
   4. is going to watch the sky tonight _____

Vocabulary: Adverbs of manner

4. Look at the pictures and the boldfaced words. These words are adverbs. You can form adverbs from adjectives. Complete the sentences with the correct adverbs. Then listen and check your answers.

quick → **quickly**	bad → **badly**
slow → **slowly**	happy → **happily**
loud → **loudly**	terrible → **terribly** ✓
quiet → **quietly**	hard → **hard**
careful → **carefully**	good → **well**

> **Spell it RIGHT!**
> To change an adjective to an adverb:
> - change *-y* to *-i* and add *-ly*:
>   happy → happ**ily**
> - change *-ble* to *-bly*:
>   terribl**e** → terri**bly**

1. Gina slept ___*terribly*___ last night.
2. The dog barked _____.
3. The snail was moving _____.
4. The archaeologist worked with the bones _____.
5. Richard plays the piano _____.
6. The plane flew by _____.
7. Carlos sings _____.
8. The children were playing _____.
9. We entered the room _____.

5. **YOUR TURN** Work with a partner. Ask and answer questions using the adverbs in Exercise 4. Use the words below or your own ideas.

| ☐ catch a ball | ☐ clean your bedroom | ☐ play tennis | ☐ sing |
| ☐ check your homework | ☐ cook | ☐ run | ☐ throw a ball |

> Do you run quickly?
>
> No, I don't. I run slowly.

46 | Unit 5

Grammar: Simple past vs. past continuous; *when* and *while*

6. Complete the chart.

> Use the past continuous for an event that was in progress.
> Use the simple past for an event that interrupted the event in progress.
> Use *when* or *while* with the phrase in the past continuous.
> Use *when* with the phrase in the simple past.
>
> I _____ **studying when** I **saw** red lights in the sky.
> (event in progress)   (event that interrupts)
>
> **While/When** I **was studying**, I _____ red lights in the sky.
> (event in progress)   (event that interrupts)
>
> **When** it **happened**, my parents _____ **sleeping**.
> (event that interrupts)   (event in progress)
>
> It _____ **while/when** my parents **were sleeping**.
> (event that interrupts)   (event in progress)

> Check your answers: Grammar reference, p. 110

7. Circle *when* or *while*. Sometimes both answers are possible.
1. Karl caught the ball (**when**) / (**while**) Sandra was running.
2. Olivia was practicing the piano **when** / **while** the phone rang.
3. I heard the loud sound **when** / **while** I was cleaning my room.
4. **When** / **While** the police officer was chasing the thief, he fell.
5. **When** / **While** someone knocked on the door, I was watching TV.

8. Complete the sentences with the simple past or past continuous.
1. Janet watched a mystery movie while she _was eating_ (eat) dinner.
2. I was running in the park when I _____ (see) a police officer.
3. When the lights _____ (go) out, Doug was working.
4. When the fire alarm rang, you _____ (take) a test.
5. While the cat _____ (hide) under the bed, we heard her meow.

Speaking: While you were . . .

9. YOUR TURN Work with a partner. Talk about things that happened while you were doing some of these things in the past.

| cooking | eating | exercising | sleeping | studying |

> My phone rang while I was sleeping last night.

> Really? When I was sleeping, I had a nightmare.

10. YOUR TURN Join another pair. Tell the pair two things that happened to your partner.

> Last night, Jake had a nightmare while he was sleeping.

→ Get it **RIGHT!**

Use the simple past, not the past continuous, for an event that interrupts an event in progress.
*Our team was playing well when I **scored** a goal.*
NOT: *Our team was playing well when I was scoring a goal.*

NOTICE IT
A *nightmare* is a very bad dream.

Workbook, pp. 32–33

REAL TALK — 5.2 WHAT'S AN UNUSUAL OR INTERESTING THING THAT HAPPENED TO YOU RECENTLY?

Strange STORIES

Conversation: An unusual dream

1. Watch or listen to the teenagers. Circle the correct words.

   1. The boy's soccer team **won** / **lost** the game.
   2. The girl's cat **chased** / **ran toward** her.
   3. **The girl** / **The teacher** gave the class some chocolate for her birthday.
   4. Two girls **wore** / **gave each other** the same shirt.
   5. Someone **made** / **took** the boy's lunch at school.
   6. Someone stole the boy's **bike** / **lock**.

2. **YOUR TURN** What's an unusual or interesting thing that happened to *you* recently? Tell your partner.

3. Dave is telling Anna about a nightmare. Listen and complete the conversation with the words from the box.

USEFUL LANGUAGE: Telling and reacting to a story

| then what happened | Did I tell you about | That's weird! | In the beginning |

Dave: ¹_____ my dream last night?

Anna: No. Tell me about it.

Dave: OK. ²_____, I was **in a park** at night. I was **walking slowly** when a **bear** jumped out at me!

Anna: Oh, no! What did you do?

Dave: I hid behind **a big tree**, and I waited quietly. But **the tree** got smaller and smaller!

Anna: ³_____

Dave: I know. Then the **bear** found me and chased me! While the **bear** was chasing me, I **screamed loudly**!

Anna: So, ⁴_____?

Dave: The **bear** caught me, and I woke up! It was scary!

4. Practice the conversation with a partner.

5. **YOUR TURN** Repeat the conversation in Exercise 3, but change the words in purple. Use the information in the chart for one conversation and your own ideas for another.

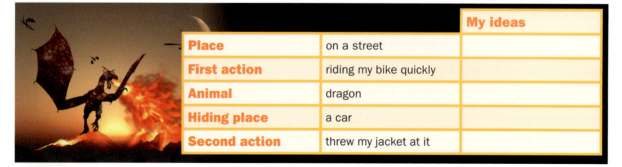

		My ideas
Place	on a street	
First action	riding my bike quickly	
Animal	dragon	
Hiding place	a car	
Second action	threw my jacket at it	

AN URBAN LEGEND
by Stacy Meyers

"Oh, no! I have to help," thought Mickey. One day last summer, he was driving slowly along a quiet road when he saw a car next to the road. A man had a flat tire, and he was trying to change it. Mickey stopped his car and helped the man. While they were changing the tire, they talked about their families. Then the man asked Mickey for his address. At first, Mickey said no, but the man asked him again and again, so Mickey gave it to him. One week later, Mickey got a letter:

> *Dear Mickey,*
> *Thanks for your help. I know a lot about computers but nothing about cars!*
> *Bill Gates*

Finally, Mickey knew who the man was – the founder of one of the world's largest computer companies. He was also one of the richest people in the world. And there was a check for $10,000 with the letter!

Reading to write: A narrative about an unusual event

6. Look at the illustration. What do you think happened? Read Stacy's story to check.

Focus on CONTENT
When you write a story, include:
- a beginning: It should get the readers' attention and make them want to read more.
- a middle: It has details about the events and is in chronological order.
- an ending: It brings the story to a close. A story can have a surprise ending.

7. Read Stacy's story again. What gets the readers' attention at the beginning? What is the surprise ending?

Focus on LANGUAGE
Sequencing words
Use sequencing words to:
- start a story: One day/night/time, . . . In the beginning, . . .
- order events: At first, . . . Next, . . . Then . . .
  After that, . . . Ten minutes later, . . .
- end a story: In the end, . . . Finally, . . .

8. Find examples of sequencing words in Stacy's story.

9. Complete the story with the correct words.

| at first | finally | later | one night | then |

¹_____, I was doing my homework quietly in my bedroom when I heard a strange noise outside. ²_____, I didn't want to go outside, but ³_____ I opened the door, and I went into the yard. There was a very small dog, and it was barking loudly. While I was playing with the dog, my mom came home. She was laughing. Five minutes ⁴_____, my dad and sister arrived. They were laughing, too. ⁵_____, I understood. The dog was my birthday present!

Writing: Your narrative

PLAN
Think of an interesting or unusual story. It can be something that really happened, or you can create the story. Write notes about the events in the order they happened.

Beginning: _____

Middle: _____
_____
_____
_____

Ending: _____

WRITE
Write your story. Use your notes to help you. Write at least 80 words.

CHECK
Check your writing. Can you answer "yes" to these questions?

- Does your story have a beginning, a middle, and an ending? Are the events in chronological order?
- Do you use sequencing words correctly?

The World's Number One
DETECTIVE

A Sherlock Holmes is famous for solving impossible crimes carefully and easily. He lived at 221B Baker Street in London. He played the violin well and was good at science. He didn't really exist, but he became famous in England more than 125 years ago, and he's famous all over the world today.

B Scottish writer Sir Arthur Conan Doyle wrote the original Sherlock Holmes stories. The first story appeared in a British magazine in 1887. It was the first of 56 stories. Doyle also wrote four Sherlock Holmes books. Doyle was working as a doctor when he wrote the first stories. He often wrote the stories while he was waiting for his patients.

C The detective's assistant, Dr. Watson, is almost as famous as Holmes, and the two always worked together. Holmes liked to explain the crimes to Watson. In the movies, Holmes answers Watson's questions with the phrase, "Elementary, my dear Watson, elementary," which means, "The answer is easy." But Holmes never really said this in any of the original stories or books.

D There are more than 200 Sherlock Holmes movies and TV shows with many different actors playing the roles of Holmes and Watson. In a recent TV series, *Elementary*, the stories take place today. Holmes lives in New York City, and his assistant, Dr. Watson, is a woman.

E Sherlock Holmes is everywhere! There are Sherlock Holmes games, toys, hats, comic books, and video games. There's even a Sherlock Holmes social networking page!

Culture: Sherlock Holmes

1. **Look at the photos. What do you know about Sherlock Holmes? What can you tell about him from the photos?**

2. **Read and listen to the article. Match the paragraphs (A–E) to the topics.**
   1. Holmes in Today's Culture ___
   2. Partners in Crime ___
   3. Holmes in Movies and on TV ___
   4. Fame: Past and Present ___
   5. Sherlock Holmes Stories ___

3. **Read the article again. Circle the correct answers.**
   1. Sherlock Holmes was **a real** / **an imaginary** detective.
   2. The writer of Sherlock Holmes was a **doctor** / **detective**.
   3. In the **movies** / **books**, Holmes's famous phrase is "Elementary, my dear Watson, elementary."
   4. There are about **125** / **200** Sherlock Holmes movies and TV shows.

4. **YOUR TURN** Work with a partner. Are there any famous fictional characters in your country? Who are they and what do they do?

   > Pascualina is a famous fictional character. There are many books about her. She travels around the world and . . .

DID YOU KNOW...?
Sherlock Holmes died in one of Doyle's stories in 1893, but the writer brought him back to life because his fans got angry!

Find out about a young woman who disappears from her home. What happened to her? (Workbook, p. 81)

5.3 THE CASE OF THE MISSING WOMAN

50 | Unit 5

AN URBAN LEGEND
by Stacy Meyers

"Oh, no! I have to help," thought Mickey. One day last summer, he was driving slowly along a quiet road when he saw a car next to the road. A man had a flat tire, and he was trying to change it. Mickey stopped his car and helped the man. While they were changing the tire, they talked about their families. Then the man asked Mickey for his address. At first, Mickey said no, but the man asked him again and again, so Mickey gave it to him. One week later, Mickey got a letter:

> Dear Mickey,
> Thanks for your help. I know a lot about computers but nothing about cars!
> Bill Gates

Finally, Mickey knew who the man was – the founder of one of the world's largest computer companies. He was also one of the richest people in the world. And there was a check for $10,000 with the letter!

Reading to write: A narrative about an unusual event

6. Look at the illustration. What do you think happened? Read Stacy's story to check.

● Focus on CONTENT
When you write a story, include:
- a beginning: It should get the readers' attention and make them want to read more.
- a middle: It has details about the events and is in chronological order.
- an ending: It brings the story to a close. A story can have a surprise ending.

7. Read Stacy's story again. What gets the readers' attention at the beginning? What is the surprise ending?

● Focus on LANGUAGE
Sequencing words
Use sequencing words to:
- start a story: *One day/night/time, . . . In the beginning, . . .*
- order events: *At first, . . .   Next, . . .   Then . . .*
  After that, . . .   Ten minutes later, . . .
- end a story: *In the end, . . .   Finally, . . .*

8. Find examples of sequencing words in Stacy's story.

9. Complete the story with the correct words.

| at first | finally | later | one night | then |

¹_____, I was doing my homework quietly in my bedroom when I heard a strange noise outside. ²_____, I didn't want to go outside, but ³_____ I opened the door, and I went into the yard. There was a very small dog, and it was barking loudly. While I was playing with the dog, my mom came home. She was laughing. Five minutes ⁴_____, my dad and sister arrived. They were laughing, too. ⁵_____, I understood. The dog was my birthday present!

▶ Workbook, pp. 34–35

Writing: Your narrative

◯ PLAN
Think of an interesting or unusual story. It can be something that really happened, or you can create the story. Write notes about the events in the order they happened.

Beginning:	_____
Middle:	_____
	_____
	_____
	_____
Ending:	_____

◯ WRITE
Write your story. Use your notes to help you. Write at least 80 words.

◯ CHECK
Check your writing. Can you answer "yes" to these questions?

- Does your story have a beginning, a middle, and an ending? Are the events in chronological order?
- Do you use sequencing words correctly?

The World's Number One
DETECTIVE

A Sherlock Holmes is famous for solving impossible crimes carefully and easily. He lived at 221B Baker Street in London. He played the violin well and was good at science. He didn't really exist, but he became famous in England more than 125 years ago, and he's famous all over the world today.

B Scottish writer Sir Arthur Conan Doyle wrote the original Sherlock Holmes stories. The first story appeared in a British magazine in 1887. It was the first of 56 stories. Doyle also wrote four Sherlock Holmes books. Doyle was working as a doctor when he wrote the first stories. He often wrote the stories while he was waiting for his patients.

C The detective's assistant, Dr. Watson, is almost as famous as Holmes, and the two always worked together. Holmes liked to explain the crimes to Watson. In the movies, Holmes answers Watson's questions with the phrase, "Elementary, my dear Watson, elementary," which means, "The answer is easy." But Holmes never really said this in any of the original stories or books.

D There are more than 200 Sherlock Holmes movies and TV shows with many different actors playing the roles of Holmes and Watson. In a recent TV series, *Elementary*, the stories take place today. Holmes lives in New York City, and his assistant, Dr. Watson, is a woman.

E Sherlock Holmes is everywhere! There are Sherlock Holmes games, toys, hats, comic books, and video games. There's even a Sherlock Holmes social networking page!

Culture: Sherlock Holmes

1. **Look at the photos. What do you know about Sherlock Holmes? What can you tell about him from the photos?**

2. **Read and listen to the article. Match the paragraphs (A–E) to the topics.**

   1. Holmes in Today's Culture ___
   2. Partners in Crime ___
   3. Holmes in Movies and on TV ___
   4. Fame: Past and Present ___
   5. Sherlock Holmes Stories ___

3. **Read the article again. Circle the correct answers.**

   1. Sherlock Holmes was **a real** / **an imaginary** detective.
   2. The writer of Sherlock Holmes was a **doctor** / **detective**.
   3. In the **movies** / **books**, Holmes's famous phrase is "Elementary, my dear Watson, elementary."
   4. There are about **125** / **200** Sherlock Holmes movies and TV shows.

4. **YOUR TURN** Work with a partner. Are there any famous fictional characters in your country? Who are they and what do they do?

   > Pascualina is a famous fictional character. There are many books about her. She travels around the world and . . .

DID YOU KNOW...?
Sherlock Holmes died in one of Doyle's stories in 1893, but the writer brought him back to life because his fans got angry!

Find out about a young woman who disappears from her home. What happened to her? (Workbook, p. 81)

5.3 THE CASE OF THE MISSING WOMA[N]

UNIT 5 REVIEW

Vocabulary

1. **Match the phrases to make sentences.**

   1. A police officer chased the thief ___
   2. The thief threw ___
   3. Then he jumped ___
   4. The thief hid ___

   a. his bag into the river.
   b. at his friend's house until the police officer finally found him.
   c. into the river and swam away.
   d. down the street for 2 kilometers.

2. **Complete the sentences with the correct adverbs of manner.**

   1. Carlos slept _____ (terrible) because of the storm.
   2. My brother sat _____ (quiet) and watched his favorite Sherlock Holmes movie.
   3. The detective studied the crime scene _____ (careful).
   4. He worked _____ (hard) to solve the crime.

Grammar

3. **Look at Gabe's calendar. Write sentences in the past continuous about what he was doing.**

   1. (last Monday night) _____
   _____
   2. (last Wednesday afternoon) _____
   _____
   3. (Friday evening) _____
   _____

4. **Write sentences using the simple past and past continuous.**

   1. he / answer / the phone / while / he / eat / dinner
   _____
   2. we / have / a picnic / when / it / start / to rain
   _____
   3. Mark / not wear / a helmet / when / he / fall / off his bike
   _____

Useful language

5. **Complete the conversation with the correct phrases.**

   | then what happened | Did I tell you about | That's weird. | In the beginning |

   Elsa: Hey, Ned. ¹_____ my vacation?
   Ned: No, you didn't. Did you have a good time?
   Elsa: ²_____, I had a great time. But then my bag was stolen at a restaurant.
   Ned: Oh, no!
   Elsa: Oh, yes! I put my bag on the back of my chair while I was eating. I didn't even see it happen.
   Ned: ³_____
   Elsa: I know. Luckily, a police officer was sitting next to me. She saw and chased the thief!
   Ned: So, ⁴_____?
   Elsa: She caught the thief and gave me back my bag!

PROGRESS CHECK: Now I can . . .

- ☐ tell a story with action verbs.
- ☐ talk about what I was doing in the past.
- ☐ talk about past events and describe how I do things.
- ☐ tell an interesting or unusual story.
- ☐ write a story about an interesting or unusual event.
- ☐ understand information and talk about fictional characters.

CLIL PROJECT

5.4 An Underwater Mystery, p. 118

Uncover Your Knowledge
UNITS 1–5 Review Game

TEAM 1
START

- In one minute, name a modern example and a traditional example of something for each of these categories: food, music, and sports.

- Ask a teammate about someone he or she knows. Ask two *Wh-* questions and two *Yes/No* questions. Your teammate answers.

- Talk with a teammate about traditions in your families, such as birthdays or weddings. See how long you can keep the conversation going by asking and answering questions.

- In one minute, name as many types of movies as you can.

- Ask a teammate five questions about people's possessions in the classroom. Use *whose*. Your teammate answers.

- In one minute, name five different characters or actors from five different types of TV shows.

- Make five statements about your movie-watching habits using the adverbs of frequency: *always, usually, often, sometimes,* and *never*.

- Role-play a conversation with a teammate about a sports team or sporting event. Keep the conversation going for two minutes.

- You want to go shopping at the mall. Ask a teammate where to buy three different things. Your teammate answers the questions.

- Look around the room. Tell a teammate five things you see happening right now.

- Ask a teammate for his/her opinion about three different TV shows. Disagree with your teammate's opinions.

INSTRUCTIONS:

- Make teams and choose game pieces.
- Put your game pieces on your team's START.
- Flip a coin to see who goes first.
- Read the first challenge. Can you do it correctly?

    Yes ➔ Continue to the next challenge.

    No ➔ Lose your turn.

The first team to do all of the challenges wins!

TEAM 2
START

- Tell a teammate five sentences about the way you do things. Use adverbs of manner, such as *carefully* and *well*.
- Start a sentence about a past event using *while* or *when* and have a teammate finish it.
- Tell your teammate about an unusual dream or story. Your teammate reacts to the story using phrases like *then what happened?* Keep the conversation going for two minutes.
- With a teammate, ask and answer four questions about what you were doing last night.
- Tell a teammate the story of an action movie or sporting event using at least four action verbs.
- Ask your teammate Wh- questions and Yes/No questions to find out about a time in the past when he or she was brave or helpful. Your teammate answers.
- Tell a teammate about one of your heroes. Your teammate asks questions for clarification.
- Tell a teammate three things about yourself that happened in the past. Use *ago* to say how far back in the past.
- In one minute, name three jobs you think are interesting and three you think are boring.
- Ask a teammate two questions using *how many* and *how much*. Your teammate answers.
- In one minute, describe a teammate using three adjectives, but don't say the person's name. Your team tries to guess who you are describing.
- Role-play shopping with a teammate. Make requests to buy objects in the classroom. Use expressions like *I'd like to buy, I'd prefer, I'll take it!* Your teammate responds.
- In one minute, make four sentences about things in the classroom using *a lot of, any, enough,* and *some*.
- In one minute, name ten different jobs.

- GRAMMAR
- VOCABULARY
- USEFUL LANGUAGE

Units 1–5 Review | 53

6 Home, Sweet HOME

Discovery EDUCATION

BE CURIOUS

- A Cool Life
- Which do you prefer – houses or apartments?
- Moving House

1. What is this house like?

2. Who do you think lives here?

3. Would you want to live in a house like this? Why or why not?

UNIT CONTENTS

Vocabulary Furniture and other household items; household appliances
Grammar Comparative and superlative adjectives and adverbs; should (not), (not) have to, must (not)
Listening A clothing emergency

54 | Unit 6

Vocabulary: Furniture and other household items

1. Match the words with the correct pictures.

| a. a bed | c. a chair | e. a dresser | g. a shower | i. a table | ✓k. an armchair |
| b. a bookcase | d. a desk | f. a mirror | h. a sofa | j. a toilet | l. cabinets |

LIVING ROOM KITCHEN BEDROOM BATHROOM

1. k   2. ☐   3. ☐   4. ☐   5. ☐   6. ☐   7. ☐   8. ☐   9. ☐   10. ☐   11. ☐   12. ☐

2. Listen, check, and repeat.

3. Answer the questions with the words in Exercise 1.

1. Which items do you sit on?
   _____

2. Which items do you put things in?
   _____

3. Which items do you put things on?
   _____

4. Which items do you get into?
   _____

5. Which item do you look into?
   _____

Say it RIGHT!

The letters **er** and **or** can make the /ər/ sound. Listen to the sentence.

*A photo of an act**or** is ov**er** my bed.*

Listen to the words in Exercise 1 again. Which words have the /ər/ sound? What letters make the sound?

4. Work with a partner. Describe the furniture and items in Exercise 1.

> The armchair is big. It's brown and blue.

Speaking: Your house

5. YOUR TURN Which things from Exercise 1 are in your house? What other things do you have? Make a list.

> *Kitchen: cabinets, two chairs, . . .*

6. Work with a partner. Tell your partner about the things in your house.

> There isn't a table in our kitchen. There are a lot of cabinets. We have two chairs by the window . . .

▶ Workbook, p. 36

Reading A Home in the Jungle; My House; Life on the Water
Conversation Asking for and offering help
Writing An email about your house

UNUSUAL Rooms

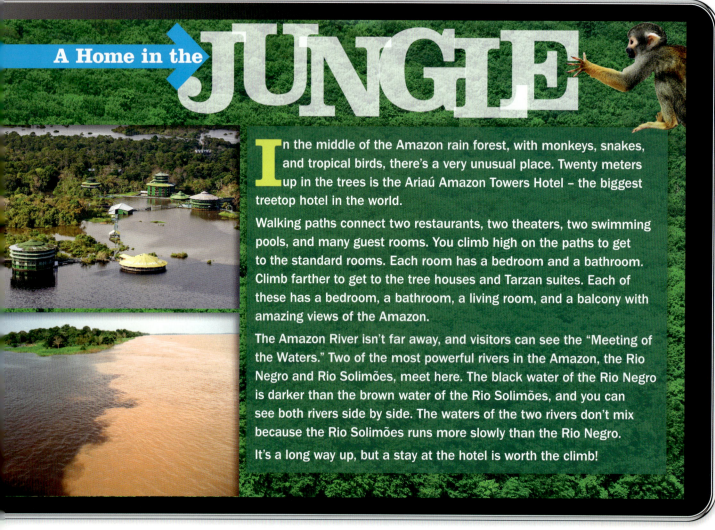

A Home in the JUNGLE

In the middle of the Amazon rain forest, with monkeys, snakes, and tropical birds, there's a very unusual place. Twenty meters up in the trees is the Ariaú Amazon Towers Hotel – the biggest treetop hotel in the world.

Walking paths connect two restaurants, two theaters, two swimming pools, and many guest rooms. You climb high on the paths to get to the standard rooms. Each room has a bedroom and a bathroom. Climb farther to get to the tree houses and Tarzan suites. Each of these has a bedroom, a bathroom, a living room, and a balcony with amazing views of the Amazon.

The Amazon River isn't far away, and visitors can see the "Meeting of the Waters." Two of the most powerful rivers in the Amazon, the Rio Negro and Rio Solimões, meet here. The black water of the Rio Negro is darker than the brown water of the Rio Solimões, and you can see both rivers side by side. The waters of the two rivers don't mix because the Rio Solimões runs more slowly than the Rio Negro.

It's a long way up, but a stay at the hotel is worth the climb!

Reading: An article about an unusual hotel

1. Look at the photos. What do you see? Where do you think it is?

2. Read and listen to the article. Why is the hotel unusual?

3. Read the article again. Answer the questions.
   1. Which animals live near the hotel?
      _____
   2. How high up in the trees is the hotel?
      _____
   3. What rooms do tree houses and Tarzan suites have?
      _____
   4. What is the "Meeting of the Waters"?
      _____

4. **YOUR TURN** Work with a partner. Would you like to stay in a treetop hotel? Why or why not?

   > I'd like to stay in a treetop hotel! I love nature and animals.

   > I wouldn't like it because . . .

DID YOU KNOW...?
The Rio Negro is home to the amazing pink dolphin, one of the rarest animals in the world.

Grammar: Comparative and superlative adjectives and adverbs

5. Complete the chart.

Use comparative adjectives and adverbs to show how two things are different from each other.
Use superlative adjectives and adverbs to compare three or more things.

	Comparative		Superlative	
Adjectives	dark → dark**er** powerful → **more** _____ good → **better**	big → _____ bad → **worse**	dark → _____ popular → _____ good → **the best**	big → **the** big**gest** bad → **the worst**
	The Rio Negro is _____ than the Rio Solimões.		The bathroom is **the darkest** room in the hotel.	
Adverbs	fast → _____ far → far**ther** well → **better**	slowly → _____ badly → **worse**	fast → **the** fast**est** far → _____ well → _____	slowly → **the most slowly** badly → **the worst**
	The Rio Solimões runs **more slowly than** the Rio Negro.		The water runs _____ in the summer.	

> Check your answers: Grammar reference, p. 111

6. Complete the sentences with the comparative adjectives or adverbs.

1. Brazil is ___*bigger than*___ (big) Mexico.
2. The Rio Negro runs _____ (fast) the Rio Solimões.
3. A vacation in the Amazon is _____ (exciting) a vacation in Antarctica.
4. The furniture in my room is _____ (good) the furniture in your room.
5. We got _____ (wet) our parents on the hike because they used umbrellas.

7. Circle the correct words.

In Spain, I toured the Guadix cave homes with my sister. They are some of the ¹**strangest** / **more strangely** homes in the world. People live in cave houses there. The houses are ²**more dark** / **darker** than normal houses because they don't have many windows.

In the summer, the caves are ³**cooler** / **coolest** than normal homes, and in winter they are ⁴**the warmer** / **warmer**.

Our tour guide spoke ⁵**quickest** / **more quickly** than most tour guides. He talked the ⁶**faster** / **fastest** near the end of the tour. My sister understood the guide ⁷**better** / **best** than I did, so she repeated everything ⁸**slower** / **more slowly** for me.

Speaking: Compare!

8. YOUR TURN Discuss the questions with a partner.

1. Who studies longer at night?
2. Who is better at sports?

> I study for an hour at night.

> I study for two hours. I study longer than you.

9. Join another pair. Compare your answers to Exercise 8. Then answer these questions.

1. Who studies the longest at night?
2. Who is the best at sports?

> Jack studies for four hours at night. He studies the longest.

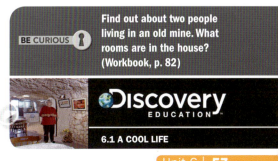

BE CURIOUS Find out about two people living in an old mine. What rooms are in the house? (Workbook, p. 82)

Discovery EDUCATION
6.1 A COOL LIFE

> Workbook, p. 37

Things That PLUG IN

Listening: A clothing emergency

1. Who washes your clothes? Do you wash your own clothes?

2. Listen to Jackie tell her sister Chloe about her clothes. What's wrong with her pants? With her sweater?

3. Listen again and circle the correct answers.

   1. Jackie washed her dark and light clothes _____.
      a. together   b. separately   c. by hand

   2. Jackie's sweater is made of _____.
      a. cotton   b. jean material   c. wool

   3. Jackie washed her clothes on _____.
      a. hot   b. warm   c. cold

   4. Jackie learned how to fix her sweater from _____.
      a. her sister   b. a website   c. a label

Vocabulary: Household appliances

4. Write the words next to the correct numbers. Then listen and check your answers.

a dishwasher	a microwave	a toaster	an alarm clock
a hair dryer	a refrigerator	a vacuum cleaner	an iron
a lamp	✓ a stove	a washing machine	an oven

NOTICE IT
Fridge is short for *refrigerator*.

1. _a stove_   5. _____   9. _____
2. _____   6. _____   10. _____
3. _____   7. _____   11. _____
4. _____   8. _____   12. _____

5. **YOUR TURN** Work with a partner. In what rooms do you use each of the household appliances in Exercise 4? How often do you use them?

> I use the stove in the kitchen. I use it two times a week.

58 | Unit 6

Grammar: should (not), (not) have to, must (not)

6. Complete the chart.

Use should not for advice and recommendations. Use have to for responsibilities.
Use not have to for things that are not required. Use must for obligation. Use must not for prohibition.

Affirmative	Negative
You _____ **wash** dark clothes separately. **She should look** at the labels.	You **shouldn't wash** darker clothes with lighter ones. She _____ **put** it in a sunny room.
You _____ **choose** the temperature first. It **has to be** cool.	You **don't have to wash** it by hand. It _____ **be** cold.
You **must use** cold water. They _____ **follow** the directions.	You _____ **use** hot water. They **must not miss** a step.

> Check your answers: Grammar reference, p. 111

7. Complete the sentences with the affirmative or negative of the words.

1. We ___shouldn't put___ (should / put) metal in the microwave. It can start a fire.
2. Sara _____ (have to / wash) her clothes today. She can do it tomorrow.
3. I _____ (should / get) a small hair dryer for my trip. My suitcase only has room for small things.
4. Jack and Paula _____ (have to / buy) a new dishwasher. Theirs broke.
5. Don _____ (must / use) his vacuum cleaner before 8:00 p.m. His parents don't like noise late at night.

8. Complete the sentences with should (not), (not) have to, or must (not).

1. Jenny _____ get a lamp for her bedroom. It's really dark.
2. The label says, "You _____ put the hair dryer in water." You will get hurt.
3. I _____ set my alarm clock on Saturday because I don't work on the weekend!
4. We _____ make the vegetables in the microwave. They're better on the stove.
5. My sister _____ wash her clothes at the laundromat. She doesn't have a washing machine at home.

> **Get it RIGHT!**
>
> Use **must** for obligation, not for things that are responsibilities.
> You **have to bring** a pencil to class.
> (= It's your responsibility to bring a pencil.)
> You **must use** a pencil on the test.
> (= It's an obligation to use a pencil. You're not allowed to use a pen or a marker.)

Speaking: Guess the appliance

9. YOUR TURN Work with a partner. Think of an appliance. Describe it, and tell your partner how you *should (not), (not) have to, must (not)* use it. Your partner guesses the appliance. Take turns.

> It's small, and it's often white. You have to plug it in. You use it in the kitchen. You shouldn't put metal in it.

> Is it a microwave?

> Yes, it is!

> Workbook, pp. 38–39

At Home

Conversation: I have to clean the house.

1. **REAL TALK** Watch or listen to the teenagers. Are these reasons for preferring houses or apartments? Write H (house) or A (apartment).

   1. ___ They're usually bigger.
   2. ___ They're quieter.
   3. ___ They usually have a garden.
   4. ___ They're usually closer to the center of a city.

> **NOTICE IT**
> Some words are different in American English and British English.
>
> | American English | British English |
> | --- | --- |
> | apartment | flat |
> | yard | garden |

2. **YOUR TURN** Which do *you* prefer – houses or apartments? Tell your partner. Give a reason for your answer.

3. Josh is helping Cara with her chores. Listen and complete the conversation.

USEFUL LANGUAGE: Asking for and offering help
- Can I ask you for a favor?
- Could you help me out?
- Would you like some help?
- I'll give you a hand.

Josh: Are you ready to go the mall?

Cara: I'm sorry, but I can't go yet. I didn't finish my chores. I have to clean **the living room**.

Josh: ¹_____

Cara: Oh, yes. That'd be great. I'll **clean the furniture**, and you can **vacuum**.

Josh: OK. Let's get started.

Cara: I need to get the cleaning supplies out of that cabinet. I can't reach them.

Josh: Wait. ²_____

Cara: Great, thanks.

Josh: Hey . . . ³_____

Cara: Of course.

Josh: I need to get a birthday present for my sister. ⁴_____

Cara: Sure. Let's finish cleaning **the living room** and then shop for your sister.

4. Practice the conversation with a partner.

5. **YOUR TURN** Repeat the conversation in Exercise 3, but change the words in **purple**. Use the information in the chart for one conversation and your own ideas for another.

		Your ideas
Room to clean	the kitchen	
Chore #1	clean the sink	
Chore #2	put the dishes in the dishwasher	

To: santiagoG@middleschool.cup.org
From: jorge.vegasrg@net.cup.org
Subject: My House

Hi Santiago,

I'm excited you're coming to stay with us in our new house for the summer! We live in a big house with four bedrooms. My parents have the biggest bedroom, and they have their own bathroom. My sister and I have our own bedrooms. There's a fourth bedroom, but now it's my mom's office. My bedroom is pretty big. I have two beds, so you can sleep in my room. There's room for your clothes in my dresser.

Downstairs there's a big living room. We have a sofa, two armchairs, and a huge TV! My favorite room is the kitchen. There's a big table where we eat, talk, and play games. There's a dishwasher, so we don't have to wash dishes by hand!

Tell me about your apartment.

Your cousin,

Jorge

Reading to write: A description of Jorge's house

6. Look at the photo of Jorge's house. How many bedrooms do you think it has? Read the email to check.

Focus on CONTENT
When you write about your house, include:
- the size, age, and kind of house
- how many bedrooms it has
- what other rooms it has
- your favorite room and why
- some of the furniture or appliances there

7. Read Jorge's email again. What information does he include for each category from the Focus on Content box?

Focus on LANGUAGE
Commas
Use commas to separate items in a list.
I have a desk, two chairs, and big bed in my bedroom.
Use commas to join two complete sentences with conjunctions like *and*, *but*, and *so*.
We usually cook in the oven, but sometimes we use the microwave.

8. Find examples in Jorge's email of the comma rules in the Focus on Language box.

9. Put commas in the correct places.
   1. My bedroom is small but it's comfortable.
   2. There are four chairs a big table and two lamps in our kitchen.
   3. The dishwasher isn't working so I have to wash the dishes by hand.
   4. I packed a hair dryer a toothbrush and shampoo in my suitcase.

Workbook, pp. 40-41

Writing: An email about your house

PLAN
Use the categories in the Focus on Content box and take notes about your home.

Size, age, and kind	
Number of bedrooms	
Other rooms	
Favorite room/why	
Furniture/appliances	

WRITE
Write an email describing your house to a friend or someone in your family. Use your notes to help you. Write at least 80 words.

CHECK
Check your writing. Can you answer "yes" to these questions?

- Is information for each category of the Focus on Content box in your description?
- Do you use commas correctly?

Unit 6 | 61

LIFE ON THE WATER

Did you know that some people live on the water? You can find houseboats on lakes, rivers, and canals all over the world. There are hundreds in Sausalito, California. Thirteen-year-old Ryan Harvey moved to a houseboat community with his family two years ago. We asked Ryan about a typical Saturday on his houseboat.

7:00 A.M. WILDLIFE WATCH
Early morning is the best time to see marine animals because it's the quietest time of the day. Sometimes, I can see seals right outside my bedroom window. They're amazing!

5:00 P.M. VISIT FRIENDS
We often go out in our kayaks to see other families on their boats. I paddle faster than my parents!

10:15 A.M. MORNING WALK
I go with Dad to get our mail at the marina. It's where all our neighbors meet. I always see my friends there.

7:00 P.M. DINNER
Dad makes dinner, and we eat on the balcony on top of our houseboat when the weather is nice. Because we're far from the town, there aren't any streetlights. You can see the stars at night!

1:00 P.M. LUNCH
The kitchen is very small, so only one person fits. Mom and I take turns making lunch. I usually cook more slowly than my mom.

"There's not much room on the houseboat, but you're closer to nature. It's also safer and quieter than the city. I love life on the water!"

Culture: Living on a houseboat

1. Look at the photos. Do you think the boy is at home or on vacation?

2. Read and listen to the article. What are some advantages to living on a houseboat? What are some disadvantages?

3. Read the article again. Number the activities in order from 1–6.
   ___ Ryan's mom cooks.
   ___ Ryan's family eats outside.
   ___ Ryan sees animals.
   ___ Ryan's family goes out on the water.
   ___ Ryan's dad cooks.
   ___ Ryan and his dad go for a walk.

4. **YOUR TURN** Work with a partner. Would you like to live on a houseboat? Why or why not? What other kind of house would you like to live in?

> I'd like to live on a houseboat because . . . I'd also like to live . . .

> I wouldn't like to live on a houseboat because . . . I'd like to live . . .

BE CURIOUS Find out about someone who buys a house. Why does he want to move it? (Workbook, p. 83)

Discovery EDUCATION
6.3 MOVING HOUSE

62 | Unit 6

UNIT 6 REVIEW
Vocabulary

1. **Write the words for the furniture, items, and appliances next to the correct numbers.**

   1. _____   7. _____
   2. _____   8. _____
   3. _____   9. _____
   4. _____   10. _____
   5. _____   11. _____
   6. _____   12. _____

Grammar

2. **Write sentences with the comparative or superlative form of the adjectives and adverbs.**

   1. these tablets / be / good / those laptops
      _____
      _____

   2. Tara / have / comfortable / bed / in the house
      _____
      _____

   3. we usually / walk / far / our cousins
      _____
      _____

   4. my dog / bark / loudly / your dog
      _____
      _____

   5. the water / move / slowly / in the winter
      _____
      _____

3. **Circle the correct words.**

   1. Look at that sign. You **must not / don't have to** eat in the library.

   2. You **have to / shouldn't** turn off the computer before you leave. It can't stay on all night.

   3. You **don't have to / shouldn't** download any computer games onto the school computers. The teacher doesn't like it.

   4. You **should / don't have to** cook tonight. I'm going to make dinner.

   5. You **must / should** ask for help if you have a problem. It's a good idea.

Useful language

4. **Look at the underlined words in the conversations. Write A if the person is asking for help. Write O if the person is offering help.**

   1. ____
   A: The iron is up so high in that cabinet. I can't reach it.
   B: <u>Would you like some help?</u>
   A: Sure. That'd be great.

   2. ____
   A: I don't understand this recipe. <u>Could you help me out?</u>
   B: Sure. Let me see it.

   3. ____
   A: Hey, Sue. Do you want to go to a movie?
   B: Sure, but, <u>can I ask you for a favor</u> first?
   A: OK.

PROGRESS CHECK: Now I can . . .

☐ identify rooms in a house and household items.   ☐ ask for and offer help.
☐ compare two or more rooms.   ☐ write an email about my house.
☐ identify and talk about household appliances.   ☐ talk about the kind of house I'd like to live in.

▶ REVIEW UNITS 5–6, Workbook, pp. 42–43

7 VISIONS of the FUTURE

Discovery EDUCATION

BE CURIOUS

A Pizza Robot

How important is your cell phone?

Music Sharing

The Secret of the Pyramids

1. What is this city like? How is it different from our cities today?

2. How do you think people communicate in this city?

3. Would you like to live in a place like this? Why or why not?

UNIT CONTENTS

Vocabulary Computers and communication; technology verbs
Grammar *Will* and *won't* for predictions; adverbs of possibility; first conditional with *will* (*not*), *may* (*not*), and *might* (*not*)
Listening They're always coming out with something new.

Vocabulary: Computers and communication

1. Match the words (a–i) with the correct pictures.

- a. a keyboard
- b. a flash drive
- c. a mouse
- d. a printer
- e. a smartphone
- f. a tablet
- g. a touch pad
- h. a touch screen
- ✓ i. Wi-Fi

1. *i* 2. ☐ 3. ☐ 4. ☐

5. ☐ 6. ☐ 7. ☐ 8. ☐ 9. ☐

2. Listen, check, and repeat.

3. Circle the correct words.
1. Do you usually use **Wi-Fi / (a touch pad)** or a mouse?
2. You can save your work on **a flash drive / a touch pad**.
3. You use **Wi-Fi / a printer** to go on the Internet.
4. You use **a mouse / a keyboard** to type an email.
5. You can carry **a smartphone / a touch screen** easily in one hand.
6. I prefer **a flash drive / a mouse** to a touch pad.

Say it RIGHT!
The letters **ou** can sound like the /uh/ or /ow/ sound. Listen to the sentence.
*My c**ou**sin has three computers in her h**ou**se.*
Which words in Exercise 1 have the letters **ou**? What sounds do they make?

Speaking: A computer quiz

4. YOUR TURN Use the words from Exercise 1 to give information about you.
Something I use:
- at school: _____
- to do homework: _____
- at home: _____
- every day: _____
- to play games: _____
- to communicate with friends: _____

5. Work with a partner. Share your answers to the quiz in Exercise 4.

> I use Wi-Fi, a printer, and a touch pad at school.

 Workbook, p. 44

Reading Computers: A Big Past, A Small Future; How do you think people will listen to music in the future?; Television Grows Up . . . and Down!
Conversation Asking for and giving instructions
Writing An opinion paragraph

The Future of Technology

Computers: A Big Past, A Small Future

Over 65 years ago, the world's first computer was "born." Scientists called it "The Baby," but it was huge. It filled an entire room! Three people made the computer and programmed math problems for it. On June 19, 1948, the computer solved its first math problem – in 52 minutes! At that time, this was amazing.

Computers are now much smaller. With touch-screen technology, many computers don't need extra things, like a keyboard or a mouse. In the future, computers probably won't need these things at all. Some computers, like the smartphone, can fit in one hand. Computers are also more powerful today. There is more computing power in a smartphone than there was in all of the computers on *Apollo 11*, the first spacecraft to take people to the moon!

How else will computers change in the future? A computer's "brain" is a chip inside the computer, and in the future, people will definitely be able to save much more information on a computer chip. So, computers will be smaller and even more powerful. Perhaps they'll even think like humans! Maybe we won't need to tell computers what to do because they'll decide for themselves!

Reading: An article about computers

1. Work with a partner. Look at the photo of an old computer. How was it different from modern computers?

2. Read and listen to the article. What was the first computer like?

3. Read the article again. Circle the correct answers.

    1. The first computer fit in _____.

        a. a hand   b. a room   c. a building

    2. The Baby found the answer to _____ math problem(s) in 52 minutes.

        a. 1   b. 3   c. 65

    3. The computers on *Apollo 11* were _____ a smartphone.

        a. more powerful than   b. less powerful than   c. as powerful as

    4. Today, many computers don't have _____.

        a. keyboards   b. chips   c. touch screens

4. **YOUR TURN** Work with a partner. Think of at least five things you think computers should do in the future.

    > Computers should clean our houses in the future. They should . . .

5. **YOUR TURN** Join another pair. Share your ideas from Exercise 4. Which idea do you think is the best?

DID YOU KNOW...?

There are more than two billion personal computers in the world today, including tablets and smartphones.

66 | Unit 7

Grammar: *will* and *won't* for predictions

6. Complete the chart.

Use will and won't to predict future events.

Wh- questions	Affirmative answers	Negative answers
What **will** my smartphone **do** in the future?	Perhaps it**'ll think** like a human.	It _____ **drive** a car.
How _____ computers **change**?	They _____ **be** smaller.	They **won't be** bigger.
Yes/No questions	**Short answers**	
_____ my smartphone **think** like a human?	Yes, it **will**.	No, it _____.
Will computers **change**?	Yes, they _____.	No, they **won't**.
Contractions: I will = I**'ll** you will = you**'ll** he will = he**'ll** she will = she**'ll** it will = _____		
we will = we**'ll** they will = _____		

> Check your answers: Grammar reference, p. 112

7. In 1900, an American engineer made these predictions. Complete them with *will* or *won't* and the correct verbs.

| buy | eat | not be | not cook | ✓ not live | not wait | talk |

1. Animals ___won't live___ in the wild.
2. People _____ on wireless phones.
3. We _____ all of our own meals. We _____ them in stores.
4. The letters *C*, *X*, and *Q* _____ in the alphabet.
5. We _____ until summer to eat vegetables. We _____ them in winter.

8. Work with a partner. Which predictions in Exercise 7 are true now?

9. Write sentences about the future with *will* and *won't*. How sure are you? Use *definitely, certainly, probably, maybe,* or *perhaps*.

1. we / have / Wi-Fi connections in our clothes
   We'll probably have Wi-Fi connections in our clothes.

2. cars / not need / human drivers
   _____

3. people / live / to be 120 years old
   _____

4. we / not use / pens and pencils
   _____

Adverbs of possibility

Sure	Pretty sure	Not as sure
definitely	probably	maybe
certainly		perhaps

Use adverbs of possibility to say how sure you are about a prediction. **Definitely**, **certainly**, and **probably** come between the subject and **will** or **won't**, or between **will** and the base form of the verb. **Perhaps** and **maybe** come before the subject.

They **definitely** will think like humans.

They'll **probably** think like humans.

Perhaps they will think like humans.

Speaking: Predictions about my future

10. YOUR TURN Work with a partner. Ask and answer questions about the future. Make predictions about the items below or your own ideas.

| your school/job | your friends/family | your town/city | your computer |

> What will you do in the future?

> I'll probably write software for computers.

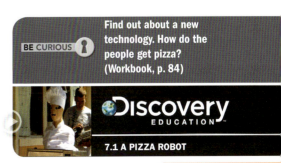

BE CURIOUS Find out about a new technology. How do the people get pizza? (Workbook, p. 84)

7.1 A PIZZA ROBOT

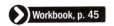
Workbook, p. 45

Unit 7 | 67

Using TECHNOLOGY

Listening: They're always coming out with something new.

1. Do you and your friends play video games? What do you play?

2. 🔊 7.04 Listen to Jenna and Karl talk about a video game. Who wants to work with computers in the future?

3. 🔊 7.04 Listen again. Are the sentences true (*T*) or false (*F*)?

   1. Karl has a new game console. ___
   2. There aren't any boy characters in Cyber Chase. ___
   3. Jenna and Karl play Ocean World. ___
   4. Jenna wants a game console for her birthday. ___
   5. Karl thinks Jenna should get a Ztron 2100. ___
   6. Karl is taking a computer class. ___

Vocabulary: Technology verbs

4. 🔊 7.05 Match the pictures with the correct sentences. Then listen and check your answers.

   1. _c_ To see the bottom of the web page, **scroll down**. To go back to the top, **scroll up**.
   2. ___ **Click on** the item you want.
   3. ___ To see more of the city on the map, **zoom out**. To look at your street, **zoom in**.
   4. ___ You can **sign into** your web page from any computer. Don't forget to **sign out** when you're done!
   5. ___ Do you **shut down** your computer at night?
   6. ___ **Turn on** your computer with the power button.
   7. ___ I **back up** my files every day.

5. **YOUR TURN** Work with a partner. Tell your partner how to do one of these things on a computer. Use the phrases in Exercise 4.

   | listen to music | read a blog | watch a video | write an email |

   > Turn on your computer. Then sign into your email account. Next, . . .

68 | Unit 7

Grammar: First conditional with *will* (*not*), *may* (*not*), and *might* (*not*)

6. Complete the chart.

Use the first conditional to show results or possible results of future actions. Use if *and the simple present in the main clause and* will (not), may (not), *or* might (not) *and the base form of a verb in the result clause.*
Statements
You**'ll see** all of the choices **if** you **zoom out**.
If I **make** games, they **won't be** boring.
_____ I **ask** my parents, they **might get** it for me for my birthday.
I **may not get** the Ztron 2100 _____ a newer model **comes** out.
Questions
What kind of games _____ you **make if** you**'re** a designer?   Action games.
If I **beat** you, **will** you **do** my homework?   Yes, I **will**. / No, I _____.

> Check your answers: Grammar reference, p. 112

NOTICE IT
The *if* clause can come at the beginning or end of the sentence. Use a comma after the *if* clause when it comes at the beginning.
If you scroll down, you'll see more characters.
You'll see more characters *if you scroll down.*

7. Circle the correct words.
1. If Joe (**learns**) / **might learn** to write code, he **gets** / **might get** a great tech job.
2. If my parents **get** / **will get** a new computer, they **don't buy** / **won't buy** a tablet.
3. You **don't lose** / **won't lose** your files if you **back** / **may back** them up.
4. I **buy** / **may buy** a new smartphone if I **get** / **will get** enough money for my birthday.
5. **Will I get** / **Do I get** to your blog if I **click on** / **will click on** this link?
6. If my computer **stops** / **will stop** working, I **don't finish** / **may not finish** my homework.
7. If you **decide** / **will decide** to get a printer, which one **do you buy** / **will you buy**?
8. Your tablet **shuts down** / **will shut down** if you **click on** / **will click on** that.

Get it **RIGHT!**
Do not use the simple present in the main clause with the first conditional.
I'll win if we play that game.
NOT: ~~I win if we play that game.~~

8. Complete the paragraph with the simple present or *will* (*not*).

If I ¹ _pass_ (pass) all of my exams, my parents ² _____ (buy) me a new tablet. If I ³ _____ (get) a new tablet, I ⁴ _____ (start) my own website. I ⁵ _____ (post) a video of my dog riding a skateboard if I ⁶ _____ (make) my own website. If one million people ⁷ _____ (like) my video, I ⁸ _____ (be) famous! I ⁹ _____ (not be) famous if no one ¹⁰ _____ (watch) my video. If I ¹¹ _____ (fail) any of my exams, my parents ¹² _____ (not buy) me a tablet. I should start studying!

Speaking: A lot of *Ifs*!

9. YOUR TURN Ask and answer questions with the ideas below or your own ideas. Use *will* (*not*), *may* (*not*), or *might* (*not*).

If I have a website in the future, . . .   If I buy a computer in the future, . . .
If I make a video in the future, . . .

> What will you post if you have a website in the future?

> If I have a website, I'll post funny videos.

Workbook, pp. 46–47

Tech TRENDS

Conversation: Using your cell phone

1. **REAL TALK** Watch or listen to the teenagers. How many think their cell phones are important? How many don't think they're important? Write the numbers.

Important	Not important

2. **YOUR TURN** How important is *your* cell phone? Tell your partner.

3. Kendra is telling her grandmother how to make a call on a smartphone. Listen and complete the conversation.

USEFUL LANGUAGE: Asking for and giving instructions

you need to | all you have to | how do I | How does it work?

Grandma: Can I borrow your phone to **call Grandpa**?
Kendra: Sure. Here's my smartphone.
Grandma: ¹_____
Kendra: First, ²_____ press the round button to turn it on.
Grandma: Like this?
Kendra: Yes. That's it. See . . . it's a touch screen. Now, click on the **phone** icon.
Grandma: OK. So, ³_____ **make a call**?
Kendra: **Click on the contacts icon and scroll down to Grandpa's name.**
Grandma: OK. Now what?
Kendra: ⁴_____ do is **click on his name**.
Grandma: I see. That was easy!

4. Practice the conversation with a partner.

5. **YOUR TURN** Repeat the conversation in Exercise 3, but change the words in purple. Use the information in the chart for one conversation and your own ideas for another.

		My ideas
Task	text Aunt Linda	
Type of icon	text message	
Task	send a text	
Step 1	scroll down to Aunt Linda's name and click on it	
Step 2	type your text and click on "send"	

70 | Unit 7

TechIt Question of the Week:

How do you think people will listen to music in the future?   Marcus Howard   posted 10/18

In my opinion, people will listen to music from computer chips in their clothing. One reason is that it will be an easy way to listen to music. People won't need to carry MP3 players or even smartphones for music. Small computer chips will be in sunglasses, hats, jackets, and shirts. Another reason is that some of this technology exists already. For example, you can buy sunglasses that play music. If this trend continues, it will be popular in the future. In conclusion, I think people will listen to music in their clothing, and it will be great!

👍 2   👎 0

Reading to write: An opinion paragraph

6. Look at the title and the photo. How does Marcus think people will listen to music in the future? Read his paragraph to check.

> ● *Focus on* **CONTENT**
> In an opinion paragraph, include:
> - **A** an introduction to the topic and your opinion
> - **B** reasons for your opinion
> - **C** facts and examples to support your reasons
> - **D** a conclusion with your opinion

7. Read Marcus's paragraph again. Label the sentences in the paragraph with the items in the Focus on Content box (A–D).

> ● *Focus on* **LANGUAGE**
> You can use these phrases in opinion pieces:
> To give opinions: **In my opinion,**   **I think (that)**
>   **I believe (that)**
> To give reasons: **One reason**   **Another reason**
>   **is (that)**   **is (that)**
> To conclude: **In conclusion,**   **For these reasons,**

8. Find examples of the phrases in the Focus on Language box in Marcus's paragraph.

9. Complete the paragraph.

| another reason is that | I believe that | one reason is that |
| for these reasons | in my opinion | |

¹_____, people will ride in cars without drivers in the future. ²_____ it will make streets safer. The cars will drive themselves with new technology. If people don't drive, accidents won't happen. ³_____ it will save people a lot of money. The cars will be electric, and people won't have to buy gas. ⁴_____ this will happen because the technology already exists. ⁵_____, people won't drive cars in the future.

✏️ Writing: Your opinion paragraph

❑ PLAN
Choose one of the topics about the future or your own idea. Write notes about it.

How do you think people will . . . in the future?

communicate with each other	listen to music
read books	shop
travel	use their smartphones

Topic and opinion: _____

Reason	Fact / Example

❑ WRITE
Write an opinion paragraph about your topic. Use your notes to help you. Write at least 80 words.

❑ CHECK
Check your writing. Can you answer "yes" to these questions?

- Is information for each category from the Focus on Content box in your paragraph?
- Do you use the expressions from the Focus on Language box correctly?

▶ Workbook, pp. 48–49

Television Grows Up... and Down!

People in every country and every culture watch television. You watch TV differently than your parents and grandparents did. And TV watching will probably be different in the future.

The story of TV started over 80 years ago. In 1936, there were only about 200 televisions. Sixty years later, there were one billion TVs worldwide. The first TVs were big, square boxes, and the TV shows were in black and white. People had to get off the couch to turn on the TV and change the channel with a button on the front of the TV. Color TVs arrived in the 1950s. Today, all TVs are in color, and people change the channel with remote controls. And there are more channels. When TV started, there were only a few channels, and now there are hundreds!

In 1973, the first big-screen TV was in stores. Today, TVs are getting bigger – and smaller. People have huge flat-screen TVs, and some have surround sound. It's like being at a movie theater at home. "TVs" are also getting smaller. Many people watch TV shows on their tablets and smartphones. Some shows are only available online.

How will people watch TV in the future? Some newer inventions are 3D television and smart TVs with Wi-Fi connections. Some people say our TVs at home will get even bigger, while the gadgets we watch TV on will get smaller; for example, there are "TV watches" and "TV glasses." Most people agree that TV watching will definitely stay popular.

DID YOU KNOW...?
The remote control arrived in 1956. Surround sound, sound that comes from speakers instead of just the TV, was first available for TVs in 1982.

Culture: How we watch TV

1. **Look at the photos. How are TVs today different than they were in the past?**

7.08

2. **Read and listen to the article. What is the main idea?**

   a. how we watch TV today

   b. the history of TV watching

   c. the future of TV watching

3. **Read the article again. Are the sentences true or false? Write *T* (true), *F* (false), or *NI* (no information).**

   1. The first TVs were in color and black and white. ___

   2. In 1996, there were about one billion TVs in the world. ___

   3. Today, there are over 500 TV channels. ___

   4. Big TVs aren't popular today because people watch shows on their phones. ___

   5. There are some shows you can only watch online. ___

   6. In the future, everyone will watch 3D TV shows. ___

4. **YOUR TURN** Work with a partner. How do you watch TV now? How do you think you'll watch TV in the future?

Workbook, p. 85

BE CURIOUS Find out about Napster. What is it? (Workbook, p. 85)

7.3 MUSIC SHARING

UNIT 7 REVIEW

Vocabulary

1. Label the photos with the correct words.

1. _____   3. _____

2. _____   4. _____

2. Circle the correct words.

1. How often do you **scroll up / back up** your files?
2. If you **zoom in / sign into**, you can see my house on the map.
3. Will you please **turn on / shut down** my computer when you're done with it?
4. **Click on / Zoom out** that link to see the photos I posted.

Grammar

3. Write sentences about the future with *will* or *won't* and the word in parentheses.

1. Everyone works at home. (probably)
   Everyone will probably work at home.
2. People have robots in their houses. (perhaps)
   _____
3. Students don't use flash drives. (definitely)
   _____
4. We go to the moon for vacation. (maybe)
   _____

4. Match the phrases to make sentences.

1. If you're going to be late, ___
2. If you get a smaller computer, ___
3. If I don't study tonight, ___
4. What will you do ___

a. if your computer breaks?
b. I won't pass my test tomorrow.
c. will you send me a text message?
d. it will be easier to carry.

Useful language

5. Circle the correct answers.

1. **A:** This is a great new video game.
   B: How does it **work / need / do**?
2. **A:** **What / How / Who** do I send an email from my phone?
   B: First, sign into your email account.
3. **A:** Can you help me download this app?
   B: Sure. First, you **need to / click on / will to** go to the app store.
4. **A:** How do I shut down my tablet?
   B: All you **like to / don't have to / have to** do is hold that button down for a few seconds.

PROGRESS CHECK: Now I can . . .

- ☐ talk about computers and technology.
- ☐ make predictions about the future.
- ☐ talk about how to use technology.
- ☐ ask for and give instructions.
- ☐ write an opinion paragraph.
- ☐ talk about how I watch TV today and in the future.

CLIL PROJECT

7.4 The Secret of the Pyramids, p. 119

Unit 7 | 73

8 The CHOICES We MAKE

BE CURIOUS

A School at Home

What are you going to do when you leave school?

Time for an Adventure!

1. What decision do you think this person has to make?

2. What decisions do you have to make in your life?

3. What do you do when you have to make a difficult decision?

UNIT CONTENTS

Vocabulary Life events; containers and materials
Grammar *be going to* and *will*; present continuous and simple present for future
Listening An eco-project

Vocabulary: Life events

1. Match the pictures (a–j) with the correct words and phrases.

1. _h_ be born
2. ___ finish school
3. ___ get a job
4. ___ get married
5. ___ get your driver's license
6. ___ go to college
7. ___ go to school
8. ___ have children
9. ___ retire
10. ___ take a year off

2. Listen, check, and repeat.

3. In which order do people usually do the life events in Exercise 1?

> First, people are born. Then they go to school. After that . . .

Speaking: About someone's life

4. **YOUR TURN** Work with a partner. Tell your partner about a parent's life or the life of another relative or adult you know. What do they have in common?

> My mother was born in 1967. She went to school in Durango, Mexico. She went to college at the University of Texas. After college, she got a job at . . .

> My Uncle Jim was born in 1967, too. But he went to school in . . .

Workbook, p. 50

Reading Life in the Outback; Farah's Application Letter; A Summer in Alaska
Conversation Agreeing and disagreeing
Writing An application letter

Unit 8 | 75

UNUSUAL LIVES

Life in the Outback

by Lauren Birch

The outback is a large area in the middle of Australia. Not many people live there, and most of them are sheep farmers. Matt Clark lives on a "sheep station" with his parents and sister. I interviewed Matt to find out about life in the outback.

Q: Do you work?

A: Yes. I help my parents on the farm and take care of the sheep. It's very hard, but I love it!

Q: Where do you go to school?

A: My sister and I go to the "school of the air." We have classes with other kids and a teacher on our computer. We can see and hear each other with web cams. We take quizzes and tests online, and we also email homework to our teacher.

Q: How do you see friends?

A: My friends live far away, but we're lucky because my family has a small airplane. We fly to the nearest town every month to see friends and go shopping. My school has special events, too. I'm going to go to a camp next month!

Q: What are you going to do after you finish school? Will you stay on the farm?

A: I'm going to study agriculture in college in Sydney. But I think I'll come back here to live. I was born here, and this is my home.

> **DID YOU KNOW...?**
> About 60,000 people live in the outback, and there are over 70 million sheep!

Reading: An interview about life in the outback

1. Look at the photos. Where do you think it is? Would you want to live there?

2. Read and listen to the article. Why does the reporter interview Matt?

   a. to find out about an unusual school

   b. to find out about life on a sheep farm

   c. to find out about his college plans

3. Read the article again. Are the sentences true (*T*) or false (*F*)? Correct the false sentences.

   1. Most Australians live in the center of Australia. ___

   2. Matt works with his parents. ___

   3. Matt flies in a plane to get to school. ___

   4. Matt's friends don't live near his sheep station. ___

   5. Matt's family goes to a town every week. ___

   6. Matt plans to leave his home and return in the future. ___

4. **YOUR TURN** Work with a partner. Answer the questions.

   1. How is Matt's life different from your life?

   > Matt's life is different from mine because he has to work, and . . .

   2. What do you think are the positive and negative things about life in the outback?

   > One positive thing is . . .

76 | Unit 8

Grammar: *be going to* and *will*

5. Complete the chart.

Use be going to to talk about plans in the future.
Use will to talk about predictions and unplanned decisions.

be going to	will
Wh- questions and answers	
What **are** you **going to do**?	Where **will** he **live**?
I'm _____ study agriculture.	He**'ll live** in the outback.
I'm **not going to study** history.	He _____ **live** in Sydney.
Yes/No questions and answers	
Is he **going to study** history?	_____ you **stay** here?
Yes, he _____. / No, he **isn't**.	Yes, I **will**. / No, I **won't**.

> Check your answers: Grammar reference, p. 113

Say it RIGHT!

The *i* in **will** is a short *i* (/ɪ/), and the *e* in **we'll** is a long *e* (/e/). However, in speaking, **will** and **we'll** often sound alike. They both can sound like /wɪl/. Listen to the sentences.
I will get married to Tom next year.
We'll get married in May.
Ask and answer the questions in Exercise 6 with a partner. Pay attention to the pronunciation of **will** and **we'll**.

6. Match the questions with the answers.

1. _e_ Will Sheila retire next year?
2. ___ When are you going to go to college?
3. ___ Will you get your driver's licenses in June?
4. ___ Are Tom and Rita getting married next month?
5. ___ When will you finish school?
6. ___ Is Lily going to have children?

a. No, they're not.
b. Yes, she is.
c. I'm going to start in September.
d. We'll be done in a year.
e. Yes, she will.
f. No, we won't. We'll get them in July.

7. Complete the conversation with the correct form of *be going to* for future plans or *will* for predictions and unplanned decisions.

Mom: I'm worried about Neil.
Dad: Why? What's the problem?
Mom: He says he ¹ *is going to get* (get) an after-school job.
Dad: That ² _____ (be) really difficult! ³ _____ he _____ (stop) playing soccer?
Mom: No, he ⁴ _____ (stay) on the team.
Dad: When ⁵ _____ he _____ (study)?
Mom: I don't know. I don't think he should get a job until the summer.
Dad: I agree! Maybe he ⁶ _____ (change) his mind. I ⁷ _____ (talk) to him tonight.
Mom: You can try, but he probably ⁸ _____ (not listen) to you.

Speaking: Future plans and predictions

8. **YOUR TURN** Work with a partner. First, tell your partner about what you are going to do or not going to do in the future. Then give predictions about what you will or won't do.

> I'm going to take a year off when I finish school. I'm not going to start college right away. I think I'll go to Brazil. I'll probably go to the rain forest. I don't think I'll go to Rio . . . .

NOTICE IT

Think, *probably*, and *maybe* are often used with **will** for predictions and unplanned events.
He **thinks** he'll live in the outback.
He **probably won't live** in Sydney.
Maybe they'll **get** married next year.

BE CURIOUS Find out about children who are homeschooled. What are some subjects they study? (Workbook, p. 86)

8.1 A SCHOOL AT HOME

> Workbook, p. 51

Cleaning UP

Listening: An eco-project

1. Do you know anyone who took a year off after finishing high school? What did he or she do?

2. Listen to Olivia tell Dan about her sister's plans for a year off. What are her sister's plans?

3. Listen again. Circle the correct answers.

   1. Olivia's sister is going to _____.
      a. Costa Rica　　　　b. Europe
   2. She's going to _____.
      a. help sea turtles　　b. pick up trash
   3. She'll probably work in _____.
      a. a surf shop　　　　b. a restaurant
   4. Olivia wants to _____ after she finishes high school.
      a. travel in Europe　　b. work in Paris
   5. Dan wants to work _____ before he goes to college.
      a. on an eco-project　b. at home

Vocabulary: Containers and materials

4. Look at the pictures. Write the phrases next to the correct numbers. Then listen and check your answers.

   | a cardboard box | a glass bottle | a metal can | a plastic bottle |
   | a cloth bag | ✓ a glass jar | a paper bag | a plastic carton |

   1. _a glass jar_　　　　5. _____
   2. _____　　6. _____
   3. _____　　7. _____
   4. _____　　8. _____

5. Work with a partner. Answer the questions.

   1. What things come in the containers in Exercise 4?

   > Peanut butter comes in a glass jar or a plastic jar.

   > Pasta sauce does, too.

   2. Do you recycle containers in your home? What do you recycle?

   > In my home, we recycle . . .

Grammar: Present continuous and simple present for future

6. Complete the chart.

As with be going to, use the present continuous to talk about future plans. Use the simple present to talk about scheduled future events.

Present continuous	Simple present
Wh- questions and answers	
Why _____ she **going** there?	When _____ she **start** the project?
She**'s taking** a year off.	She **starts** next week.
She**'s not traveling**.	She **doesn't start** tomorrow.
Yes/No questions and answers	
_____ they **helping** the turtles?	**Does** class **start** in five minutes?
Yes, they **are**. / No, they _____.	Yes, it _____. / No, it **doesn't**.

> Check your answers: Grammar reference, p. 113

7. Complete the sentences with the present continuous or simple present.

I ¹ _'m going_ (go) to a class at the recycling center next week. The class ² _____ (be) on Tuesday. It ³ _____ (start) at 10:00 a.m., and it ⁴ _____ (end) at 4:00 p.m. My friend Vic ⁵ _____ (take) the class with me. We ⁶ _____ (not drive) to the recycling center. We ⁷ _____ (walk). Two people ⁸ _____ (teach) how to make chairs out of recycled cardboard boxes. I ⁹ _____ (not collect) boxes for the class because the recycling center ¹⁰ _____ (provide) the boxes next week.

Get it RIGHT!

Use the present continuous, not *will*, to talk about future arrangements.
I'm going to Italy on July 15.
NOT: ~~I'll go to Italy on July 15.~~

8. Correct the mistakes in the underlined words.

1. My roommate and I <u>recycle</u> our metal cans tomorrow.

2. The class <u>started</u> at 8:00 a.m. tomorrow.

3. I'm excited because I<u>'ll volunteer</u> at a recycling center next month.

4. We <u>are having</u> a meeting for the eco-project at 11:00 next Tuesday.

5. My sister and I <u>will go</u> to Costa Rica on May 10.

Speaking: Reuse it!

9. YOUR TURN Choose a container from the Vocabulary on page 78, and think of something you can make out of it. Then plan a class to teach people how to make the object. Fill out the chart.

Type of container	
What you will make	
Date of the class	
Where the class is	
When the class will start	
When the class will end	

10. Work with a partner. Tell your partner about your class. Your partner asks questions.

> In my class, I'm teaching people how to make flower vases out of plastic bottles.

> How many vases are you making?

Workbook, pp. 52–53

REAL TALK
8.2 WHAT ARE YOU GOING TO DO WHEN YOU LEAVE SCHOOL?

Our FUTURES

Conversation: I'm going to get a degree.

1. **REAL TALK** Watch or listen to the teenagers. Check (✓) the things they are going to do when they leave school.

   ☐ be the leader of a country   ☐ play a sport
   ☐ buy something   ☐ study a language
   ☐ get a driver's license   ☐ visit someone
   ☐ have children   ☐ volunteer somewhere
   ☐ marry someone   ☐ work

2. **YOUR TURN** What are *you* going to do when you leave school? Tell your partner.

3. Listen to Lenny and Katie talking about their plans for when they finish school. Complete the conversation.

USEFUL LANGUAGE: Agreeing and disagreeing

Absolutely!   I disagree   I suppose you're right.   Maybe, but I think

Katie: I can't believe we'll finish school **in two years**! What are you going to do then?

Lenny: I'm definitely going to college.

Katie: What are you going to study?

Lenny: I think I'll study **marine biology**!

Katie: Wow! That's going to be difficult.

Lenny: ¹_____ I'll love the **science** classes, so it won't be too hard. What about you?

Katie: I'm going to take a year off. I want to volunteer at **a recycling center.** I think it's important.

Lenny: ²_____ Not enough people care about helping **the environment**.

Katie: Well, ³_____. A lot of people do things to help **the environment**.

Lenny: ⁴_____

4. Practice the conversation with a partner.

5. **YOUR TURN** Repeat the conversation in Exercise 3, but change the words in purple. Use the information in the chart for one conversation and your own ideas for another.

		Your ideas
Finish school	in May	
Subject to study	engineering	
Type of classes	math	
Where to volunteer	an animal shelter	
Who/What to help	animals	

80 | Unit 8

To: Morton@net.cup.org
From: FarahA@net.cup.org
Subject: Application letter

Dear Mr. Morton:

I am interested in volunteering at Clinton Hospital this summer. One day, I want to be a doctor and get a job in a hospital. I'm going to college in the fall, and I'm going to study medicine.

I'd like to help sick people. My mother was sick last year, and she had wonderful doctors. This inspired me to become a doctor. I want to help people have healthier lives.

For these reasons, I'd like to volunteer at your hospital. I'd work in any area, but I'd rather work with patients. Thank you for considering me for this volunteer position.

Sincerely,

Farah Ajam

Reading to write: An application letter

6. Look at the photo of Farah. What kind of job do you think she wants in the future? Read the email to check.

> ◉ *Focus on* **CONTENT**
> When you write an application letter, include this information:
> - **1** The position you're interested in
> - **2** Your long-term goals
> - **3** Your motivation for wanting the position
> - **4** Repeat the position you're interested in
> - **5** Thank the person you're writing to

7. Read Farah's letter again. What information does she include for each step in the Focus on Content box? Write the numbers by the sentences.

> ◉ *Focus on* **LANGUAGE**
> *want, would like ('d like), would rather ('d rather)*
> Use the infinitive form of a verb after **want** and **would like** to talk about things you want in the future.
> - He **wants to be** a scientist. He**'d like to work** with animals.
> Use the base form of a verb after **would rather** to talk about a preference.
> - I don't want to work in a hospital. **I'd rather work** in a doctor's office.
> - **I'd rather work** in a doctor's office **than** in a hospital.

8. Find examples in Farah's letter of the expressions in the Focus on Language box.

9. Complete the sentences with the infinitive or base form of the verbs.

1. Dina and Marcos want _____ (get) married in the spring.
2. I'd rather _____ (use) these cardboard boxes than throw them away.
3. Jenny would like _____ (retire) at age 60.
4. We don't want _____ (go) to college right away. We'd rather _____ (take) a year off first.
5. I'd like _____ (help) people learn about recycling.

Writing: Your application letter

◻ PLAN

First, think about a volunteer position that interests you. Choose one of these volunteer opportunities or use your own idea. Take notes.

a day-care center	a park
a library	a sea turtle program
a recycling center	

The position: _____

Your long-term goals	Your motivation
_____	_____
_____	_____
_____	_____

◻ WRITE

Write an application letter for the volunteer opportunity. Use your notes to help you. Write at least 80 words.

◻ CHECK

Check your writing. Can you answer "yes" to these questions?

- Is information for each category from the Focus on Content box in your letter?
- Do you use *want*, *would like*, and *would rather* correctly?

Workbook, pp. 54–55

A SUMMER IN ALASKA

Do you have summer plans? Are you looking for an interesting experience? Then do something different and discover Alaska. We organize summer activities for young people. Help others and gain experience in a possible future career! Here are our three most popular programs.

A MARINE VOLUNTEER
Work with professional ocean scientists at an aquarium and wildlife rescue center. You'll learn about octopuses, sea lions, and other ocean animals. You'll learn from the scientists as they study these animals. Volunteers help with research and animal rescue, and they teach others about marine life. This is a great first step to a career in marine biology!

B PARK VOLUNTEER
Work in one of the many parks in Alaska. You'll stay in a cabin right in the park and use public showers and a dining room near your cabin. You'll help keep the park clean, and you'll learn a lot about Alaska's wild animals, like bears and moose. Many volunteers will take park visitors on hikes and tell them about Alaska's plants and animals. This is an excellent experience for people interested in a job in conservation.

C COMMUNITY VOLUNTEER
Work and live in a local Alaskan community. You can work at a school and help children with their schoolwork and teach them computer skills. You'll even have the chance to start your own program. For example, you could start a recycling program or an afterschool club. You'll teach others, and you'll also learn about life in the community. It is a good experience for people interested in a teaching career.

Culture: Volunteer programs in Alaska

1. **Look at the photos of volunteer activities in Alaska. What do you see? What do you think the volunteers do for each job?**

2. **Read and listen to the article. Match the volunteer programs in the article (A–C) with the future careers (1–3).**

   1. a conservationist ___
   2. a teacher ___
   3. a marine biologist ___

3. **Read the article again. Answer the questions.**

   1. Who are the volunteer projects for? _____
   2. Where do park volunteers live? _____
   3. In which program can you start your own project? _____
   4. Which programs involve animals? _____
   5. Which programs involve teaching others? _____

4. **YOUR TURN** Work with a partner. Which place would you like to volunteer? Why? Do you know of any similar projects in your city or country?

   > I'd like to volunteer at a park because I love nature.

   > In my country, there's a . . .

DID YOU KNOW...?
Some high schools in the United States, Canada, and other countries require students to do volunteer work before they finish school.

BE CURIOUS Find out about someone who wants to have an adventure. What are some things she might do? (Workbook, p. 87)

Discovery EDUCATION
8.3 TIME FOR AN ADVENTURE!

82 | Unit 8

UNIT 8 REVIEW

Vocabulary

1. Complete the sentences with the words and phrases.

   | finish school | get a job |
   | get a driver's license | go to college |

   1. My sister is going to _____ in Boston next year.
   2. You have to take a test before you can _____ and have a car.
   3. Amy would like to _____ at a computer design company.
   4. I'll _____ in May. Then I'm going to work during the summer.

2. Complete the name of each container and the material it is made from.

   1. M _ _ _ _   C _ _   2. P _ _ _ _   B _ _

   3. G _ _ _ _   J _ _   4. C _ _ _ _   B _ _

Grammar

3. Circle *be going to* for future plans or *will* for predictions.

   Mark: What ¹**will you / are you going to** do this summer?

   Jenny: My cousin from Canada ²**will / is going to** visit us in June, and we ³**will / are going to** go on a trip to the mountains.

   Mark: Do you think you'll go hiking?

   Jenny: Yes, we ⁴**will / are**.

   Mark: That sounds nice. I think it ⁵**will / is going to** be fun.

   Jenny: Yeah, I know we ⁶**will / are going to** have a good time.

4. Write sentences. Use the present continuous or simple present.

   1. we / go / to a restaurant / tonight

      _____

   2. the volunteer program / start / on June 15

      _____

   3. the recycling center / close / at 10:00 p.m. tonight

      _____

   4. they / get married / in April

      _____

Useful language

5. Circle the correct answers.

   1. **A:** I think it's a good idea to volunteer somewhere before college.

      B: I suppose you're _____. It's a great experience.

      a. right   b. true   c. false

   2. **A:** That table made of plastic bottles is cool.

      B: _____. I think it's sort of ugly.

      a. I agree   b. I disagree   c. Absolutely

   3. **A:** People should retire when they're 60.

      B: _____, but I think some people like to keep working, and that's OK, too.

      a. I disagree   b. Never   c. Maybe

   4. **A:** I think everyone should recycle plastic, paper, and glass.

      B: _____!

      a. Absolutely   b. Never   c. Not now

PROGRESS CHECK: Now I can . . .

☐ identify and talk about life events.

☐ discuss future plans and predictions.

☐ talk about future plans and scheduled events.

☐ agree and disagree with someone.

☐ write an application letter.

☐ talk about places I'd like to volunteer.

REVIEW UNITS 7–8, Workbook, pp. 56–57

9 Watch OUT!

BE CURIOUS

Danger in Our Food

Have you ever had an accident?

A Deadly Job

1. What is the teen going to do?

2. Why do you think this is exciting? Do you think it's dangerous?

3. What exciting activities do you or your friends do?

UNIT CONTENTS

Vocabulary Accident and injury verbs; parts of the body
Grammar Present perfect statements with regular and irregular verbs; present perfect questions; present perfect vs. simple past
Listening I'm accident-prone.

Vocabulary: Accident and injury verbs

1. Complete the sentences with the words in the box.

bang	burn	cut	hurt	sprain
break	crash	fall off	slip	✓ trip

1. We need to move the computer cord, so I don't _____trip_____ over it.
2. Be careful! Don't _____ your finger with the knife.
3. If you _____ your leg, you'll have to use crutches.
4. Watch out! You can _____ on the ice.
5. This road is dangerous. Be careful you don't _____ your car.
6. The stove is hot. Don't _____ your hand.
7. Always wear a helmet in case you _____ your bike.
8. Look out! You're going to _____ your head!
9. If you _____ your back, you might need to see a doctor.
10. Put ice on your finger if you _____ it.

2. Listen, check, and repeat.

3. Work with a partner. Where are some common places that the accidents and injuries in Exercise 1 happen?

> People often trip over things at school.

> Yes, and they trip over things at home, too.

Speaking: It happened to me!

4. **YOUR TURN** Work with a partner. When was the last time the accidents and injuries in Exercise 1 happened to you or someone you know?

> I tripped over my dog yesterday!

> My dad cut his finger last week.

Workbook, p. 58

Reading It's Hard Being a Teen!; Your Invitation; Beware of the Amazon!
Conversation Reacting to good and bad news
Writing An email to refuse an invitation

STAY Safe!

It's Hard Being a Teen!

Being a teenager can be difficult – *and dangerous!* The most common injuries for teens are breaking their bones, banging their heads, and getting cuts and burns. Here are some common ways these injuries happen.

Bicycle Accidents

Many teens fall off their bikes. This can cause minor or serious injuries. Many bicycle injuries have happened when teens weren't wearing helmets. If you ride a bike, always wear a helmet!

Car Crashes

Teens have had more car crashes than any other age group. One problem is texting. In the United States, over 30 percent of teens have texted while driving. This causes many accidents. Don't text and drive! And always wear a seatbelt!

Kitchen Accidents

It's easy to cut a finger with a knife. However, burns are the most common kitchen injury. People have burned themselves on the stove or with hot liquids when they weren't careful. Teens need to be careful in the kitchen!

Sports Injuries

Exercise is good for you, but it can also be dangerous. Many teens get injuries when they play sports. Injuries in winter sports, like snowboarding and skiing, are very common. In the past, most snowboarding injuries have happened to people under 30. If you play sports, you'll want to wear protective equipment.

So, be careful and be safe . . . on the street, at home, and on the soccer field!

DID YOU KNOW...?
The younger you are, the faster you heal! Children and teens recover from injuries more quickly than adults.

NOTICE IT
Many accident and injury words are both nouns and verbs.
I **burned** my finger.
It was a bad **burn**.

Reading: Common teen injuries and accidents

1. Work with a partner. Look at the title, subtitles, and photos. What do you think the article is about?

2. Read and listen to the article. Where do teens often get hurt?

3. Read the article again. Check the common injuries and accidents for teens.

Common injuries	Common accidents
☐ spraining their hands	☐ crashing a car
☐ head injuries	☐ falling off a bike
☐ cuts	☐ falling down the stairs
☐ hurting their backs	☐ getting hurt playing a sport
☐ broken bones	☐ burning their hands on a stove
☐ burns	☐ tripping over something

4. **YOUR TURN** Work with a partner. Can you think of other common injuries and accidents?

> Many people bang their heads.

Grammar: Present perfect statements with regular and irregular verbs

5. Complete the chart.

Use the present perfect to talk about experiences that happened at an indefinite time in the past. Use has/have + the past participle to form the present perfect.

	Affirmative statements	Negative statements
Regular verbs	Liv **has slipped** on the ice many times. Most snowboard injuries _____ **happened** to people under 30.	Kyle _____ **burned** his hand in years. Eva**'s never burned** her hand. They **haven't crashed** a car before. I**'ve** _____ **crashed** a car.
Irregular verbs	Martin _____ **broken** his arm twice. Teens **have had** more crashes than any other age group.	Julia **hasn't cut** her finger before. Teens _____ **worn** helmets. We**'ve never seen** an accident.

Contractions   has = 's   _____ = 've

> Check your answers: Grammar reference, p. 114

6. Complete the sentences with the present perfect. The verbs in blue are irregular. Check the correct forms of these verbs on p. 121.

1. I ____'ve broken____ (broke) my arm before.
2. My parents _____ (travel) to many countries.
3. I _____ (sing) in a band for five years.
4. I _____ (slip) and _____ (fall) on the ice before.
5. My best friend _____ (write) a blog since July.
6. My cousins _____ (live) in Mexico since 2012.
7. My brother _____ (trip) over our cat many times.
8. I _____ (take) a safety class before.

7. Work with a partner. Are the sentences in Exercise 6 true for you? If not, make them negative.

> I've broken my arm before.

> Really? I've never broken my arm.

Speaking: True or false?

8. YOUR TURN Work with a partner. Say two true and two false things you have and haven't done before. Your partner guesses if they are true or false. Take turns.

> I've eaten snake.

> I think that's false.

> No, it's true!

9. Join another pair. Tell the pair what your partner has and hasn't done.

> Dan has eaten snake. He hasn't flown in a plane. He's never . . .

Spell it RIGHT!

Past participles For regular verbs:
+ **-ed**: bang → bang**ed**
+ **-d**: live → live**d**
-y → **-i** + **-ed**: study → stud**ied**
double consonant + **-ed**: trip → trip**ped**
For irregular verbs: See p. 121.

Get it RIGHT!

Do not put **never** before the verb. It goes between **has/have** and the past participle in the present perfect.
You **have never broken** your arm.
NOT: ~~You **never have broken** your arm.~~

Find out about *E. coli*. What foods can you get *E. coli* from? (Workbook, p. 88)

9.1 DANGER IN OUR FOOD

Actions and ACCIDENTS

Listening: I'm accident-prone.

1. Do you and your friends do any dangerous sports or activities? What are they?

 2. Listen to Angie and Franco talk about accidents and injuries. Who gets hurt easily?
   a. Franco
   b. Angie
   c. both Franco and Angie

 3. Listen again. Are the sentences true (*T*) or false (*F*)?
   1. Angie has broken her arm in the past. ____
   2. She has fallen off her bike. ____
   3. She doesn't wear a helmet when she rides her bike. ____
   4. She fell off a swing when she was a baby. ____
   5. She slipped in the kitchen once. ____
   6. Franco has broken his arm. ____

Vocabulary: Parts of the body

4. Match the words (a–i) with the correct parts of the body. Then listen and repeat.

   a. an ankle
   b. an elbow
   c. a foot
   d. a knee
   ✓ e. a neck
   f. a shoulder
   g. a stomach
   h. toes
   i. a wrist

1. e
2. ☐
3. ☐
4. ☐
5. ☐
6. ☐
7. ☐
8. ☐
9. ☐

5. What other parts of the body do you know? Make a list.

   eyes, a head, fingers . . .

6. **YOUR TURN** Work with a partner. Tell your partner what parts of the body you've injured. Use these verbs and your own ideas.

   | break | burn | cut | hurt | sprain |

   I've broken my wrist, and I've sprained my knee. I've also burned my fingers.

NOTICE IT
The plural of *foot* is *feet*.

88 | Unit 9

Grammar: Present perfect questions; present perfect vs. simple past

7. Complete the chart.

Use the present perfect to ask questions about experiences that happened at an indefinite time in the past. Ever is often used in Yes/No questions.

Yes/No questions	Wh- questions
Have you **ever broken** an arm? Yes, I _____. / No, I **haven't**.	What bones _____ you **broken**? My wrist, my arm, and my leg.
_____ she **ever fallen** off her bike? Yes, she **has**. / No, she _____.	Why **has** she **had** accidents? Because she's clumsy.

Remember: Use the simple past, not the present perfect, for experiences that happened at a definite time in the past.

Have you ever fallen off your bike?	Yes, I have. I **fell** off my bike yesterday.
What happened the second time?	I **slipped** and **fell**. I **broke** my wrist.

> Check your answers: Grammar reference, p. 114

8. Write questions with the present perfect. The verbs in blue are irregular. Check the correct forms of these verbs on p. 121.

1. you / ever / lose / your keys — *Have you ever lost your keys?*
2. your parents / ever / live / in another city _____
3. your / best friend / fall off / a bike _____
4. you / ever / slip on something _____
5. what bones / you / break _____
6. where / your teacher / travel _____

9. Work with a partner. Ask and answer the questions in Exercise 8.

> Have you ever lost your keys?
>
> Yes, I have.

10. Circle the correct words.

1. (It's stopped) / It stopped raining. Let's ride our bikes.
2. I've never tried / I didn't try snowboarding. I'd love to do that.
3. My mom has read / read a good book last week.
4. When have you hurt / did you hurt your foot?
5. My brother has banged / banged his knee a lot. He's accident-prone.

Say it RIGHT!

In *Wh-* questions, **have** often sounds like /əv/. Listen to the questions.

Where **have** *you been?*
What **have** *you seen?*

Pay attention to the way you pronounce **have** in Exercise 11.

Speaking: Have you ever . . . ?

11. YOUR TURN Work with a partner. Ask and answer questions in the present perfect. Use the phrases from the box or your own ideas. Add additional information in the simple past.

| climb a mountain | have a pet | try an adventure sport | try Mexican food |

> Have you ever tried an adventure sport?
>
> What sport have you tried?
>
> Yes, I have.
>
> I went globe riding two years ago. I loved it!

A Dangerous TRIP?

Conversation: Good news, bad news

 1. **REAL TALK** Watch or listen to the teenagers. Check the accidents and injuries they've had.

☐ broken an arm   ☐ cut a foot   ☐ fell out of a tree   ☐ tripped over a skateboard
☐ broken a leg   ☐ cut a hand   ☐ sprained a wrist
☐ burned a hand   ☐ fell off a bike   ☐ sprained an ankle

2. **YOUR TURN** Have *you* ever had an accident? Tell your partner.

 3. Holly is telling Theo some news. Listen and complete the conversation.

USEFUL LANGUAGE: Reacting to good and bad news
I'm sorry to hear that.   That's too bad.   That sounds like fun.   That's cool!

Theo: Hi, Holly. How's it going?
Holly: Well . . . I have good news, and I have bad news.
Theo: What happened?
Holly: I'll start with the bad news. I **fell on a ski trip** and **sprained my ankle**.
Theo: ¹_____ So, what's the good news?
Holly: I met a new friend at the hospital. She's really nice.
Theo: ²_____ But, what happened to her?
Holly: She **tripped over some shoes** and **broke her arm**.
Theo: Oh, no! ³_____
Holly: I know. But we've texted each other a lot, and we're **going to the beach** this weekend.
Theo: ⁴_____

4. Practice the conversation with a partner.

5. **YOUR TURN** Repeat the conversation in Exercise 3, but change the words in purple. Use the information in the chart for one conversation and your own ideas for another.

		My ideas
First accident	fell off my skateboard at a competition	
First injury	cut my leg	
Second accident	slipped on the stairs	
Second injury	hurt her knee	
Activity	seeing a movie	

Hi Ted,

Thanks for inviting me to the amusement park on Saturday. I'm sorry, but I can't go with you. My family is going on a trip with real danger. We're going to swim with sharks this weekend! Have you ever done that?

I've taken diving classes for two years. I've been on a lot of dives, but I've never seen sharks. Actually, it will be safe. We're going with a diving instructor, and we'll be in cages. But it's still scary! Look at the photo I sent from the diving website.

Again, I'm really sorry. Have a great time! Maybe we can go to the amusement park together in July.

Your friend,

Gary

Reading to write: An email to refuse an invitation

6. Look at the photo. What do you think Gary is going to do? Read his email to check.

⊙ Focus on CONTENT

When you refuse an invitation:
- thank the person for the invitation
- apologize at the beginning of the note
- explain why you can't accept the invitation
- apologize again at the end of the note
- suggest another time to do something

7. Read Gary's email again. Why can't he go to the amusement park? When does he suggest going to the amusement park with Ted?

⊙ Focus on LANGUAGE

You can use these phrases to refuse an invitation.
To thank someone:
Thanks for inviting me to . . .
Thank you for the invitation to . . .
To apologize and refuse:
I'm sorry, but I . . .   *I'd love to come, but . . .*
Sorry, but I'm busy . . . *I'm really sorry.*
To suggest another time:
Could we go . . . ?   *Maybe we can . . .*
How about another time?

8. Which phrases in the Focus on Language box does Gary use in his email?

9. Circle the correct words.

¹**Thanks / Sorry** for the invitation to your pool party. ²**Maybe we can / I'd love to** come, but I broke my leg last week. I can't get my cast wet, and the doctor said I have to stay off my leg for several weeks.
I'm really ³**busy / sorry**. I hope you have a great birthday and party. ⁴**How about / Thanks for** another time? ⁵**Sorry / Maybe** I can come over and swim in a few months.

Writing: Your email to refuse an invitation

▢ PLAN

Your friend invited you to an event, and you can't go. Write notes about it with your own ideas.

The event	
Why you can't go	
Another time you could go	

▢ WRITE

Write your email. Use your notes to help you. Write at least 80 words.

▢ CHECK

Check your writing. Can you answer "yes" to these questions?

- Is information for each category from the Focus on Content box in your email?

- Do you use expressions from the Focus on Language box correctly?

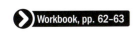

BEWARE OF THE AMAZON!

Millions of people have visited the Amazon rain forest, and more will visit in the future. They have seen tiny insects, beautiful birds, and playful monkeys. But some Amazon animals are very dangerous!

HOME | Virtual Tour | About Us | Contact Us | FAQs

BRAZILIAN WANDERING SPIDERS aren't very big, but they are very dangerous! Some say they are the most poisonous spiders in the world! Don't let this scary creature bite your hands or feet.

As you can tell from the name, **POISON DART FROGS** are also poisonous. They don't bite, but these cute and colorful frogs have poisonous skin. Their bright colors tell other animals, "Watch out! I'm poisonous. Don't eat me!" The golden poison dart frog is only about five centimeters long, but its skin has enough poison to kill 10 people!

ANACONDAS aren't small. They're very big snakes, and they never stop growing. People have seen anacondas up to 6.5 meters long. They aren't poisonous, but they are definitely dangerous. They squeeze animals and then eat them whole! People have found birds, pigs, and jaguars in their stomachs!

JAGUARS are big and beautiful cats, and they can kill. They are the third biggest cat in the world, after lions and tigers. They eat more than 80 different kinds of animals. They've even eaten anacondas!

So, who would win a fight between an anaconda and a jaguar? Either animal could win. But it's the tiny **MOSQUITO** that is the most dangerous animal in the rain forest. You can become very sick or even die from a mosquito bite.

Watch out for these dangerous Amazon animals – big and small!

Culture: Dangerous rain forest animals

1. **Look at the title and the photos. How do you think these animals are similar? How are they different?**

2. **Read and listen to the article. Which Amazon animals are small? Which ones are big?**
   9.08

3. **Read the article again. Answer the questions.**
   1. Which animals are poisonous? _____
   2. Why is the poison dart frog's skin colorful?
      _____
   3. What are some animals that anacondas have eaten?
      _____
   4. Which cats are bigger than jaguars? _____
   5. Which animal is the most dangerous?
      _____

4. **YOUR TURN** Work with a partner. What are some dangerous animals in your country? What do you know about them? Have you or has someone you know ever had an experience with a dangerous animal?

DID YOU KNOW...?
Some people in the Amazon use the poison from the poison dart frog's skin in blow darts. They use the darts to hunt and kill other animals.

BE CURIOUS Find out about some animals in Australia. Which ones are dangerous? (Workbook, p. 89)

9.3 A DEADLY JOB

UNIT 9 REVIEW

Vocabulary

1. Match the warnings with the situations.

1. The floor is wet. ___
2. That box is heavy. ___
3. The pan is hot. ___
4. This knife is very sharp. ___
5. That trail has a lot of rocks on it. ___
6. There's a book on the floor. ___
7. The ceiling is low. ___
8. The road is dangerous. ___

a. Don't fall off your bike.
b. Don't bang your head.
c. Don't hurt your back.
d. Don't crash your car.
e. Don't slip!
f. Don't cut your finger.
g. Don't trip!
h. Don't burn your hand.

2. Write the name for each part of the body.

1. _____
2. _____
3. _____
4. _____
5. _____
6. _____
7. _____
8. _____
9. _____

Grammar

3. Write negative sentences two ways.

1. I / not slip / on ice _I haven't slipped on ice._
   I've never slipped on ice.

2. Jake / not burn / his arm
   _____
   _____

3. we / not fall / off our bikes
   _____
   _____

4. my parents / not crash / their car
   _____
   _____

5. you / not hurt / your back
   _____
   _____

4. Complete the conversation with the present perfect or the simple past.

Jim: ¹_____ you ever _____ (be) scuba diving?
Lia: No, I ²_____. Have you?
Jim: Yes, I ³_____. I ⁴_____ (go) scuba diving last week.
Lia: Cool! ⁵_____ you _____ (like) it?
Jim: Yes. I ⁶_____ (love) it!
Lia: I ⁷_____ never _____ (do) any adventure sports.
Jim: Do you want to?
Lia: Not really.

Useful language

5. Circle the correct words.

1. **A:** I fell off a ladder last week.
   B: That sounds like fun. / That's too bad. Are you OK?

2. **A:** I'm going to the Amazon rain forest next month.
   B: That's cool! / That's too bad!

3. **A:** My mother slipped and broke her arm.
   B: I'm sorry to hear that. / That's cool.

4. **A:** My family is going to go hiking this weekend.
   B: I'm sorry to hear that. / That sounds like fun.

PROGRESS CHECK: Now I can . . .

☐ talk about accidents and injuries.
☐ talk about things I have and haven't done.
☐ ask, answer, and give details about things I've done.
☐ react to good and bad news.
☐ write an email to refuse an invitation.
☐ talk about dangerous animals.

10 Have Fun!

Discovery EDUCATION
BE CURIOUS

- A New York City Food Tour
- How do you celebrate your birthday?
- Punkin Chunkin!
- An Ancient Answer

1. Where are the teens?
2. What are they doing? Are they having fun?
3. What do you do for fun?

UNIT CONTENTS
Vocabulary Free-time activities; adjectives of feeling
Grammar Indefinite pronouns; *too* and *enough*
Listening I'll never forget . . .

Vocabulary: Free-time activities

1. Label the pictures with the correct phrases.

celebrate your birthday	have a party	play video games	spend time with your family
go to a dance	listen to music	read books	take photos
✓ hang out with friends	play an instrument		

1. _____ 2. _____ 3. _____

4. _____ 5. _____ 6. _____

7. <u>hang out with friends</u> and _____   8. _____ and _____

 2. Listen, check, and repeat.

3. Work with a partner. Where do you usually do the activities in Exercise 1? Are there any activities you don't do?

> I listen to music alone in my room. I don't go to dances.

Speaking: Top 5

4. **YOUR TURN** **Work with a group. What are your top five favorite activities from Exercise 1? Which one is the most popular with the group?**

> My top five favorite activities are taking photos, celebrating . . .

▶ Workbook, p. 64

Reading Jodi's Blog; Your Invitation; April Fool's!
Conversation Making and responding to suggestions
Writing An invitation

Unit 10 | 95

Weekend FUN

JODI'S BLOG

I want to go somewhere fun this weekend. I'll go anywhere in the city or close by. Does anyone have a good idea? Please post a picture if you have one!

VERONICA RAMIREZ
Go to the outdoor community swimming pool. It's a great place to spend time with your family or hang out with friends. There's something for everyone there! You can swim, sit in the sun and read a book, or go to the café for a snack. I always have a good time there!

MIKE BENSON
Why don't you listen to music on Saturday – live music! I'm in a band with my friends, and we're playing at Roks Café at 9:00 p.m. We all play different instruments. I play the drums, my friend Joe plays the piano, and Cassandra plays the guitar and sings. Come and listen to us and bring someone with you. Hey – if anyone knows about future gigs, we'll play anywhere! :)

JASON PETERS
You could go power kiting in the park. It's a cool, new sport, and it's a lot of fun! I went last weekend, and I've never done anything like it before. It's a combination of skateboarding and kite flying. It looks hard, but it's actually pretty easy. The guide helps you with everything and even takes your photo while you're in the air!

> **DID YOU KNOW...?**
> The world's largest outdoor swimming pool is in Chile. It's more than 1 km long. That's the size of 20 Olympic swimming pools.

Reading: Weekend plans

1. Work with a partner. Look at the photos. Which activity looks like the most fun?

2. Read and listen to the article. What does each person suggest for Jodi?

3. Read the article again. Who does or did these things? Check (✓) the correct names. Sometimes more than one answer is possible.

	Veronica	Mike	Jason
does an outdoor activity			
spends time with his/her family			
plays an instrument			
does a sport			
does an activity with friends			

4. **YOUR TURN** Work with a partner. What fun things can you do on the weekend in your city or in other areas?

> You can go to an amusement park and . . .

96 | Unit 10

Grammar: Indefinite pronouns

5. Complete the chart.

Use indefinite pronouns for people, places, and things that are not specific.

	People	Places	Things
some-	_____	somewhere	something
every-	everyone	everywhere	_____
no-	no one	nowhere	nothing
any-	anyone	_____	anything
	Bring **someone** with you.	I want to go **somewhere** fun.	He helps you with **everything**.
	No one has an idea.	We'll play **anywhere**.	I've never done **anything** like it.

> Check your answers: Grammar reference, p. 115

6. Replace the underlined words with an indefinite pronoun.

1. I think there's <u>a person</u> at the door. — *someone*
2. Where's Jack? He's <u>in a room</u> in the house, I think.
3. I've looked for my bag <u>in all the places</u> in my room. I can't find it <u>in any place</u>.
4. There's <u>no food</u> in the fridge.
5. Ouch! I have <u>a small object</u> in my shoe!
6. There's <u>not one place</u> to listen to music in this town.

7. Circle the correct words.

Edinburgh, Scotland, is an amazing city. ¹(**Anyone**) / **Anything** could have fun there. It's the world capital of festivals. There's a festival for ²**everything** / **everywhere**, and there's always ³**something** / **somewhere** to do. In the summer, it has the biggest arts festival in the world. There are thousands of events ⁴**everything** / **everywhere** in the city. Many of the outdoor shows are free. In the winter, the Scottish New Year party is a three-day festival that ⁵**everything** / **everyone** goes to. ⁶**Nowhere** / **No one** wants to miss it! If you don't have ⁷**nothing** / **anything** better to do this summer, go to Edinburgh!

Speaking: Fun in my town

8. **YOUR TURN** Work with a partner. Think of the following things for your town.

- an area where there's nothing to do
- a place everyone likes to go
- a place no one likes to go
- a place that sells everything for computers
- a place you can buy anything you need
- someone famous from your town
- something to do on the weekend
- somewhere to play sports

> Clinton Park is somewhere you can play sports.

> So is City Stadium.

Get it RIGHT!

Use indefinite pronouns with **any-**, not **no-**, in negative sentences.
I **didn't show anyone** the photo.
NOT: I ~~didn't show no one~~ the photo.
I **didn't go anywhere** on vacation.
NOT: I ~~didn't go nowhere~~ on vacation.
I **didn't do anything** with my friends.
NOT: I ~~didn't do nothing~~ with my ~~friends.~~

BE CURIOUS Find out about food in New York City. What is something each restaurant is famous for? (Workbook, p. 90)

Discovery EDUCATION
10.1 A NEW YORK CITY FOOD TOUR

> Workbook, p. 65

Exciting
TRIPS

Listening: I'll never forget . . .

1. Have you ever been on an interesting or exciting school trip? What did you do?

2. Listen to three teens talk about school trips. Match the people with the trips.

   1. Kate ___   a. an adventure camp
   2. Hannah ___   b. a party at a zoo
   3. Toby ___   c. a classroom at a museum

3. Listen again. Choose the correct answers.

   1. _____ got angry at the zoo.
      a. Hannah   b. A zoo guide   c. A monkey
   2. A monkey threw _____ at a party.
      a. food   b. a hat   c. a chair
   3. In the 1900s, girls and boys sat _____ of the classroom.
      a. together   b. alone   c. on different sides
   4. Hannah didn't answer _____.
      a. a math problem b. her friend   c. a boy's question
   5. Toby climbed _____ on his trip.
      a. a mountain   b. a tree   c. a tower

Vocabulary: Adjectives of feeling

4. Match the words (a–j) with the correct pictures. Then listen and repeat.

   | a. embarrassed | c. stressed | ✓e. afraid/scared | g. excited | i. angry |
   | b. surprised | d. nervous | f. tired | h. upset | j. bored |

   1. *e*   3. ☐   5. ☐   7. ☐   9. ☐
   2. ☐   4. ☐   6. ☐   8. ☐   10. ☐

5. **YOUR TURN** Work with a partner. Look at the adjectives in Exercise 4. When do you feel this way? Ask and answer questions with your partner.

> When are you afraid?

> I'm afraid when I see a spider! When are you afraid?

98 | Unit

Grammar: too and enough

6. Complete the chart.

Use **too** + adjective + infinitive to show something is more than what we want or need.
Use adjective + **enough** + infinitive to show something is what we want or need. **Not enough** shows something is less than we want or need.

too	enough
I was **too scared** _____ answer.	I was **strong** _____ **to do** it.
They were _____ **nervous to try** something.	The monkey was**n't big enough** _____ **reach** the food.

> Check your answers: Grammar reference, p. 115

7. Complete the sentences with too + adjective + infinitive.

angry   cold   ✓ scared   stressed   tired

1. Yolanda is _too scared to watch_ (watch) the horror movie!
2. I don't want to go in the water because it's _____ (swim).
3. We rode bikes all morning. We're _____ (go) on a hike.
4. You're _____ (talk) to me now. Call me when you're calmer.
5. Jeff is _____ (have) fun; he needs to relax.

8. Complete the sentences with (not) enough + the adjectives and verbs.

1. We can't have a picnic because it's _not warm enough to eat_ (warm / eat) outside.
2. Lilly is _____ (young / get) into the museum for free. She has to buy a ticket.
3. I was _____ (tired / fall) asleep on the train. I missed my stop!
4. My sister is _____ (old / drive). Maybe she can take us to the mall.
5. I'm _____ (tall / reach) my suitcase. Can you get it for me, please?

9. Circle the correct words.

1. Don't go in the ocean. It's **not dangerous enough / (too dangerous)** to swim.
2. I'm going to bed. I'm **tired enough / too tired** to watch TV.
3. Victor was sick yesterday, but he's **well enough / too well** to go to school today.
4. You can't move that box. You're **not strong enough / too strong**.
5. Jan is **not embarrassed enough / too embarrassed** to sing in the musical.

Speaking: Are you old enough?

10. YOUR TURN Work with a partner. Use these phrases to describe yourself or someone you know.

(not) hungry enough to . . .   too embarrassed to . . .
(not) old enough to . . .   too scared to . . .
(not) strong enough to . . .   too tired to . . .

> I'm not old enough to drive.

> My little brother's too scared to go snowboarding.

Say it RIGHT!

The letters **gh** can be silent or make the /f/ sound. They make the /f/ sound in **enough**. Listen to the sentence.

/haɪ/ /ɪnʌf/

The ladder isn't **high enough** to reach the window.

Pay attention to the way you pronounce **enough** in Exercise 10.

REAL TALK | 10.2 HOW DO YOU CELEBRATE YOUR BIRTHDAY?

Let's CELEBRATE!

Conversation: Birthday plans

1. **REAL TALK** Watch or listen to the teenagers. How do, did, or will they celebrate their birthdays? Number the activities in the order you hear them.

   ___ took an exam   ___ has a big party
   ___ is going to have a dance party   ___ had a pink party
   ___ prefers to celebrate at home   ___ goes on a trip

2. **YOUR TURN** How do *you* celebrate *your* birthday? Tell your partner.

3. Molly and Paul are talking about birthday plans. Listen and complete the conversation.

> **USEFUL LANGUAGE: Making and responding to suggestions**
> I'd rather | That's a great idea! | How about | Why don't we

Molly: What should we do for your birthday?
Paul: I don't know. I want to have a party and do something fun.
Molly: OK. Who are you inviting?
Paul: My **friends and a few people in my family**.
Molly: [1]_____ **go to the beach**? We can **have a picnic**.
Paul: [2]_____ do something more exciting.
Molly: OK. Let's see . . . we could **go to the water park**.
Paul: Hmm . . . I've done that several times before. I want to do something really different.
Molly: Hey, here's an idea . . . [3]_____ **paintball**?
Paul: [4]_____ Everyone will like that.
Molly: Great. I'll email the invitations.
Paul: Cool. Thanks.

4. Practice the conversation with a partner.

5. **YOUR TURN** Repeat the conversation in Exercise 3, but change the words in purple. Use the information in the chart for one conversation and your own ideas for another.

		My ideas
Who you're inviting	my cousins and my best friend	
First suggestion	go to the mountains	
Activity for first suggestion	go horseback riding	
Second suggestion	ice-skating	
Third suggestion	miniature golf	

100 | Unit 10

To: LolaP@net.cup.org
From: sara98@net.cup.org
Subject: An invitation

Hi Lola,

How were your exams? I'm glad to be done with <u>them</u>. I did well enough to pass, but the math and history <u>ones</u> were really hard.

Anyway, I'm having a party to celebrate the end of the school year, and I'd like you to come. It's on June 23 at Mario's Restaurant. It's the <u>one</u> behind the movie theater. We're meeting <u>there</u> at 7:00 p.m. We'll have pizza and listen to live music after dinner.

I invited 20 people. I hope <u>everyone</u> can come! The room is big enough for 25 people, so you can invite a friend.

On Thursday, I have to tell the restaurant how many people are coming. Please let me know by <u>then</u> if you can come.

Your friend,
Sara

Reading to write: An invitation

6. Look at the photo. What do you think Sara is inviting Lola to do? Read Sara's email to check.

> ◉ *Focus on* **CONTENT**
> When you write an invitation:
> - give the event
> - give the reason for the event
> - give the details of the event
> - ask for a response

7. Read Sara's email again. What is the event? Why is she having it? Where and when is it? What activities will there be?

> ◉ *Focus on* **LANGUAGE**
> You can use *referencing* words when you don't want to repeat a noun.
> Pronouns:
> *I bought **a guitar**, but I haven't learned to play **it**.*
> One/Ones:
> *You take great **photos**. I like the black and white **ones**.*
> Then:
> *Joe's birthday is on **Friday**. I need to buy him a gift. I hope I have time to buy something before **then**.*
> There:
> *We're meeting at the **ice-skating rink**. See you **there**!*

8. What nouns do the underlined referencing words in Sara's email refer to?

9. Circle the correct words.

1. I need a new book to read. Can you suggest any good **them / ones**?
2. I like to hang out with friends at The Get Away Café. Have you been **it / there**?
3. I have six cousins. I love to spend time with **them / then**.
4. Here's an invitation to my party. I'm sorry I didn't give **it / then** to you sooner.

 Writing: Your invitation

◯ **PLAN**
You are going to invite your friend to a fun event. Think of an event and write notes about it.

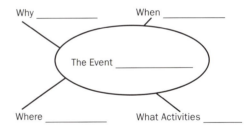

◯ **WRITE**
Write your invitation. Use your notes to help you. Write at least 80 words.

◯ **CHECK**
Check your writing. Can you answer "yes" to these questions?

- Is information for each category from the Focus on Content box in your invitation?
- Do you use referencing words correctly?

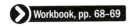

APRIL FOOL'S!

Be careful! Today is April 1. Don't listen to your friends when they say school's closed for a week. Don't run to the window if your brother tells you it's snowing. And don't believe everything you see on TV and the Internet.

It's April Fool's Day, and you don't want to be a fool!

April Fool's Day probably began in the 1500s in France when New Year's Day moved from April 1 to January 1. Of course, there wasn't any TV or Internet then, so some people didn't know about this change. People called anyone who still celebrated New Year's Day on April 1 a fool.

Playing jokes on April 1 became popular, and in the 1700s, this tradition spread to England, Scotland, and eventually the United States. Today, people celebrate April Fool's Day in many countries around the world. News shows and Internet sites enjoy the fun, too!

A British TV station has made many April Fool's jokes. In 1957, it showed a program about spaghetti growing on trees. A lot of people thought it was true and called the station to ask where they could buy the trees. In 1980, reporters said that Big Ben, the famous clock in London, had a new digital face. Everyone was angry until the reporters told them it was an April Fool's joke!

An Internet company is also famous for its April Fool's Day jokes. In 2014, it advertised a keyboard for cats to use so they could type on computers. That same year, the company said it was making a "magic hand" – a robot that types on your cell phone for you. Both inventions were jokes!

Have you ever been foolish enough to believe an April Fool's Day joke?

Culture: April Fool's Day

1. **Look at the photos. What do you see? Which ones do you think are pictures of real things?**

2. **Read and listen to the article. Which is NOT an April Fool's Day joke in the article?**

   a. A clock gets a digital face.
   b. You can buy a keyboard for your cat.
   c. You can smell things on the Internet.
   d. Spaghetti grows on trees.

3. **Read the article again. Choose the correct answers to the questions.**

   1. On April Fool's Day, people _____.
      a. don't go to school
      b. play jokes on each other
      c. have a party

   2. Before the 1500s, New Year's Day was on _____.
      a. April 1
      b. January 1
      c. two different days

   3. _____ believed the joke about spaghetti growing on trees.
      a. Everyone
      b. No one
      c. Some people

4. **YOUR TURN** Work with a partner. Think of two April Fool's Day jokes to tell people.

   > We can tell people that monkeys can talk.

   > Yes. And we can make a video . . .

DID YOU KNOW...?
One of the first April Fool's Day jokes was to send people to parties that weren't really happening.

BE CURIOUS Find out about a pumpkin-throwing competition. What are the rules? (Workbook, p. 91)

10.3 PUNKIN CHUNKIN!

UNIT 10 REVIEW

Vocabulary

1. Label the pictures with the correct phrases.

celebrate a birthday	play video games
go to a dance	read books
listen to music	take photos

1. _____

2. _____

3. _____

4. _____

5. _____

6. _____

2. Complete the sentences.

| angry | nervous | tired |
| embarrassed | scared | |

1. Susan's really _____. She went to bed late last night.
2. Tim is _____ of spiders, especially the big ones!
3. Nina is _____ about playing in her first concert tonight.
4. Julie's teacher was very _____ because Julie was late for class again.
5. Brett was _____ because he forgot his grandma's birthday.

Grammar

3. Complete the sentences with the words in parentheses and -one, -thing, or -where.

1. I like _____ (every) in this store. I want to buy it all!
2. We didn't see Ken _____ (any).
3. _____ (every) at the park had fun.
4. There is _____ (no) to eat here.

4. Complete the sentences with enough or too + adjectives and verbs.

1. I'm _____ (scared / go) into the ocean.
2. We're not _____ (strong / lift) that box.
3. He felt _____ (sick / go) to school this morning.
4. My brother runs _____ (fast / win) the race.

Useful language

5. Complete the conversation.

| How about | I'd rather | That's a great idea | Why don't we |

Shel: What do you want to do today?
Andy: ¹_____ horseback riding?
Shel: I don't think so. ²_____ do something inside.
Andy: OK. ³_____ go to the mall?
Shel: ⁴_____! We can shop and then eat lunch.

PROGRESS CHECK: Now I can . . .
- ☐ talk about free-time activities.
- ☐ talk about weekend plans.
- ☐ describe feelings and situations with *too* and *enough*.
- ☐ make and respond to suggestions.
- ☐ write an invitation.
- ☐ talk about April Fool's Day and jokes.

▶ REVIEW UNITS 9–10, Workbook, pp. 70–71

CLIL PROJECT

10.4 An Ancient Answer, p. 120

Uncover Your Knowledge
UNITS 6–10 Review Game

TEAM 1 — START

- GRAMMAR
- VOCABULARY
- USEFUL LANGUAGE

1. Tell a teammate three sentences about how to use an appliance. Use *should (not)*, *have (not)*, and *must (not)*.

2. In 30 seconds, name five appliances you can find in a kitchen.

3. Role-play a conversation with a teammate. Ask for and offer to help clean the house.

4. What technology will we have in the future? Make five predictions. Use adverbs of possibility, such as *definitely*, *certainly*, *probably*, *maybe*, and *perhaps*.

5. In 30 seconds, give five examples of computers and communications devices people use today.

6. Role-play a conversation with a teammate. Pretend one of you has never used a smartphone to text. Ask for and give instructions on how to send a text.

7. In one minute, name 10 life events.

8. Think of your favorite website. Tell a teammate how to find it on the Internet and use it. Use technology verbs.

9. Pretend you aren't familiar with today's technology. Ask a teammate for instructions on how to use a computer or tablet.

10. Have a conversation with a teammate. Talk about what you will be doing in five years. Use *be going to* and *will*.

11. Make three statements about your future using the first conditional. Use *will (not)*, *may (not)*, or *might (not)*.

TEAM 2
START

Role-play a conversation with a teammate. For every suggestion about something to do, offer a counter-suggestion. See how long you can keep the conversation going.

Role-play with a teammate. Act out five different feelings, and your teammate guesses the adjective.

Role-play a conversation with a teammate. Take turns telling each other about an accident or injury you had. Use expressions like *That's too bad* or *I'm sorry to hear that* to react to the bad news.

Tell a teammate six of your favorite free-time activities.

Give clues using indefinite pronouns to get your teammate to name a person, a place, or a thing (for example, *it's something many people enjoy watching*; *this year it will take place somewhere fun*.)

Play good news/bad news. Tell a teammate something good or bad that happened. Your teammate has to respond quickly to the news. See how many you can say in two minutes.

Point to and name nine parts of the body.

Ask a teammate four questions about his/her past. Use the question *Have you ever . . . ?* Your teammate answers.

With a teammate, make three statements about the environment and recycling. Agree and disagree with each other.

In 30 seconds, name five ways someone can get hurt. Use accident verbs.

Use the present continuous to ask a teammate about his/her future plans. Then use the simple present to ask when the events will happen.

How can you agree or disagree in a conversation? Give two examples of each.

INSTRUCTIONS:
- Make teams and choose game pieces.
- Put your game pieces on your team's START.
- Flip a coin to see who goes first.
- Read the first challenge. Can you do it correctly?

  Yes → Continue to the next challenge.

  No → Lose your turn.

The first team to do all of the challenges wins!

Units 6–10 Review | 105

Simple present review with *be* and *have*, p. 5

Use the simple present of be to identify people and give locations and dates.
Use the simple present of have to talk about possessions, characteristics, and relationships.

be	have
Wh- questions and answers	
Where **am** I? You'**re** in Quito. You'**re not** in Otavalo.	Where **do** I **have** art class? You **have** art in room 9. You **don't have** art in room 10.
Where **are** you? I'**m** in Otavalo. I'**m not** in Quito.	When **do** you **have** art class? I **have** art at 10:00. I **don't have** art at 9:00.
How old **is** he/she/it? He'**s**/She'**s**/It'**s** 14. He'**s**/She'**s**/It'**s not** 17.	What **does** he/she/it **have** for dinner? He/She/It **has** meat. He/She/It **doesn't have** fish.
Who **are** we/they? We/They **are** Maria's parents. We'**re**/They'**re** her grandparents.	What **do** we/they **have**? We/They **have** a computer. We/They **don't have** a desk.
Yes/No questions and answers	
Am I in Quito? Yes, you **are**. / No, you **aren't**.	**Do** I **have** art in room 9? Yes, you **do**. / No, you **don't**.
Are you in Otavalo? Yes, I **am**. / No, I'**m not**.	**Do** you **have** art at 10:00? Yes, I **do**. / No, I **don't**.
Is he/she/it 14? Yes, he/she/it **is**. / No, he/she/it **isn't**.	**Does** he/she/it **have** meat for dinner? Yes, he/she/it **does**. / No, he/she/it **doesn't**.
Are we/they Maria's parents? Yes, we/they **are**. / No, we/they **aren't**.	**Do** we/they **have** a computer? Yes, we/they **do**. / No, we/they **don't**.

1. Complete the sentences with the correct form of *be* or *have*. Write affirmative sentences for items with a ✔. Write negative sentences for items with an ✗.

1. We _____ dinner at 6:00 p.m. (✔)
2. Lydia _____ 17 years old. (✔)
3. Dan and Lia _____ a music class. (✗)
4. You _____ my sister. (✗)
5. _____ they at school? (✔)
6. When _____ she _____ lunch? (✔)

whose and possessives, p. 7

Use whose to ask about possession.
Use a name/noun + 's, a possessive adjective, or a possessive pronoun to show possession.

Whose	Possessive 's or s'
Whose computer is it? / **Whose** is it?	It's Dad**'s** computer.
Whose shoes are they? / **Whose** are they?	They're our grandmother**'s** shoes.
Whose house is that? / **Whose** is that?	That's our grandparents**'** house. That's Lois**'s** house.
Possessive adjectives	**Possessive pronouns**
It's **my/your/his/her/our/their** computer.	It's **mine/yours/his/hers/its/ours/theirs**.
They're **my/your/his/her/our/their** shoes.	They're **mine/yours/his/hers/its/ours/theirs**.
That's **my/your/his/her/its/our/their** house.	That's **mine/yours/his/hers/its/ours/theirs**.

2. Circle the correct words to complete the sentences.

1. This photo is **my** / **mine**.
2. **Who's** / **Whose** car is that?
3. I have **Sheila's** / **hers** pen.
4. **Yours** / **Your** phone is small.
5. That house is **our** / **ours**.
6. Look at **their** / **theirs** faces.

106 | Unit 1

Simple present review, p. 15

Use the simple present to talk about routines, habits, and facts.

Wh- questions	Affirmative answers	Negative answers
What movies **do** you **like**?	I **like** horror movies.	I **don't like** musicals.
How often **does** he/she **go** to the movies?	He/She **goes** to the movies three times a week.	He/She **doesn't go** to the movies on Sundays.
Yes/No questions	**Short answers**	
Do you **like** horror movies?	Yes, I/we **do**.	No, I/we **don't**.
Does he/she **go** to the movies?	Yes, he/she **does**.	No, he/she **doesn't**.
Contractions do not = **don't**	does not = **doesn't**	

1. **Complete the conversation with the simple present.**

   Dan: Hey, Jim. ¹ _Do_ you _work_ (work) at the movie theater on Elm Street?
   Jim: Yes, I ² _____.
   Dan: ³ _____ it _____ (show) animated movies?
   Jim: Yes, it ⁴ _____. There is one there now, *Super Kid*. Why?
   Dan: My brother ⁵ _____ (like) animated movies. Let's all go see it!
   Jim: OK. When?
   Dan: On Sunday. My brother ⁶ _____ (study) in the morning, so let's go at noon.
   Jim: Great. I ⁷ _____ (not work) on Sundays.

Verb + infinitive or *-ing* form (gerund), p. 17

Verb + infinitive	Verb + gerund
have, hope, need, plan, want	dislike, don't mind, enjoy, finish
They **want to watch** a drama.	Sheldon **dislikes trying** new things.
He **needs to see** who gets voted off *Big Brother*.	Leonard **enjoys trying** different things.
I **plan to go** to a movie on Saturday.	We **don't mind watching** commercials.
Verb + infinitive or *-ing* form (gerund)	
hate, like, love, prefer, start	
I **like to read** comic books. I **like reading** comic books.	
They **love to read** comic books. They **love reading** comic books.	
She **hates to watch** reality TV shows. She **hates watching** reality TV shows.	
He **prefers to get** the news online. He **prefers getting** the news online.	

2. **Put the words in the correct order to make sentences. Use the infinitive or gerund form of the underlined word. Sometimes more than one answer is possible.**

   1. about documentaries / <u>read</u> / we / like
      We like to read about documentaries. OR _We like reading about documentaries_.

   2. <u>work</u> / Denny / at 6:00 / finishes
      _____

   3. starts / in the afternoon / it / often / <u>rain</u>
      _____

   4. after school / hopes / <u>watch</u> / her favorite show / Ann
      _____

   5. movies / <u>watch</u> / on my computer / hate / I
      _____

Unit 2 | 107

GRAMMAR REFERENCE

Present continuous review; simple present vs. present continuous, p. 25

Use the present continuous to talk about activities that are happening now.

Wh- questions	Affirmative answers	Negative answers
What **am** I **doing**?	You're **playing** soccer.	You're **not playing** baseball.
What **are** you **doing**?	I'm **writing** about my life.	I'm **not writing** about my job.
What **is** he/she **doing**?	He/She **is skating**.	He/She **isn't running**.
What **are** we/they **doing**?	We/They **are watching** the fish.	We/They **aren't skating**.
Yes/No questions	**Short answers**	
Am I **playing** soccer?	Yes, you **are**.	No, you **aren't**.
Are you **writing** about Dubai?	Yes, I **am**.	No, I'm **not**.
Is he/she **skating**?	Yes, he/she **is**.	No, he/she **isn't**.
Are we/they **shopping**?	Yes, we/they **are**.	No, we/they **aren't**.

Remember: Use the simple present for facts, habits, and routines.

At night, the water **changes** color. = routine
Look! The water **is changing** color. = activity happening now

1. Circle the correct words to complete the sentences.

   1. Margot **shop / shops / is shopping / are shopping** in a sporting goods store right now.
   2. Dan and Eduardo **play / plays / is playing / are playing** soccer every Saturday.
   3. Where **do / does / am / are** you usually **go / goes / going / to go** after class?
   4. **Do / Does / Is / Are** she **buy / buys / buying / to buy** a tablet right now?
   5. We **eat / eats / am eating / are eating** at the food court in the mall now.
   6. **Do / Does / Is / Are** Lexi usually **buy / buys / buying / to buy** her books online?

Quantifiers, p. 27

Use quantifiers to show the amount of something.

With countable plural nouns	With uncountable nouns
How **many** T-shirts do you have?	How **much** money do you have?
I have **some / a lot of / enough** T-shirts.	I have **some / a lot of / enough** money.
I don't have **many / any / a lot of / enough** T-shirts.	I don't have **much / any / a lot of / enough** money.
Are there **many / any / a lot of / enough** T-shirts in your dresser?	Is there **much / any / a lot of / enough** money in your bank account?
Yes, there are. / No, there aren't.	Yes, there is. / No, there isn't.

2. Circle the correct words to complete the conversation.

   A: Do you have [1]**many / any** money I can borrow?
   B: Yes, I do. How [2]**many / much** money do you need?
   A: I need [3]**any / enough** money to buy books for my class.
   B: How [4]**many / much** books do you need?
   A: I need [5]**a lot of / much** books! About 10.
   B: Well, how [6]**many / much** do they cost?
   A: I think about $300 in total.
   B: Oh, OK. Well, I can't lend you $300, but I can lend you [7]**enough / some** money. It's [8]**not a lot of / not enough**, but I can lend you $100.
   A: A: That really helps. Thanks! I can pay you back in two weeks.

Simple past statements review and *ago*, p. 35

Use simple past statements to describe things in the past and to talk about past events and activities.
Use ago to say how far back in the past something happened or was.

	Affirmative statements	Negative statements
be	I/He/She **was** MVP in 2011.	I/He/She **wasn't** MVP in 2010.
	They/We/You **were** in Brazil a week **ago**.	They/We/You **weren't** in Spain last week.
Regular verbs	I/He/She/They/We/You **played** for Mexico.	I/He/She/They/We/You **didn't play** for Spain.
	I/He/She/They/We/You **moved** a month **ago**.	I/He/She/They/We/You **didn't move** last week.
Irregular verbs	I/He/She/They/We/You **made** a solo album in 2003.	I/He/She/They/We/You **didn't make** an album in 2001.
	I/He/She/They/We/You **got** a tablet a year **ago**.	I/He/She/They/We/You **didn't get** a laptop.

For regular verbs: + -ed: work → work**ed**   + -d: live → liv**ed**
                       -y → -i + -ed: try → tr**ied**   double consonant + -ed: shop → shop**ped**

For irregular verbs: See p. 121.

1. Write statements in the simple past.

1. we / win / two medals a year ago   *We won two medals a year ago.*
2. Dennis / grow up / in Guatemala   _____
3. Cassie / be / Player of the Year in 2014   _____
4. my friends / not sing / at the party last night   _____
5. you / be / funny at the party last weekend   _____

Simple past questions review and *ago*, p. 37

Use simple past questions to ask about past things, events, and activities.
Use ago to ask how far back in the past something happened or was.

	Wh- questions and answers	*Yes/No* questions and answers
be	How **was** he/she an hour **ago**? He/She **was** happy.	**Was** he/she happy an hour **ago**? Yes, he/she **was**. / No, he/she **wasn't**.
	Where **were** they/we? They/We **were** at home.	**Were** they/we/you at home? Yes, they/we/you **were**. / No, they/we/you **weren't**.
Regular verbs	How long **ago did** I/he/she/it/they/we/you **start**? I/He/She/It/They/We/You **started** an hour **ago**.	**Did** I/he/she/it/they/we/you **start** an hour **ago**? Yes, I/he/she/it/they/we/you **did**. / No, I/he/she/it/they/we/you **didn't**.
	Why **did** I/he/she/they/we/you **carry** him? I/He/She/They/We/You **carried** him because he was hurt.	**Did** I/he/she/they/we/you **carry** him? Yes, I/he/she/they/we/you **did**. / No, I/he/she/they/we/you **didn't**.
Irregular verbs	What **did** I/he/she/they/we/you **see**? I **saw** a fire.	**Did** I/he/she/they/we/you **see** a fire? Yes, I/he/she/they/we/you **did**. / No, I/he/she/they/we/you **didn't**.
	Where **did** I/he/she/they/we/you **put** the ladder? I/He/She/They/We/You **put** it against the house.	**Did** I/he/she/they/we/you **put** the ladder against the house? Yes, I/he/she/they/we/you **did**. / No, I/he/she/they/we/you **didn't**.

2. Write questions for the answers.

1. **A:** *Where did you go last night?*   **B:** I went to a soccer game.
2. **A:** _____   **B:** I saw a famous writer at the restaurant.
3. **A:** _____   **B:** No, I wasn't at the concert. I was at home.
4. **A:** _____   **B:** Yes, I did. I studied for two hours last night.
5. **A:** _____   **B:** I wrote about my aunt because I admire her.

Past continuous, p. 45

Use the past continuous to talk about activities that were in progress in the past.

Wh- questions	Affirmative answers	Negative answers
Who **was** I **talking** to?	You **were talking** to the butler.	You **weren't talking** to the maid.
What **were** you **doing**?	I **was talking** on the phone.	I **wasn't talking** to Max.
What **was** he/she **reading**?	He/She **was reading** a newspaper.	He/She **wasn't reading** a book.
What **were** they/we **doing**?	They/We **were playing** tennis.	They/We **weren't playing** soccer.
Yes/No questions	Short answers	
Was I **talking** to the teacher?	Yes, you **were**.	No, you **weren't**.
Were you **talking** to Max?	Yes, I **was**.	No, I **wasn't**.
Was Max **reading**?	Yes, he **was**.	No, he **wasn't**.
Were they **playing** tennis?	Yes, they **were**.	No, they **weren't**.

1. Complete the questions and answers with the past continuous.

1. **A:** What _____ you _____ (do) last night at 9:00 p.m.?
   B: I _____ (listen) to music, but I _____ (not listen) to it loudly.

2. **A:** _____ Rosa _____ (watch) a detective show this afternoon?
   B: No, she _____. She _____ (clean) her bedroom.

3. **A:** _____ they _____ (chasing) their dog at 8:00 a.m.?
   B: Yes. They _____ (chase) it in the park, but they _____ (not run) very fast.

4. **A:** _____ you _____ (study) for the science test yesterday?
   B: Yes, I _____. I _____ (work) with Jorge.

Simple past vs. past continuous; *when* and *while*, p. 47

Use the past continuous for an event that was in progress.
Use the simple past for an event that interrupted the event in progress.
Use when *or* while *with the phrase in the past continuous.*
Use when *with the phrase in the simple past.*

I **was studying** (event in progress)	**when** I **saw** red lights in the sky. (event that interrupts)
While/When I **was studying**, (event in progress)	I **saw** red lights in the sky. (event that interrupts)
When it happened, (event that interrupts)	my parents **were sleeping**. (event in progress)
It **happened** (event that interrupts)	**while/when** my parents **were sleeping**. (event in progress)

2. Circle the correct words to complete the sentences.

1. Don **took / was taking** photos when a thief **stole / was stealing** his camera.
2. The phone **rang / was ringing** while Britney **watched / was watching** TV.
3. When the detective **entered / was entering** the room, the maid **cleaned / was cleaning** the house.
4. While I **read / was reading** about Easter Island, someone **knocked / was knocking** on the door.
5. Someone **screamed / was screaming** loudly when Sara and Maria **walked / were walking** their dog.

Comparative and superlative adjectives and adverbs, p. 57

Use comparative adjectives and adverbs to show how two things are different from each other.
Use superlative adjectives and adverbs to compare three or more things.

	Comparative	Superlative
Adjectives	dark → dark**er** big → big**ger** powerful → **more** powerful good → **better** bad → **worse** The Rio Negro is **darker** than the Rio Solimões.	dark → **the** dark**est** big → **the** big**gest** popular → **the most** popular good → **the best** bad → **the worst** The bathroom is **the darkest** room in the hotel.
Adverbs	fast → fast**er** slowly → **more** slowly far → far**ther** well → **better** badly → **worse** The Rio Solimões runs **more slowly than** the Rio Negro.	fast → **the** fast**est** slowly → **the most** slowly far → **the farthest** well → **the best** badly → **the worst** The water runs **the most slowly** in the summer.

1. Complete the sentences with comparative or superlative adjectives or adverbs.

1. My bedroom is *smaller than* (small) my sister's room.
2. Ramon fits _____ (well) in that chair than his father does.
3. We all eat quickly in my family, but my older brother eats _____ (quickly).
4. We stayed at _____ (bad) hotel in the city.
5. I run _____ (fast) my brother.
6. Scott is _____ (powerful) player on the team.

should (not), (not) have to, must (not), p. 59

Use should (not) for advice and recommendations. Use have to for responsibilities.
Use not have to for things that are not required. Use must for obligation. Use must not for prohibition.

Affirmative	Negative
You **should wash** dark clothes separately.	You **shouldn't wash** darker clothes with lighter ones.
She **should look** at the labels.	She **shouldn't put** it in a sunny room.
You **have to choose** the temperature first.	You **don't have to wash** it by hand.
It **has to be** cool.	It **doesn't have to be** cold.
You **must use** cold water.	You **must not (mustn't) use** hot water.
They **must follow** the directions.	They **must not (mustn't) miss** a step.

2. Complete the conversations with *should (not), (not) have to,* or *must (not)* and the verb.

stay

1. You _____ in the Hotel Flores. It's wonderful!
2. Carla _____ in a hotel on her trip. She's staying with a friend.
3. We _____ in a hotel downtown. It's really dangerous.

put

4. I _____ the dishes in the dishwasher before I go out.
5. She _____ her full name on the form. She's not allowed to use a nickname.
6. You _____ that information on the Internet. It's against the law.

will and *won't* for predictions, p. 67

Use will and won't to predict future events.

Wh- questions	Affirmative answers	Negative answers
What **will** my smartphone **do** in the future?	Perhaps it**'ll think** like a human.	It **won't drive** a car.
How **will** you/I/he/she/it/they/we **change**?	You/I/He/She/It/They/We **will be** smaller.	You/I/He/She/It/They/We **won't be** bigger.
Yes/No questions	**Short answers**	
Will my smartphone **think** like a human?	Yes, it **will**.	No, it **won't**.
Will you/I/he/she/it/they/we **change**?	Yes, you/I/he/she/it/they/we **will**.	No, you/I/he/she/it/they/we **won't**.
Contractions	I will = I'**ll** you will = you'**ll** he will = he'**ll** she will = she'**ll** it will = it'**ll** we will = we'**ll** they will = they'**ll**	

1. Complete the sentences with *will* or *won't* and the verbs in parentheses.

1. Where _____ you _____ (live) in the future?
2. Computers _____ (be) faster in five years.
3. We _____ (not buy) big phones in the future.
4. _____ Janelle _____ (study) computer science?
5. Most people _____ (not use) keyboards in a few years.

First conditional with *will (not)*, *may (not)*, and *might (not)*, p. 69

Use the first conditional to show results or possible results of future actions. Use if and the simple present in the main clause, and will (not), may (not), or might (not) and the base form of a verb in the result clause.

Statements
You**'ll see** all of the choices **if** you **zoom out**.
If I **make** games, they **won't be** boring.
If I **ask** my parents, they **might get** it for me for my birthday.
I **may not get** the Ztron 2100 **if** a new model **comes** out.
Questions
What kind of games **will** you **make if** you**'re** a designer?   Action games.
If I **beat** you, **will** you **do** my homework?   Yes, I **will**. / No, I **won't**.

2. Write sentences in the first conditional with the phrases in the box.

Main clause	Result
1. I / take / the bus / to school	I / might / be / late
2. John / buy / a computer	he / will not / get / a tablet
3. you / zoom out	you / will / see / the entire town
4. Mia and Sara / share / a computer	they / may not / finish / their homework
5. I / back up / my files	I / will not / worry

1. _____
2. _____
3. _____
4. _____
5. _____

be going to and will, p. 77

Use be going to to talk about plans in the future.
Use will to talk about predictions and unplanned decisions.

be going to	will
Wh- questions and answers	
What **are** you/we/they **going to do**? I**'m**/We**'re**/You**'re**/They**'re going to study** agriculture. He/She/It **is not going to study** history.	Where **will** you/I/he/she/it/we/they **live**? I/You/He/She/It/We/They **will live** in the outback. I/You/He/She/It/We/They **won't live** in Sydney.
Yes/No questions and answers	
Are you/we/they **going to go** to Sydney? Yes, I **am**. / Yes, we/you/they **are**. No, I**'m**/we**'re**/you**'re**/they**'re not**. **Is** he/she/it **going to study** history? Yes, he/she/it **is**. / No, he/she/it **isn't**.	**Will** you/I/he/she/it/we/they **stay** here? Yes, you/I/he/she/it/we/they **will**. No, you/I/he/she/it/we/they **won't**.

1. Write questions for the answers. Use *be going to* or *will*.

1. **A:** (when / you / study) _____
   B: I'm going to study after school.

2. **A:** (they / get married / in March) _____
   B: Yes, they will.

3. **A:** (we / drive / to the library) _____
   B: No, we aren't.

4. **A:** (where / Lea / go / to college) _____
   B: She'll go to the University of Chicago.

Present continuous and simple present for future, p. 79

As with be going to, use the present continuous to talk about future plans.
Use the simple present to talk about scheduled future events.

Present continuous	Simple present
Wh- questions and answers	
What **are** you/they/we **doing** next week? I**'m**/We**'re**/You**'re**/They**'re (not) collecting** trash.	What time **do** I/you/they/we **start**? I/We/You/They **start** at 9:00 a.m. tomorrow. I/We/You/They **don't start** at 9:00 a.m. tomorrow.
Why **is** he/she **going** there? He**'s**/She**'s taking** a year off. He**'s**/She**'s not traveling**.	When **does** he/she **start** the project? He/She **starts** next week. He/She **doesn't start** tomorrow.
Yes/No questions and answers	
Are we/you/they **helping** the turtles? Yes, we/you/they **are**. No, we**'re**/you**'re**/they**'re not**.	**Do** I/you/they/we **start** at 9:00 a.m. tomorrow? Yes, I/you/they/we **do**. No, I/you/they/we **don't**.
Is he/she **taking** a year off? Yes, he/she **is**. No, he/she **isn't**.	**Does** he/she/it **start** in five minutes? Yes, he/she/it **does**. No, he/she/it **doesn't**.

2. Circle the correct words.

1. John **is working / works** on an eco-project next summer.

2. Carla and Sammy **are making / make** jewelry from old metal cans tomorrow.

3. The store **is opening / opens** at 10:00 a.m. tomorrow.

4. **Is the class starting / Does the class start** at noon on Monday?

5. Where **are they going / do they go** tomorrow?

Unit 8 | 113

Present perfect statements with regular and irregular verbs, p. 87

Use the present perfect to talk about experiences that happened at an indefinite time in the past. Use has/have + the past participle to form the present perfect.

	Affirmative statements	Negative statements
Regular verbs	He/She/It **has slipped** on the ice many times. Most snowboard injuries **have happened** to people under 30. I/We/They/You **have crashed** a car.	He/She **hasn't burned** his/her hand in years. He/She **has never burned** his/her hand. I/We/They/You **haven't crashed** a car before. I/We/They/You **have never crashed** a car.
Irregular verbs	He/She/It **has broken** his/her/its arm twice. I/You/We/They **have had** more crashes than any other age group.	He/She **hasn't cut** his/her finger before. Teens **haven't worn** helmets. I/You/We/They **have never seen** an accident.
Contractions	has = 's have = 've	

1. Circle the correct words.

1. Marcy **has had / has have** three broken bones.
2. Ronaldo **has gone / has went** on many exciting vacations.
3. We **have slip / have slipped** on ice in front of our house.
4. I've **haven't seen / I've never seen** an anaconda before.
5. She **haven't burned / hasn't burned** her finger.

Present perfect questions; present perfect vs. simple past, p. 89

Use the present perfect to ask questions about experiences that happened at an indefinite time in the past. Ever is often used in Yes/No questions.

Yes/No questions	Wh- questions
Have I/you/we/they **ever broken** an arm? Yes, I/you/we/they **have**. No, I/you/we/they **haven't**.	What bones **have** I/you/we/they **broken**? My wrist, my arm, and my leg.
Has he/she **ever fallen** off his/her bike? Yes, he/she **has**. / No, he/she **hasn't**.	Why **has** he/she/it **had** accidents? Because he/she/it is clumsy.
Remember: Use the simple past, not the present perfect, for experiences that happened at a definite time in the past.	
Have you ever fallen off your bike? What happened the second time?	Yes, I have. I **fell** off my bike yesterday. I **slipped** and **fell**. I **broke** my wrist.

2. Circle the correct answers.

1. Have you ever ___ off your bike?
   a. fall   b. fell   c. fallen

2. Elsa ___ a poison dart frog at the museum yesterday.
   a. saw   b. has seen   c. has saw

3. ___ you snowboard in the mountains on your trip?
   a. Do   b. Did   c. Have

4. What bones ___ you broken?
   a. did   b. has   c. have

5. Luke ___ his cousins in months.
   a. didn't see   b. hasn't seen   c. haven't seen

Indefinite pronouns, p. 97

Use indefinite pronouns for people, places, and things that are not specific.

	People	Places	Things
some-	**someone** Bring **someone** with you.	**somewhere** I want to go **somewhere** fun.	**something** I see **something** in the water.
every-	**everyone** I invited **everyone** in my class.	**everywhere** Lilly takes her phone **everywhere**.	**everything** He helps you with **everything**.
no-	**no one** **No one** has an idea.	**nowhere** Jason is **nowhere** to be found.	**nothing** We have **nothing** ready for the party.
any-	**anyone** Does **anyone** have a good idea?	**anywhere** We'll play **anywhere**.	**anything** I've never done **anything** like it.

1. Complete the sentences with *some-*, *every-*, *no-*, or *any-* + the word in parentheses.

1. I looked _____ (where) in my room for my keys.
2. _____ (one) came to the party because Ted put the wrong date on the invitation.
3. Kate didn't say _____ (thing) about the party, so I was really surprised.
4. I have _____ (thing) to do on Saturday, but I can meet you on Sunday.
5. We are _____ (where) near Jeff's house. How did we get so lost?
6. _____ (one) is at the door, but I don't know who it is.

too and *enough*, p. 99

Use *too* + adjective + infinitive to show something is more than want we want or need.
Use adjective + *enough* + infinitive to show something is what we want or need.
Not enough shows something is less than we want or need.

too	enough
I/He/She was **too scared to answer**.	I/He/She was **strong enough to do** it. You/They/We were **old enough to know** better.
You/They/We were **too nervous to try** something.	I/He/She/It was**n't big enough to reach** the food. You/They/We were**n't tall enough to get** on the ride.

2. Circle the correct word to complete each sentence.

1. Vinny is **too / enough** excited to sleep.
2. Melanie is good **too / enough** to play on the team.
3. It's **too / enough** hot to play outside.
4. My parents aren't old **too / enough** to retire.
5. Are you bored **too / enough** to leave the party?
6. It isn't **too / enough** late to see a movie.

CLIL PROJECT

ROBOTS *in the Real* WORLD

1. **Complete the sentences with the correct words.**

   communicate   computer   create   design   machine   professor   teacher

   1. A _____ is a higher-level _____ in a university.
   2. A _____ is a thinking _____. It can _____ with other ones.
   3. To _____ something is to make or draw plans for it. Next, you _____ it.

2.4 WHO'S REAL?

2. **Watch the video. Are the sentences true (*T*) or false (*F*)?**

   1. Professor Ishiguro is wearing a blue shirt. ____
   2. The robot is wearing a watch. ____
   3. Professor Ishiguro's first name is Hitoshi. ____
   4. One of the three students is a woman. ____
   5. They sit at a round table. ____
   6. The white robot can run and turn around. ____

3. **Complete the paragraph with the correct words.**

   color   glasses   hair   move   same   shy   strange   think   twins

   Look at these two men. What looks the [1]_____? What looks different? Now look at their faces and look at their [2]_____. It's the same [3]_____, isn't it? And they both have [4]_____. So what do you [5]_____? Are they [6]_____? OK, now watch how they [7]_____. What's [8]_____ here? This man isn't talking. Is he very [9]_____?

 PROJECT   Plan your own robot – what do you want your robot to do? Answer the questions below. Then draw or make a model of your robot. Show your robot to the class and tell them about it.

- What three things do you want your robot to do for you?
- Do you think you will enjoy life with a robot? Why or why not?
- What do you think robots will do in the next few years?
- Will robots make life better or worse for people? Why?

Unsolved MYSTERIES

1. **Amelia Earhart was a famous female pilot from the United States. Label the places from Amelia's last flight.**

   Howland Island   Lae, Papua New Guinea   North Africa   Pacific Ocean   South America   South Asia

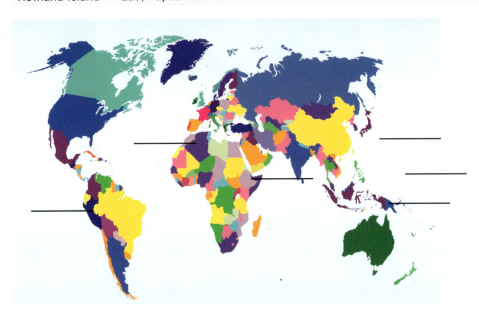

2. **Watch the video. Number the sentences in the order that you hear them from 1–6.**

   ____ a. Next, they went across North Africa and South Asia.

   ____ b. She was one of the first female pilots.

   ____ c. She traveled with a navigator.

   ____ d. We are on the line 157–337.

   ____ e. In 2001, a team looked for clues.

   ____ f. But the island was very small and difficult to find.

4.4 AMELIA EARHART: FAMOUS FLYER

 PROJECT Here are some famous mysteries. Choose the most interesting one and find out more about it. Write an explanation of what you think happened.

MYSTERY:	Sailors found the ship *Mary Celeste* abandoned with one lifeboat missing
WHEN:	December 1872
WHERE:	Atlantic Ocean, near Africa
FACTS:	Weather was good, plenty of food and water on ship
WHAT HAPPENED?	

MYSTERY:	Building Stonehenge
WHEN:	3000–2000 BCE
WHERE:	The south of England
FACTS:	Made from stones weighing 45 tons from 40 kilometers away and stones weighing almost 4 tons from 390 kilometers away
WHAT HAPPENED?	

MYSTERY:	The Yeti, a large animal, like an ape
WHEN:	First spotted in the 1800s
WHERE:	The Himalayas, in Nepal and Tibet
FACTS:	Many people believe it exists, but there are no photographs of it.
WHAT HAPPENED?	

Unit 4 | CLIL project | 117

Life below the SURFACE

1. Label the pictures with the correct words.

diver   storyteller   Tokyo   tower   Yonaguni

1. _____   2. _____   3. _____   4. _____   5. _____

Discovery EDUCATION
5.4 AN UNDERWATER MYSTERY

2. Watch the video. Complete the sentences with the correct conjunctions.

and   but   so   when

1. Not many people live on these islands, _____ it's quiet and calm.
2. Yonaguni is part of Japan, _____ it has its own language and culture.
3. In the 1980s, he was diving near the island of Yonaguni _____ he found something amazing.
4. It had streets, steps, _____ tall towers.

3. Are the sentences true (T) or false (F)?

1. Yonaguni is to the north of Japan. ____
2. About a hundred people live on Yonaguni. ____
3. The people here tell old stories to their children. ____
4. Kihachiro Aratake is a driver. ____
5. It looked like a large city under the water. ____
6. Some scientists think the structure was once above the water. ____

PROJECT

Do you know the story of the Lost City of Atlantis? Some people believe Atlantis was an underwater city, like the structures around Yonaguni.

Find out more about Atlantis and complete the chart below. Then compare the stories of Atlantis and Yonaguni and make a presentation about these two places.

	Atlantis	Yonaguni
Possible location(s)?		off the coast of Japan
When did the city exist?		10,000 years ago
What do people believe happened to the city?		
What do you believe?		

118 | CLIL project | Unit 5

Wonders of the WORLD

1. **Label the pictures with the correct words.**

   Cairo   stone blocks   tomb   pyramid

1 _____   2 _____   3 _____   4 _____

2. **Watch the video. Complete the sentences with the correct numbers.**

   2   3   8   20   147

   a. There are ____ giant pyramids near Cairo.

   b. ____ million people live in Cairo.

   c. People worked for ____ years to build each pyramid.

   d. The pyramid of Khufu is ____ meters tall.

   e. There are ____ million stone blocks in this pyramid.

   7.4 THE SECRET OF THE PYRAMIDS

3. **Circle the correct answers.**

   1. They are called the pyramids of ____.
      a. Cairo
      b. Giza
      c. Khufu

   2. The builders covered the top of the tallest pyramid with ____.
      a. gold
      b. silver
      c. paint

   3. Each stone block weighs as much as ____.
      a. a small car
      b. a large car
      c. a bus

   4. The pyramids were ____.
      a. homes
      b. castles
      c. tombs

PROJECT

People started building the Seven Wonders of the World more than 4,000 years ago. The only one still standing is the Pyramid of Khufu. What are the names of the other six Wonders of the World?

Choose one of the Seven Wonders of the World and find out seven interesting facts about it. Create a poster of your Wonder and present it to your class.

Inventions from the PAST

1. **Look at this picture of a step well. What do you think it does? Label the picture with the correct words:**

   arches   roof   stairs   walkway

   1. _____
   2. _____
   3. _____
   4. _____

10.4 AN ANCIENT ANSWER

2. **Watch the video. Are the sentences true (*T*) or false (*F*)?**
   1. In northern India, the monsoon season lasts for six months every year. _____
   2. Step wells are a system for collecting water. _____
   3. People built step wells to collect water when it rained. _____
   4. People still build step wells today. _____
   5. The animals don't get enough water. _____

3. **How did people build step wells? Number the events in order 1–5.**
   _____ a. They cut steps into the earth.
   _____ b. They made a hole near the tree.
   _____ c. They looked for a tall tree.
   _____ d. They covered these steps with stones.
   _____ e. They made the hole wider at the top.

PROJECT

Read the list below. Number the inventions and discoveries from what you think are the least important (1) to the most important (10).

_____ the wheel   _____ clothes
_____ rope   _____ houses
_____ musical instruments   _____ fire
_____ the boat   _____ knives
_____ paint   _____ spears

Then imagine selling one of these inventions to your classmate. How will it make his or her life better? Write three reasons your classmate should buy your invention.

120 | CLIL project | Unit 10

Irregular verbs

Base Verb	Simple Past	Past Participle
be	was, were	been
become	became	become
break	broke	broken
bring	brought	brought
build	built	built
buy	bought	bought
catch	caught	caught
choose	chose	chosen
come	came	come
cut	cut	cut
do	did	done
draw	drew	drawn
drink	drank	drunk
drive	drove	driven
eat	ate	eaten
fall	fell	fallen
feel	felt	felt
find	found	found
fit	fit	fit
fly	flew	flown
forget	forgot	forgotten
get	got	gotten
give	gave	given
go	went	gone
grow	grew	grown
hang	hung	hung
have	had	had
hear	heard	heard
hide	hid	hidden
hold	held	held
hurt	hurt	hurt
keep	kept	kept
know	knew	known
leave	left	left

Base Verb	Simple Past	Past Participle
lend	lent	lent
lose	lost	lost
make	made	made
meet	met	met
pay	paid	paid
put	put	put
read	read	read
ride	rode	ridden
ring	rang	rung
run	ran	run
say	said	said
see	saw	seen
sell	sold	sold
send	sent	sent
shut	shut	shut
sing	sang	sung
sit	sat	sat
sleep	slept	slept
speak	spoke	spoken
spend	spent	spent
stand	stood	stood
steal	stole	stolen
swim	swam	swum
take	took	taken
teach	taught	taught
tell	told	told
think	thought	thought
throw	threw	thrown
understand	understood	understood
wear	wore	worn
win	won	won
withdraw	withdrew	withdrawn
write	wrote	written

Answer to p. 44 #4 (Who stole the painting?)

The butler and Ray stole the painting. The butler told Clarissa there was a phone call. When she went to answer, he stayed in the garden and then climbed through the living room window. He took the painting and came back out through the window. He passed it to Ray. Ray climbed over the wall and gave it to someone waiting in the street.

Irregular verbs | 121

Credits

The authors and publishers acknowledge the following sources of copyright material and are grateful for the permissions granted. While every effort has been made, it has not always been possible to identify the sources of all the material used, or to trace all copyright holders. If any omissions are brought to our notice, we will be happy to include the appropriate acknowledgements on reprinting.

p. 2-3 (B/G): Getty Images/Lonely Planet Images; p. 3 (a): Alamy/© Imagebroker/Klaus-Werner Friedrich; p. 3 (b): Alamy/©Radius Images; p. 3 (c): Shutterstock Images/Melis; p. 3 (d): Getty Images/Chicago History Museum; p. 3 (e): Shutterstock Images/Gurgen Bakhshetsyan; p. 3 (f): Alamy/©2d Alan King; p. 3 (g): Getty Images/Retrofile/George Marks; p. 3 (h): Shutterstock Images/Ferenc Szelepcsenyi; p.3 (i): Alamy/©Bon Appetit; p. 3 (j): Shutterstock Images/Subbotina Anna; p. 3 (k): Alamy/©Greg Vaughn; p. 3 (l): Alamy/©Russell Gordon/Danita Delimont; p. 4 (BL): Corbis/Guillermo Granja; p. 4 (BR): Alamy/©Mo Fini; p. 4 (TR): Alamy/©Maria Grazia Casella; p. 5 (BR): Shutterstock Images/Blend Images; p. 6 (TL): Shutterstock Images/Jenoche/A; p. 6 (a): Shutterstock Images/James Steidl; p. 6 (b): Alamy/©Old Paper Studios; p. 6 (c): Shutterstock Images/Nataliya Hora; p. 6 (d): Shutterstock Images/Adrio Communications Ltd; p. 6 (e): Shutterstock Images/Marc Dietrich; p. 6 (f): Alamy/©Yvette Cardozo; p. 6 (g): Getty Images/De Agostini; p. 6 (h): Alamy/©Museum of London; p. 6 (i): Shutterstock Images/Balefire; p. 6 (j): Shutterstock Images/Rob Stark; p. 8 (BR): Shutterstock Images/PhotoNan; p. 8 (BL): Shutterstock Images/Doomu; p. 9 (TR): Getty Images/Adrian Weinbrecht/Digital Vision; p. 10 (B/G): Shutterstock Images/illustrart; p. 10 (TL): Getty Images/Joe Petersburger; p. 10 (TC): Getty Images/GDT; p. 10 (B): Alamy/©Chris Lewington; p. 10 (C): Alamy/©ImageDB; p. 11 (CR): Shutterstock Images/Manczurov; p. 11 (TL): Shutterstock Images/AlexMaster; p. 11 (TR): Shutterstock Images/Zybr78; p. 11 (CL): Shutterstock Images/Mike Flippo; p. 11 (CR): Shutterstock Images/WBB; p. 11 (BR): Alamy/©Urbanmyth; p. 11 (BL): Shutterstock Images/Samuel Borges Photography; p. 12-13 (B/G): Getty Images/John Eder; p. 13 (1): Getty Images/Movie Poster Image Art; p. 13 (2): Alamy/AF Archive; p. 13 (3): ©DISNEY CHANNEL/THE KOBAL COLLECTION; p. 13 (4): REX/Courtesy Everett Collection; p. 13 (5): REX/Col Pics/Everett; p. 13 (6): Alamy/©Moviestore Collection; p. 13 (7): ©20TH CENTURY FOX/PARAMOUNT/THE KOBAL COLLECTION; p. 13 (8): REX/Courtesy Everett Collection; p. 13 (9): Alamy/©AF Archive; p. 14 (T): Shutterstock Images/Bertrand Benoit; p. 14 (B/G): Shutterstock Images/Krivosheev Vitaly; p. 14 (CL): Alamy/©AF Archive; p. 14 (C): THE KOBAL COLLECTION/LUCASFILM/20TH CENTURY FOX; p. 14 (CR): Alamy/©Moviestore Collection Ltd; p. 15 (CR): Shutterstock Images/Adrian Weinbrecht; p. 16 (TL): Shutterstock Images/Szocs Jozsef; p. 16 (1): Getty Images/Jasin Boland/NBC/NBCU Photo Bank; p. 16 (2): Alamy/©Jochen Tack; p. 16 (3): Getty Images/Steve Mort/AFP; p. 16 (4): Alamy/©AF Archive; p. 16 (5): Getty Images/Sonja Flemming/CBS; p. 16 (6): Getty Images/Alexander Tamargo; p. 16 (7): Alamy/©Pictoria Press Ltd; p. 16 (8): Alamy/©Zuma Press; p. 16 (9): Getty Images/Steve Granitz/WireImage; p. 17 (CR): Shutterstock Images/Vovan; p. 18 (TL): Shutterstock Images/Mayakova; p. 18 (BL): Alamy/©Newscast; p. 19 (B/G): Shutterstock Images/Made-in-China; p. 19 (TL): Summit Entertainment/The Kobal Collection; p. 20 (TR): Alamy/©Archives Du 7e Art/Ashutosh Gowariker Productions 12; p. 20 (CR): REX/Everett Collection; p. 20 (BR): ©DHARMA PRODUCTIONS//THE KOBAL COLLECTION; p. 20 (B/G): Shutterstock Images/Loke Yek Mang; p. 20 (TL): Shutterstock Images/Majcot; p. 21 (BR): Shutterstock Images/Kurhan; p. 22-23 (B/G): Getty Images/John Giustina; p. 23 (1): Getty Images/JupiterImages; p. 23 (2): Alamy/©Patti McConville; p. 23 (3): Alamy/©David R.Frazier; p. 23 (4): Alamy/©Alex Segre; p. 23 (5): Alamy/©Patti McConville; p. 23 (6): Alamy/©Lain Masterton; p. 23 (7): Alamy/©P.D.Amedzro; p. 23 (8): Alamy/©Jader Alto; p. 23 (9): Alamy/©Thomas Cockrem; p. 23 (10): Alamy/©Kim Kaminski; p. 23 (11): Shutterstock Images/Racorn; p. 24 (TL): Alamy/©Robert Harding Picture Library Ltd; p. 24 (a): Alamy/©Caro; p. 24 (b): Alamy/©D. Hurst; p. 24 (c): Getty Images/Richard I'Anson/Lonely Planet Images; p. 24 (d): Alamy/©Laborant; p. 25 (BR): Corbis/2/Jack Hollingsworth/Ocean; p. 26 (TL): Corbis/Image Source; p. 27 (B): Shutterstock Images/Mark Poprocki; p. 28 (TL): Shutterstock Images/Dmitry Kalinovsky; p. 28 (BL): Shutterstock Images/Elnur; p. 29 (TR): Shutterstock Images/Sashkin; p. 29 (TL): Shutterstock Images/John Kasawa; p. 30 (T): Alamy/©ZUMA Press, Inc; p. 30 (C): Shutterstock Images/Dragi52; p. 30 (TR): Shutterstock Images/Joost Van Uffelen; p. 30 (B): Shutterstock Images/Angela Waye; p. 31 (1): Shutterstock Images/Diplomedia; p. 31 (2): Shutterstock Images/Lendy16; p. 31 (3): Alamy/©D. Hurst; p. 31 (4): Shutterstock Images/Studio Smart; p. 31 (5): Shutterstock Images/MTrebbin; p. 31 (6): Shutterstock Images/Julian Rovagnati; p. 32 (C): Corbis/Blue Images; p. 32-33 (B/G): Shutterstock Images/Neirfy; p. 33 (1): Thinkstock/mark wragg/iStock; p. 33 (2): Shutterstock Images/Brocreative; p. 33 (3): Shutterstock Images/Monika Wisniewska; p. 33 (4): Shutterstock Images/yamix; p. 33 (5): Getty Images/ Maria Pereira Photography/Flickr; p. 33 (6): Corbis/Beau Lark; p. 33 (7): Alamy/©Shotshop GmbH; p. 33 (8): Shutterstock Images/Dmitry Yashkin; p. 33 (9): Alamy/©IE235/Image Source Plus; p. 33 (10): Shutterstock Images/mezzotint; p. 34 (TL): Getty Images/Stephen Dunn; p. 34 (TC): Getty Images/Matthew Lloyd/Bloomberg; p. 34 (TR): REX/Theo Kingma; p. 35 (TR): Alamy/©Photos 12; p. 36 (T): Shutterstock Images/Nils Petersen; p. 36 (a): Alamy/©Jack Hollingsworth/Blend Images; p. 36 (b): Shutterstock Images/Oliveromg; p. 36 (c): Alamy/©KidStock/ Blend Images; p. 36 (d): Alamy/©Leah Warkentin/Design Pics Inc; p. 36 (e): Alamy/©Ron Dahlquist/Pacific Stock; p. 36 (f): Shutterstock Images/Piotr Marcinski; p. 36 (g): Alamy/©Kalle Singer/ Beyond Fotomedia GmbH; p. 36 (h): Shutterstock Images/Aleksandr Markin; p. 36 (i): Alamy/©Arco Images/De Meester; p. 37 (TR): Shutterstock Images/Shvak; p. 37 (TCR): Shutterstock Images/Rarach; p. 37 (BCR): Getty Images/Image Source; p. 37 (BR): Shutterstock Images/Murengstockphoto; p. 38 (BL): Alamy/©David Grossman; p. 38 (TL): Alamy/©Rosanne Tackaberry; p. 39 (B/G): Getty Images/Jerritt Clark/Stringer; p. 39 (TR): Alamy/©Zuma Press Inc; p. 40 (TL): Getty Images/Pascal Le Segretain; p. 40 (B): Shutterstock Images/Kjersti Joergensen; p. 40 (C): Getty Images/Cameron Spencer; p. 41 (1): Shutterstock Images/Wavebreakmedia; p. 41 (2): Alamy/©PCN Photography; p. 41 (3): Getty Images/Darren Baker; p. 41 (4): Alamy/©[apply pictures]; p. 42-43 (B/G): Getty Images/Marko Stavric Photography; p. 46 (T): Shutterstock Images/Mindscape Studio; p. 46 (1): Alamy/©Agencja Free; p. 46 (2): Alamy/©Blickwinkel; p. 46 (3): Shutterstock Images/Khwi; p. 46 (4): Getty images/Danita Delimont; p. 46 (5): Shutterstock Images/Catalin Petolea; p. 46 (6): Shutterstock Images/Jarry; p. 46 (7): Alamy/©Phovoir; p. 46 (8): Shutterstock Images/Golden Pixels LLC; p. 46 (9): Shutterstock Images/Gow27; p. 47 (1): Corbis/Erik Isakson/Blend Images; p. 48 (BL): Alamy/©MasPix; p. 48 (CL): Alamy/©Blickwinkel; p. 50 (TR): REX/Courtesy Everett Collection; p. 50 (CR): Getty Images/Jeff Neumann/CBS; p. 50 (B/G): Shutterstock Images/Richard Peterson; p. 54-55 (B/G): Corbis/Anna Stowe/LOOP IMAGES; p. 52-52 (B/G): Corbis/Elli Thor Magnusson; p. 56 (TL): Shutterstock Images/guentermanaus; p. 56 (CL): Alamy/©Hemis; p. 56 (TR): Shutterstock Images/Marina Jay; p. 56 (B/G): Shutterstock Images/KayaMe; p. 57 (CL): Alamy/©blickwinkel; p. 58 (TL): Getty Images/Chip Simons; p. 58 (1): Shutterstock Images/Big Pants Production; p. 58 (2): Alamy/©Incamerastock; p. 58 (3): Corbis/Ken Kaminesky/Take 2 Productions; p. 58 (4): Shutterstock Images/Shell114; p. 58 (5): Shutterstock Images/Kamil Macniak; p. 58 (6): Shutterstock Images/Ramona Heim; p. 58 (7): Shutterstock Images/Maxim Ibragimov; p. 58 (8): Shutterstock Images/Sergemi; p. 58 (9): Shutterstock Images/HomeArt; p. 58 (10): Getty Images/J.R.Ball; p. 58 (11)Shutterstock Images/Andrey Armyagov; p. 58 (12): Shutterstock Images/Africa Studio; p. 59 (CR): Shutterstock Images/Jaroslav74; p. 60 (TL): Shutterstock Images/Africa Studio; p. 60 (BL): Shutterstock Images/Gemenacom; p. 61 (BR): Shutterstock Images/Romakoma; p. 62 (T): Shutterstock Images/FCG; p. 62 (TL): Alamy/©Radius Images; p. 62 (CL): Shutterstock Images/EggHeadPhoto; p. 62 (CR): Thinkstock/Stockbyte; p. 62 (BL): Alamy/©Randy Duchaine; p. 62 (B): Shutterstock Images/View Apart; p. 64-65 (B/G): Shutterstock Images/Diversepixel; p. 65 (1): Shutterstock Images/Archiwiz; p. 65 (2): Shutterstock Images/Maksym Dykha; p. 65 (3): Shutterstock Images/AG-PHOTO; p. 65 (4): Shutterstock Images/Alexey Boldin; p. 65 (5): Alamy/©keith morris; p. 65 (6): Shutterstock Images/GeorgeMPhotography; p. 65 (7): Shutterstock Images/Joris van den Heuvel; p. 65 (8): Shutterstock Images/Bloom Design; p. 65 (9): Shutterstock Images/Goldyg; p. 66 (CR): Getty Images/SSPL; p. 66 (T): Shutterstock Images/Sergey Nivens; p. 66 (BR): Shutterstock Images/Joris van den Heuvel; p. 68 (TL): Shutterstock Images/CandyBox Images; p. 68 (a): Shutterstock Images/Showcake; p. 68 (b): Shutterstock Images/Modella; p. 68 (c): Alamy/©Pumkinpie; p. 68 (d): Shutterstock Images/Rob Marmion; p. 68 (e): Alamy/©Mark Sykes; p. 68 (f): Shutterstock Images/Valeri Potapova; p. 68 (g): Alamy/©Maxim Images; p. 69 (CR): Alamy/©Ralph Talmont/Aurora Photos; p. 70 (B): Alamy/©Peter Alvey People; p. 70 (CL): Shutterstock Images/Siberia - Video and Photo; p. 71 (TR): Shutterstock Images/Olga Popova; p. 72 (TL): Shutterstock Images/James Steidl; p. 72 (BR): Alamy/©Ian Dagnall Computing; p. 72 (TC): Shutterstock Images/Fad82; p. 72 (BL): Shutterstock Images/Kitch Bain; p. 72 (B/G): Shutterstock Images/Concept Photo; p. 73 (1): Shutterstock Images/Luis Carlos Torres; p. 73 (2): Shutterstock Images/Maksym Dykha; p. 73 (3): Shutterstock Images/BigKnell; p. 73 (4): Shutterstock Images/Volodymyr Krasyuk; p. 74-75 (B/G): Corbis/Werner Dieterich/Westend61; p. 75 (a): Shutterstock Images/Monkey Business Images; p. 75 (b): Alamy/©Driver's License; p. 75 (c): Alamy/©Cultura Creative; p. 75 (d): Shutterstock Images/Nikola Solev; p. 75 (e): Shutterstock Images/razihusin; p. 75 (f): Shutterstock Images/Joe Gough; p. 75 (g): Shutterstock Images/Karen Grigoryan; p. 75 (h): Alamy/©Ben Molyneux People; p. 75 (i): Corbis/Mark Edward Atkinson/Tracey Lee/Blend Images; p. 75 (j): Shutterstock Images/Monkey Business Images; p. 76 (TL): REX/Bruce Adams; p.76 (TC): Alamy/©Bill Bachman; p. 77 (BL): Shutterstock Images/MTrebbin; p. 77 (TL): Shutterstock Images/GeniusKp; p. 77 (TR): Shutterstock Images/Arman Zhenikeyev; p. 77 (BR): Shutterstock Images/Irin-k; p. 78 (T): Alamy/©VStock; p. 78 (1): Shutterstock Images/Carsten Reisinger; p. 78 (2): Shutterstock Images/Rob Hyrons; p. 78 (3): Shutterstock Images/Molodec; p. 78 (4): Shutterstock Images/Molodec; p. 78 (5): Shutterstock Images/jocic; p. 78 (6): Shutterstock Images/Worker; p. 78 (6): Shutterstock Images/R. Gino Santa Maria; p. 78 (7): Shutterstock Images/Nikkytok; p. 78 (8): Shutterstock Images/Donatas1205; p. 79 (BR): Getty images/Muammer Mujdat Uzel; p. 80 (TL): Shutterstock Images/Bloomua; p. 80 (BL): Alamy/©Denise Hager Catchlight Visual Services; p. 81 (TR): Getty Images/Juanmonino; p. 82 (BL): Getty Images/Steve Skjold; p. 82 (CL): Alamy/©Alaska Stock; p. 82 (B/G): Shutterstock Images/Galyna Andrushko; p. 82 (TL): Alamy/©Gail Mooney-Kelly; p. 82 (T): Shutterstock Images/Galyna Andrushko; p. 83 (1): Shutterstock Images/Roman Samokhin; p. 83 (2): Shutterstock Images/Hal_P; p. 83 (3): Shutterstock Images/EZeePics Studio; p. 83 (4): Alamy/©Mike Kemp; p. 84-85 (B/G): Corbis/Corey Rich/Aurora Open; p. 85 (1): Getty Images/Tammy Bryngelson; p. 85 (2): Alamy/©Rob Stark; p. 85 (3): Shutterstock Images/Apples Eyes Studio; p. 85 (4): Alamy/©Nik Taylor; p. 85 (5): Shutterstock Images/Robert Crum; p. 85 (6): Alamy/©Imagebroker; p. 85 (7): Getty Images/Jason Weddington; p. 85 (8): Corbis/Burger/phanie/Phanie Sarl; p. 85 (9): Shutterstock Images/Piotr Marcinski; p. 85 (10): Shutterstock Images/Mahathir Mohd Yasin; p. 86 (TR): Alamy/©Trekandshoot; p. 86 (TR): Shutterstock Images/Dan Thornberg; p. 86 (TL): Shutterstock Images/Ilya Andriyanov; p. 86 (CL): Shutterstock Images/Filatov Alexey; p. 86 (T): Shutterstock Images/Endeavor; p. 87 (TR): Getty Images/Ebby May; p. 88 (TR): Shutterstock Images/Varuna; p. 88 (B): Alamy/©Image Source Plus; p. 88 (BC): Alamy/©Enigma; p. 89 (BR): REX/Andrew Price; p. 90 (TL): Shutterstock Images/Wonderisland; p. 90 (BL): Shutterstock Images/HomeArt; p. 91 (TR): Shutterstock Images/Stefan Pircher; p. 92 (TL): Shutterstock Images/Dr.Morley Read; p. 92 (TC): Shutterstock Images/Kletr; p. 92 (BR): Shutterstock Images/Decha Thapanya; p. 92 (T): Shutterstock Images/Foxy; p. 92 (B/G): Shutterstock Images/Brodtcast; p. 92 (BL): Alamy/©Robert M. Vera; p. 92 (T): Getty Images/Murray Cooper/Minden Pictures; p. 93 (1,2,3,4): Shutterstock Images/Goa Novi; p. 93 (5,6,7): Shutterstock Images/Flashon Studio; p. 93 (8,9): Shutterstock Images/Iko; p. 94-95 (B/G): Corbis/Tim Pannell; p. 95 (1): Shutterstock Images/Claudia Paulussen; p. 95 (2): Shutterstock Images/Golden Pixels LLC; p. 95 (3): Getty Images/Jupiter Images; p. 95 (4): Shutterstock Images/Christine Langer-Pueschel; p. 95 (5): Shutterstock Images/BlueSkyImage; p. 95 (6): Alamy/©Radius Images; p. 95 (7): Alamy/©Frederic Cirou/PhotoAlto sas; p. 95 (8): Getty Images/Rob Lewine; p. 96 (TL): Alamy/©Zuma Press Inc; p. 96 (TR): Shutterstock Images/Fuse; p. 96 (TR): Alamy/©Gregory James; p. 97 (CL): Alamy/©South West Images Scotland; p. 98 (TL): Shutterstock Images/Mbbirdy; p. 98 (1): Shutterstock Images/PathDoc; p. 98 (2): Shutterstock Images/Guillermo Del Olmo; p. 98 (3): Shutterstock Images/Patrick Foto; p. 98 (4): Shutterstock Images/PathDoc; p. 98 (5): Shutterstock Images/Arvydas Kniuksta; p. 98 (6): Shutterstock Images/Sabphoto; p. 98 (7): Shutterstock Images/Sashahaltam; p. 98 (8): Shutterstock Images/Tracy Whiteside; p. 98 (9): Shutterstock Images/Elena Elisseeva; p. 98 (10): Shutterstock Images/Jeka; p. 100 (TL): Getty Images/Nancy R.Cohen; p. 100 (BL): Getty Images/SW Productions/Photodisc; p. 101 (TR): Alamy/©View Pictures Ltd; p. 102 (B): Alamy/©Roman Sigaev; p. 102 (TR): Shutterstock Images/Focuslight; p. 103 (1): Shutterstock Images/Denise Kappa; p. 103 (2): Shutterstock Images/Studio Vin; p. 103 (3): Alamy/©Niehoff/Imagebroker; p. 103 (4): Shutterstock Images/Taelove7; p. 103 (5): Shutterstock Images/ Artiis; p. 103 (6): Shutterstock Images/Aerogondo2; p. 104-105 (B/G): Shutterstock Images/Alexander Vershinin; p. 116 (T): Getty Images/Javier Pierini; p. 117 (T): Shutterstock Images/Jktu_21; Back cover: Shutterstock Images/Vibrant Image Studio.

Front cover photography by Alamy/©Marc Hill.

The publishers are grateful to the following illustrators:

David Belmonte p. 44; Nigel Dobbyn p. 43, 49, 102; Q2A Media Services, Inc. p. 7, 55, 63, 118; Jose Rubio p. 26, 119; Sean Tiffany p. 7.

All video stills by kind permission of:

Discovery Communications, LLC 2015: p. 2 (1, 3), 5, 10, 12 (1, 3, 4), 15, 20, 21, 22 (1, 3), 25, 30, 32 (1, 3, 4), 35, 40, 41, 42 (1, 3, 4), 45, 50, 51, 54 (1, 3), 57, 62, 64 (1, 3, 4), 67, 72, 73, 74 (1, 3), 77, 82, 84 (1, 3), 87, 92, 94 (1, 3, 4), 97, 102, 103, 116, 117, 118, 119, 120; Cambridge University Press: p. 2 (2), 8, 12 (2), 18, 22 (2), 28, 32 (2), 38, 42 (2), 48, 54 (2), 60, 64 (2), 70, 72 (2), 80, 84 (2), 90, 94 (2), 100.

Uncover 2 Combo
Lynne M. Robertson

Workbook

Table of Contents

1	Traditions	2
2	What's Playing?	8
	Review: Units 1 and 2	14
3	Spending Habits	16
4	Our Heroes	22
	Review: Units 3 and 4	28
5	It's a Mystery!	30
6	Home, Sweet Home	36
	Review: Units 5 and 6	42
7	Visions of the Future	44
8	The Choices We Make	50
	Review: Units 7 and 8	56
9	Watch Out!	58
10	Have Fun!	64
	Review: Units 9 and 10	70
	Video worksheets	72

1 Traditions

VOCABULARY Categories

1 Write the letters in the correct categories.

a.	b.
c.	d.
e.	f.
g.	h.
i.	j.
k.	l.

1. music ____d____, _____
2. sports _____, _____
3. food _____, _____
4. places _____, _____
5. art _____, _____
6. clothing _____, _____

2 Look at the pictures in Exercise 1. Circle the correct answer.

1. Which one is modern?
   d   f   (e)
2. Which one do people wear today?
   a   b   c
3. Which one is a modern place?
   e   g   h
4. Which one is traditional art?
   a   h   j
5. Which one is traditional?
   e   f   l

3 Complete the sentences with the six category words from Exercise 1.

1. My mother won't listen to modern ____music____.
2. They like modern _____ like photography.
3. He sells jeans and T-shirts in a _____ store.
4. She knows how to cook traditional _____.
5. You can learn traditional _____ like karate.
6. We like to visit traditional _____ with old buildings.

4 Answer the questions with your own information.

1. What kind of music do you like?
   I like dance music.
   Is it traditional or modern?
   ____modern____

2. What food do you like?
   _____
   Is it traditional or modern?
   _____

3. What clothing do you like?
   _____
   Is it traditional or modern?
   _____

4. What sport do you like?
   _____
   Is it traditional or modern?
   _____

2 | Unit 1

GRAMMAR Simple present review with *be* and *have*

1 Circle the correct simple present forms of *be* and *have*.

1. **A:** Who **is** / **are** you?
   B: I **'s** / **'m** Maya's brother.
2. **A:** Where **is** / **are** they?
   B: They **'s** / **'re** at the swimming pool.
3. **A:** What **do** / **does** she **have** / **has**?
   B: She **have** / **has** a laptop. She **don't have** / **doesn't have** a tablet.
4. **A:** When do they **have** / **has** science?
   B: They **have** / **has** science in the afternoon.
5. **A:** **Is** / **Are** he good at soccer?
   B: No, he **isn't** / **aren't**.
6. **A:** **Is** / **Are** we in the same English class?
   B: Yes, we **is** / **are**.
7. **A:** **Do** / **Does** you **have** / **has** a new bike?
   B: No, I **don't** / **doesn't**.
8. **A:** **Do** / **Does** she **have** / **has** traditional clothes?
   B: Yes, she **do** / **does**.

2 Match the questions with the correct answers.

1. Are they in the same class? __f__
2. Do you have a bike? ____
3. What's the date today? ____
4. Where are my parents? ____
5. What does he have in his bag? ____
6. Do they have a pet snake? ____

a. They're at the store.
b. He has a tablet. He doesn't have a book.
c. No, they don't. They have a rabbit.
d. It's the 18th.
e. No, I don't. I have a car.
f. Yes, they are.

3 Rewrite the sentences as *Wh-* questions and *yes/no* questions.

1. I am in Ecuador.
   Where are you? / Are you in Ecuador?
2. They are on the football team.
   _____
   _____
3. I have English in the morning.
   _____
   _____
4. She has a new computer.
   _____
   _____
5. He's at the party today.
   _____
   _____
6. They have an old car.
   _____
   _____

4 Complete the questions with *be* or *have*. Then answer the questions with your own information.

1. Where ___are___ you now?
   I'm in the library.
2. When do you _____ dinner?
   _____
3. How old _____ your friend?
   _____
4. _____ you at the beach now?
   _____
5. Does your friend _____ a cold?
   _____
6. _____ it sunny today?
   _____

Unit 1 | 3

VOCABULARY Clothes and objects

1 Put the letters in the correct order to make words.

1. TAH _____hat_____
2. NEP _____
3. EHOSS _____
4. SREDS _____
5. HATCW _____
6. CAKTEJ _____
7. OVEENIITSL _____
8. OPHNEELET _____
9. TPOECMUR _____
10. ROHHATGPOP _____

2 Label the pictures with the correct words from Exercise 1.

1. _____dress_____

2. _____

3. _____

4. _____

5. _____

6. _____

7. _____

8. _____

9. _____

10. _____

3 Circle the correct answers.

1. Which one is a traditional object?
   a. television
   b. pen *(circled)*
   c. computer

2. Which one is clothing?
   a. photo
   b. phone
   c. dress

3. Which one do people wear on their feet?
   a. phone
   b. shoes
   c. TV

4. Which one DON'T you use to write?
   a. pen
   b. jacket
   c. computer

5. Which one do you wear on your head?
   a. hat
   b. dress
   c. watch

4 Complete the sentences with the correct words.

| pen | phone | photo | ✓TV | watch |

1. They have a new flat screen ____TV____.
2. I have an old black-and-white _____ of my great-grandparents.
3. I use a computer to send emails, but my grandfather uses a _____ to write letters.
4. My mother wears a _____, but I use my phone to tell time.
5. My grandmother sent me a text from her new _____.

4 | Unit 1

GRAMMAR *whose* and possessives

1 Circle the correct answers.

1. **Whose** / Who's hat is that?
2. Whose / Who's Alex's sister?
3. Whose / Who's sister is that?
4. Whose / Who's are those?
5. Whose / Who's photos are they?
6. Whose / Who's on the phone?

2 Complete the chart with the correct possessive adjectives and pronouns.

Possessive adjectives	Possessive pronouns
It's ____my____ phone.	It's mine.
That's your hat.	That hat is _____.
That's _____ photo.	That's hers.
They're his shoes.	They're _____.
They're _____ pens.	They're ours.
It's their TV.	It's _____.

3 Complete the sentences with possessive 's or s'.

1. That's my uncle_'s_ motorcycle.
2. It's my three cousin____ house.
3. That's my grandparent____ computer.
4. They're his mother____ books.
5. It's my parent____ car.
6. They're the school____ cameras.

4 Complete the conversation with *whose* and possessives.

Meg: Are these ¹___your___ photos from your trip?

Robert: Yes, they are. Look. That's my grandparent²_____ house. And that's my grandfather³_____ new motorcycle.

Meg: Really?

Robert: Yes, it's ⁴_____. Look at this photo.

Meg: ⁵_____ bicycles are those?

Robert: They're my cousin⁶_____ bikes.

Meg: ⁷_____ riding the skateboard?

Robert: That's my mom. It's ⁸_____ skateboard.

Meg: Wow! That's cool.

Unit 1 | 5

CONVERSATION A cool tradition

1 **Put the sentences in the correct order to make a conversation.**

  ____ Hiro: Well, we have a party, of course. But my cousins and I have a new tradition.

  ____ Lena: That's a cool idea!

  ____ Hiro: It is. We email it to my grandparents, too. They love it.

  ____ Lena: Really? How do you do that?

  ____ Hiro: We use family photos.

  ____ Lena: That's interesting. What is it?

  ____ Hiro: We go to the computer lab and make a video.

  ____ Lena: Tell me about it.

  __1__ Hiro: It's my aunt's birthday on Saturday.

2 **Circle the phrases in Exercise 1 that keep the conversation going.**

3 **Circle the correct answer to keep the conversation going.**

  1. **A:** Did you know that brides in India paint their hair red?
     B: a. That's interesting.   b. OK.

  2. **A:** I think rock stars are cool.
     B: a. I'm sorry to hear that.   b. Really?

  3. **A:** My sister works on TV.
     B: a. Tell me about it.   b. How are you?

  4. **A:** I'm in the math competition. We go to Chicago on Monday!
     B: a. See you later.   b. Then what?

4 **Keep the conversations going with the correct phrases.**

  | Really? | That's interesting. |
  | ✓Tell me about it. | Then what? |

  1. **A:** The library has a movie night for teens on Fridays. It's really fun.
     B: *Tell me about it.*

  2. **A:** My aunt works at the park. She sees bears a lot.
     B: _____
     A: Yes. There are a lot of bears.

  3. **A:** The new mall is open. It has an ice cream shop next to a gym.
     B: _____

  4. **A:** There's a band competition in the park on Saturday. My band thinks we can win it.
     B: _____
     A: Then we win some money!

READING TO WRITE

1 Complete the invitation with the correct question words.

Who   ✓What   Where   When   Why

Tim's Party!

What	Graduation party!
_____	Tim's family and friends
_____	Celebrate Tim's graduation from school!
_____	Stow Lake Golden Gate Park, CA
_____	Saturday, June 15 Noon

3 Circle the correct answers.

1. There is / **There are** a lot of people in my family.
2. There is / There are many interesting traditions in the world.
3. There is / There are a museum with traditional Asian art on Larkin Street.
4. There is / There are a new sport called "snow kiting."
5. There isn't / There aren't a professional women's baseball team.

4 Write sentences about Tim's party. Use the word web from Exercise 2. Use *There is / There are*.

1. *There is a birthday party for Tim in the park.*
2. _____
3. _____
4. _____
5. _____

2 Complete the word web with information about Tim's party.

cake, music
lots of games, activities
many friends, grandparents, cousins
Saturday noon
✓the park

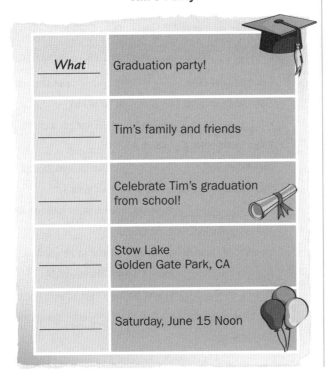

Unit 1 | **7**

2 What's Playing?

VOCABULARY Types of movies

1 Complete the crossword puzzle.

ACROSS

3.

6.

7.

8.

9.

DOWN

1.

2.

4.

5.

2 Complete the paragraph with words from Exercise 1.

My Post

I love movies! I like ¹ _____action_____ movies the best. They are so exciting. I do karate, so I also like ² _____ movies to see the kung fu experts. When I want to laugh, I watch a ³ _____ or sometimes an ⁴ _____ movie, even though they are for kids. My mom likes the love stories in ⁵ _____ movies so I watch them with her. My dad is very serious, and we watch ⁶ _____ together. My brother likes special effects, so he watches ⁷ _____ movies. I don't like to watch ⁸ _____ movies because I get scared. And I don't like to watch ⁹ _____, even though the singing is good.

Comment

3 Complete the sentences with your own ideas.

1. My favorite type of movie is ___horror movies___ because _I like scary stories_.

2. The name of my favorite movie is _____.

3. My favorite movie villain is _____ because _____.

4. I don't like _____ movies because _____.

5. I never watch _____.

8 | Unit 2

GRAMMAR Simple present review

1 Match the questions with the correct answers.

1. Do you like action movies? _c_
2. Does Helen like romance movies? ____
3. Do they watch "Bollywood" movies? ____
4. What type of movies do you watch? ____
5. Where do they watch movies? ____
6. How often does Maria go to the movies? ____

a. They watch movies at home.
b. Yes, she does.
c. No, I don't.
d. I watch horror movies.
e. She never goes to the movies.
f. Yes, they do.

2 Complete the chart. Use the simple present.

	Questions	Affirmative	Negative
1. I	What movies do you like?	I _like_ musicals.	I _don't like_ dramas.
2. They	What ____ they ____ her?	They call her "J.Lo."	They ____ her Jennifer Muñiz.
3. She	How often ____ Sally ____ to the movies?	She ____ to the movies two times a week.	She doesn't go to the movies on Fridays.
4. I	Do you like documentaries?	Yes, I ____.	No, I ____.
5. They	____ they watch movies at school?	____.	____.
6. He	Owen ____ to the movies?	____.	____.

GRAMMAR Adverbs of frequency

3 Complete the chart with adverbs of frequency.

✓always   never   often   sometimes   usually

always
_____
_____
_____

4 Put the words in the correct order to make sentences.

1. watch / at / never / movies / night / horror / I / .
   I never watch horror movies at night.

2. with / I / watch / sisters / my / romance / usually / movies / .
   _____

3. movies / on / her / sometimes / watches / computer / She / .
   _____

4. always / animated / brother / movies / My / on / the / watches / weekends / .
   _____

5 Answer the questions with your own information.

1. How often do you watch movies at school?
   We sometimes watch movies at school.

2. When do you watch movies with your friends?
   _____

3. What types of movies do you never watch?
   _____

4. Where do you usually watch movies?
   _____

5. Do you go to the movie theater? How often?
   _____

Unit 2 | 9

VOCABULARY Types of TV shows

1 Find the words for TV shows.

cartoon	crime series	documentary
game show	reality TV show	sitcom
soap opera	talk show	✓ the news

H	T	H	E	N	E	W	S	O	E	N	U	J
R	E	A	L	I	T	Y	T	V	S	H	O	W
R	P	C	A	R	T	O	O	N	S	T	Y	Z
P	C	R	I	M	E	S	E	R	I	E	S	U
E	Z	V	X	H	I	N	R	Y	Z	R	H	G
O	R	Q	E	B	I	P	N	L	V	K	K	T
M	X	D	O	C	U	M	E	N	T	A	R	Y
R	D	K	W	F	O	M	V	E	L	H	P	M
D	S	I	T	C	O	M	K	U	R	S	R	T
J	S	O	A	P	O	P	E	R	A	N	L	W
J	J	N	S	V	P	Y	O	K	Q	E	S	Q
L	G	A	M	E	S	H	O	W	C	R	P	Y
Z	T	H	I	T	A	L	K	S	H	O	W	K

2 Label the pictures with the correct types of TV shows from Exercise 1.

1. _____reality TV show_____

2. _____

3. _____

4. _____

5. _____

6. _____

7. _____

8. _____

9. _____

3 Write the types of TV shows from Exercise 1.

1. This type of TV show has funny situations that make you laugh. _____sitcom_____

2. You see real events that happen in the world every day on these shows. _____

3. This type of show often has police officers chasing villains. _____

4. In this type of show, people compete to win prizes and money. _____

5. This is usually a serious show that talks about one issue or topic. _____

6. This is an animated TV show, usually made for children. _____

7. You can watch strong characters and stories full of romance and drama in this type of show. _____

8. This show features several people sitting around talking. _____

9. People who aren't actors get into drama or competition in this type of show. _____

4 Choose three people you know. Write sentences about the TV shows they watch.

1. _My parents watch the news._
2. _____
3. _____
4. _____
5. _____

GRAMMAR Verb + infinitive or -ing form (gerund)

1 Does each sentence have a verb + infinitive or a verb + -ing form (gerund)? Underline verb + infinitive. Circle verb + -ing form.

1. She <u>loves to read</u> comic books. / She (loves reading) comic books.
2. My brother dislikes buying new clothes.
3. Ellen prefers watching movies to reading movie reviews.
4. Henry needs to get money to buy a bike.
5. Mila enjoys watching all types of movies.
6. They want to write a movie script together.

2 Use the phrases to complete the chart with verb + infinitive or verb + -ing form (gerund).

dislikes being	dislikes reading	hates being
hates to be	✓need to see	prefer eating
prefer to eat	wants to go	

Verb + infinitive
You ____need to see____ this TV show.
Howie _____ to outer space.

Verb + -ing form (gerund)
Sheldon _____ wrong.
Penny _____ comic books.

Verb + infinitive or -ing form (gerund)
Raj _____ shy. / Raj _____ shy.
They _____ Thai food on Monday night. / They _____ Thai food on Monday night.

3 Correct the sentences.

1. I dislike ~~to go~~ *going* to bed late.
2. They enjoy to washing the dog.
3. We need seeing the map.
4. Helen likes study science at school.
5. Hank wants to watching sports on TV.
6. She hates get up late.

4 Write sentences with your own information. Use *love*, *enjoy*, *want*, *prefer*, *dislike*, and *hate* plus the infinitive or -ing forms of the verbs in the box.

| get | ✓play | read | study | watch | work |

1. (love) *I love to play video games.*
   I love playing video games.
2. (enjoy) _____
3. (dislike) _____
4. (want) _____
5. (hate) _____
6. (prefer) _____

Unit 2 | 11

CONVERSATION It's really funny!

1 Put the words in the correct order to make sentences.

1. do / feel / you / How / about / reality TV shows / ?

   How do you feel about reality TV shows?

2. my / In / they're / opinion, / boring / .

   _____

3. about / you / sitcoms / do / think / What / ?

   _____

4. OK / I / they're / think / .

   _____

5. about / you / soap operas / do / How / feel / ?

   _____

2 Put the sentences in the correct order to make a conversation.

_____ **Paul:** Well, I watch for the story, not the acting.

_____ **Erika:** In my opinion, they're really awful. The actors who play the villains are so bad.

_____ **Paul:** I think they're boring. I prefer to read a book.

_____ **Erika:** Oh, well, then what do you think of documentaries?

__1__ **Paul:** Hey, Erika. What do you think about crime series?

_____ **Erika:** I think they're great. You can learn a lot.

3 Ask for and give opinions. Use the phrases and your own opinions.

| How do you feel about | In my opinion, |
| I think | What do you think about |

1. *How do you feel about* soap operas?

   _____
   _____

2. _____ crime series?

   _____
   _____

3. _____ reality TV shows?

   _____
   _____

4. _____ sitcoms?

   _____
   _____

12 | Unit 2

READING TO WRITE

1 Read Tim's movie review. Then complete the chart.

This review is of Disney's *Maleficent*. It is an action/adventure movie based on the villain from the old fairy tale, "Sleeping Beauty." It has the same director as *The Hunger Games*, Robert Stromberg.

Angelina Jolie stars as Maleficent, a beautiful fairy from a long time ago in a peaceful forest. But one day, a human army invades the forest and threatens the peace. Maleficent becomes a strong leader, but someone betrays her (so) her heart turns to stone. She *curses the human king's new baby, Aurora, to die before she is 16. As the baby grows older, Maleficent learns that Aurora (actor Elle Fanning) may be the key to peace in the forest.

I like this movie because it is a new story about an old villain. Angelina Jolie is beautiful and mysterious as Maleficent, so she makes the character very interesting. The fairy tale really comes to life because the director did a good job with the camerawork and costumes.

*__curse__ – to use magical words that make something bad happen

Main characters and actors	Director
	Robert Stromberg
Type of movie	Time and place
Short description of the story	
Why you like it or don't like it	

2 Complete the chart about a movie you like.

Main characters and actors	Director
Type of movie	Time and place
Short description of the story	
Why you like it or don't like it	

3 Circle the examples of the connectors *so* and *because* in Exercise 1. Then use your notes from Exercise 2 to write sentences using *so* and *because*.

1. *I liked this movie because the animation looked very real.*
2. _____
3. _____
4. _____

REVIEW UNITS 1–2

1 Put the words in the correct columns.

| basketball | hip-hop | jazz |
| meat with corn | pizza | sumo wrestling |

Food	Music	Sports

2 Write one traditional thing for each category from Exercise 1.

1. Food: _____
2. Music: _____
3. Sports: _____

3 Complete the questions and answers with the correct forms of *be* or *have*. Then match the questions with the correct answers.

1. What _____ he _____ for lunch? ____
2. How old _____ Ken? ____
3. Do they _____ a tablet? ____
4. _____ they your cousins? ____

a. Yes, they are.
b. He's 15. He _____ 17.
c. He _____ sushi. He doesn't have a burger.
d. No, they don't.

4 Look at the picture. Complete the sentences with the correct possessives.

1. It's my _____ house.
2. It's my _____ car.
3. It's my _____ skateboard.
4. They're my _____ kites.

5 Rewrite the sentences in Exercise 4 in two different ways. Use possessive adjectives and possessive pronouns.

1. It's _____ house. It's _____.
2. It's _____ car. It's _____.
3. It's _____ skateboard. It's _____.
4. They're _____ kites. They're _____.

6 Complete the sentences with *always*, *usually*, *often*, *sometimes*, or *never*. More than one answer may be possible.

Jean	Michelle	Ella
Watches TV every day from 7:00–9:00 p.m.	Watches TV most Mondays from 4:00–6:00 p.m. and watches movies every other weekend	Watches movies once in a while on Sundays

1. Michelle _____ watches TV on Tuesdays.
2. Jean _____ watches TV from 7:00 to 9:00 p.m.
3. Ella _____ watches movies on Sundays.
4. Michelle _____ watches movies on the weekends.

7 Rewrite the sentences and questions to make them correct.

1. When types of movies does your parents likes?
   _____

2. Does they likes comedies?
   _____

3. They doesn't call him Mr. Sparrow.
   _____

4. She teach at my school three times a week.
   _____

8 Complete the conversation.

always	so
hate watching	Tell me about it.
horror	That's interesting.
I think	want to watch
need to see	Whose
Really	

Mark: Let's go see *Godzilla* at the theater.

Anna: Maybe. ¹_____

Mark: Well, it's a ²_____ movie about a big monster.

Anna: I dislike those types of movies. I ³_____ a comedy on TV. *Modern Family* is on tonight.

Mark: ⁴_____? You can ⁵_____ watch TV. But the movie is only at the theater this week.

Anna: ⁶_____ we can rent *Godzilla* and watch it at home.

Mark: I ⁷_____ movies on a TV! You ⁸_____ horror movies on a big screen!

Anna: ⁹_____ ¹⁰_____ flat screen TV is it? Don't you have this big TV ¹¹_____ that you can watch movies?

9 Answer the questions about your favorite movies and TV shows. Write complete sentences.

1. What is your favorite movie? What type of movie is it?
   _____
   _____

2. How often do you watch TV?
   _____
   _____

3. What types of movies or TV shows do you dislike? Why do you dislike them?
   _____
   _____
   _____

4. How do you feel about documentaries? Why?
   _____
   _____
   _____

Review 1 | 15

3 Spending Habits

VOCABULARY Places to shop

1 Find 10 more words for places to shop.

ATM   bank   ✓bookstore   clothing store
department store   electronics store
food court   jewelry store   music store
pharmacy   shoe store   sporting goods store

T	Z	G	V	U	E	W	U	F	P	G	O	C	X	F	H	N	L	J
A	G	E	L	E	C	T	R	O	N	I	C	S	S	T	O	R	E	Q
Q	Z	A	T	M	W	P	D	J	B	P	M	U	N	N	A	E	J	K
N	M	U	S	I	C	S	T	O	R	E	N	D	P	A	F	G	R	
D	N	N	D	E	P	A	R	T	M	E	N	T	S	T	O	R	E	A
F	Y	V	L	J	E	W	E	L	R	Y	S	T	O	R	E	N	T	P
(B	O	O	K	S	T	O	R	E)	X	T	B	A	N	K	Y	R	M	V
F	S	P	O	R	T	I	N	G	G	O	O	D	S	S	T	O	R	E
I	S	H	O	E	S	T	O	R	E	C	P	H	A	R	M	A	C	Y
V	N	W	D	M	I	C	L	O	T	H	I	N	G	S	T	O	R	E
Y	I	Q	M	S	Z	D	L	B	F	O	O	D	C	O	U	R	T	P

2 Put the places from Exercise 1 in the correct columns. Use each word only once.

Where to get . . .			
things you can wear	things you can play	things you need to pay for things	many different types of things
shoe store			
things you need to be healthy	things to read	things to eat	

3 Where can you do these things? Write places from Exercise 1.

1. My sister bought a new MP3 player at the _electronics store_.

2. I like to read. I want to go to the _____.

3. We can eat lunch at the _____.

4. She saw a pretty necklace at the _____.

5. They went to the _____ to buy a new tennis racket.

6. We can find a wedding gift at the _____. They sell everything.

7. When my little brother is sick, I buy medicine from the _____.

8. I take money out from the _____ to go to my favorite stores.

4 Complete the sentences with your own information.

1. My favorite type of store is _a clothing store. I like to buy jeans._

2. I always shop at the _____

3. I never shop at the _____

4. On the weekend, I dislike going to the _____

5. I sometimes go to the _____

16 | Unit 3

GRAMMAR Present continuous review

1 Complete the chart using the present continuous.

Affirmative	Negative
1. I _'m getting_ lunch at the café. (get)	I _'m not getting_ lunch at the food court.
2. My friend Hal _____ at the bank now. (wait)	He _____ at the electronics store.
3. My teacher _____ at the clothing store today. (shop)	My teacher _____ at the bookstore.
4. My sister _____ a book bag online for school. (buy)	She _____ a backpack at the department store.
5. The class _____ in their notebooks right now. (write)	They _____ on their laptops.

GRAMMAR Simple present vs. present continuous

2 Complete the questions and answers. Use the present continuous or the simple present.

1. What _____are_____ you _____watching_____ right now? (watch)

   I'm watching a movie. I _'m not watching_ TV. (not watch)

2. What _____ she _____ today? (do)

   She's not running in a race. She _____ on Mondays. (study)

3. Where _____ they _____ right now? (go)

   They _____ to the beach. (go) They _____ when it's sunny. (not hike)

4. _____ you _____ about a mall in Dubai today? (write)

   Yes, I am. But I usually _____ about shopping malls. (not write)

5. _____ he _____ clothes now? (change)

   No, he's not. He usually _____ his basketball uniform home. (wear)

3 Complete the conversation with the correct forms of the verbs.

| ✓ are | buy | do | look | study |
| are | ✓do | get | shop | walk |

Alana: Hello, Vivian. What ¹_____are_____ you ²_____doing_____?

Vivian: Hi. I ³_____ with my sister, Haley. We ⁴_____ at hats.

Alana: Hats?

Vivian: Well, Haley is. But I'm ⁵_____ a hat. I need to buy sneakers for basketball. ⁶_____ you ⁷_____ your dog outside?

Alana: I wish! I'm ⁸_____ for the science test.

Vivian: Oh, too bad. I hate ⁹_____ homework on the weekend.

Alana: Me, too. But I hate ¹⁰_____ bad grades more.

4 Write sentences about you. Use the present continuous or the simple present.

1. What are you doing right now?

   I'm studying English.

2. Where are you right now?

   _____

3. Do you usually study English at this time?

   _____

4. What are you writing with right now?

   _____

Unit 3 | 17

VOCABULARY Money verbs

1 Circle the seven money verbs.

(save) earn borrow spend lend deposit withdraw

2 Match each word with its opposite.

1. borrow — a. spend
2. deposit — b. save
3. earn — c. lend
4. spend — d. withdraw

3 Correct the sentences.

1. When he needs money, he ~~lends~~ *withdraws* it at the ATM.
2. I earn my allowance by putting it in the bank.
3. My cousin deposits money from me.
4. We work after school to withdraw money to buy a bike.
5. I prefer to borrow my money on concerts, not on clothes.

4 Write sentences describing a good friend or someone in your family. Use the money verbs.

1. (save) *My friend Bill saves his money every month.*
2. (earn) _____
3. (deposit) _____
4. (withdraw) _____
5. (spend) _____
6. (borrow) _____
7. (lend) _____

18 | Unit 3

GRAMMAR Quantifiers

1 Circle the correct quantifiers.

1. I don't have **many** / **any** money until Friday.
2. Are there **much** / **many** T-shirts on sale?
3. She's not old **enough** / **some** to babysit.
4. How **a lot of** / **much** time do you have to study tonight?
5. Kevin earns **some** / **any** money selling cookies.
6. They don't have **much** / **a lot of** people on their team.

2 Complete the chart with quantifiers. More than one answer may be possible.

With countable plural nouns
1. How ____many____ sweaters do you have?
2. I have _____ sweaters.
3. I don't have _____ sweaters.
4. Are there _____ sweaters in your closet?

With uncountable nouns
5. How ____much____ money do you save every month?
6. I save _____ money every month.
7. I don't save _____ money every month.
8. Is there _____ money for the trip?

3 Complete the conversation with the correct quantifiers.

| any | How many | some |
| enough | ✓ How much | |

Jackie: The concert tickets are on sale now. Do you want to buy one?

Andrew: I want to buy two. ¹____How much____ is a ticket?

Jackie: They're $25.00 each.

Andrew: Oh no! I don't have ²_____ money. Can I borrow ³_____ money?

Jackie: Sorry. I don't have ⁴_____ money either. Who is the other ticket for?

Andrew: It's for Erika.

Erika: Andrew! I'll buy our tickets. ⁵_____ times do I have to tell you that?!?

4 Complete the questions with quantifiers. Then answer the questions with your own information.

1. How ____many____ tests do you have this week?

   I don't have any tests this week.

2. Are there _____ cafés in your town?

   _____
   _____

3. How _____ time do you spend online every day?

   _____
   _____

4. How _____ students are in your class?

   _____
   _____

5. Do you have _____ time to watch movies on the weekend?

   _____
   _____

6. How _____ times do you text each day?

   _____
   _____

CONVERSATION Shopping time

1 Put the words in the correct order to make sentences a shopper might say. Then match the sentences to the responses.

1. like / some / to / sneakers / I'd / buy / .
   I'd like to buy some
   sneakers. __d__

2. Can / on / try / I / them / ?
   _____
   ____

3. ones / prefer / red / I'd / those / .
   _____
   ____

4. them / I'll / take / !
   _____
   ____

a. The red ones are very nice. Here, try them on.

b. Of course. Here you are.

c. OK. That'll be $39.

d. OK. How about these green ones?

2 Put the sentences in order to make a conversation.

__1__ **Brandon:** I'd like to buy <u>some sneakers</u>, please.

____ **Clerk:** OK. That'll be $59.

____ **Brandon:** <u>Good. They're big enough.</u> I'll take them.

____ **Clerk:** OK. How <u>about these blue basketball sneakers</u>?

____ **Brandon:** Hmm. I'd prefer <u>ones to play basketball in</u>.

____ **Clerk:** OK. Try <u>these</u>. How do they fit?

____ **Brandon:** <u>Size 11</u>.

____ **Clerk:** Of course. What size do you wear?

____ **Brandon:** Can I try <u>them</u> on?

____ **Clerk:** OK. How about <u>these black ones? They're great for running</u>.

3 Rewrite the conversation in Exercise 2 in order. Change the underlined words to use your own ideas.

1. **You:** I'd like to buy _____, please.
2. **Clerk:** _____
3. **You:** _____
4. **Clerk:** _____
5. **You:** _____
6. **Clerk:** _____
7. **You:** _____
8. **Clerk:** _____
9. **You:** _____
10. **Clerk:** _____

20 | Unit 3

READING TO WRITE

1 Read the review. Label the information with the words and phrases.

don't like   like   ✓name of product   recommendation   the price   where to buy

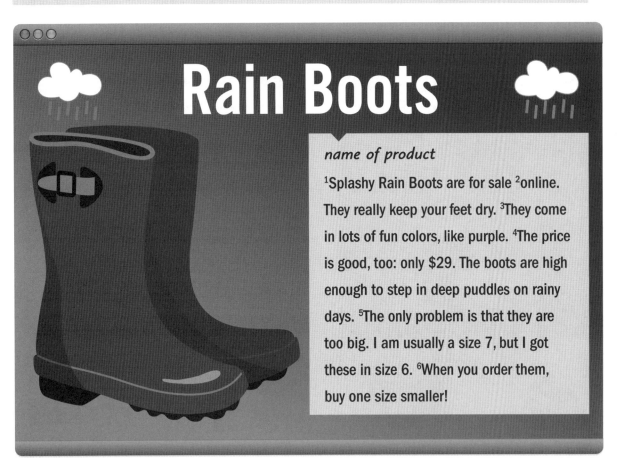

name of product
¹Splashy Rain Boots are for sale ²online. They really keep your feet dry. ³They come in lots of fun colors, like purple. ⁴The price is good, too: only $29. The boots are high enough to step in deep puddles on rainy days. ⁵The only problem is that they are too big. I am usually a size 7, but I got these in size 6. ⁶When you order them, buy one size smaller!

2 Circle the correct answers.

1. My cell phone is great. **Buy** / **Don't buy** one like mine.
2. **Get** / **Don't get** these T-shirts today. Wait until Saturday and save $10.
3. The hotel is very pleasant. **Spend** / **don't spend** your next vacation here!
4. The fruit at this store is old. **Shop** / **Don't shop** here if you want fresh fruit!
5. These sweaters come in many colors. **Buy** / **Don't buy** more than one if you can.
6. The concert seats aren't very good. Let's **get** / **not get** the tickets.

3 Write recommendations about products you use. Use imperatives.

1. _Don't buy the newest cell phone._
2. _____
3. _____
4. _____
5. _____

Unit 3 | 21

4 Our Heroes

VOCABULARY Cool jobs

1 Use the pictures to complete the crossword.

ACROSS   DOWN

2.   1.

4.   3.

6.   5.

8.   7.

9.

10.

2 Circle the correct answers.

1. Which job is a sports job?
   a. painter   b. writer   c. soccer player

2. Which job is an academic job?
   a. scientist   b. runner   c. singer

3. Which job is a job in the arts?
   a. scientist   b. soccer player   c. writer

4. Which is NOT a job in the arts?
   a. dancer   b. painter   c. runner

3 Write a sentence about a famous person for each of the jobs listed below.

1. scientist *Neil deGrasse Tyson is a famous scientist.*
2. tennis player _____
3. soccer player _____
4. actor _____
5. singer _____

4 Complete the sentences with the jobs from Exercise 1.

I think a lot about what type of job I would like. I love sports! I'm a ¹ *soccer player* on the school team. I'm also a ² _____, but I'm not on the team. I just play my brother. I'm not a very fast ³ _____. I like sports, but I don't think I want to do sports as a job.

I don't want to work in arts or entertainment. I'm not good at making pictures, so I don't want to be a ⁴_____. I don't have a good voice, so I can't be a ⁵_____. And I don't like to talk in front of an audience, so I don't want to be an ⁶_____. I'm athletic, but I don't move well, so I can't be a ⁷_____.

I like rules, but I don't like to argue, so I wouldn't want to be a ⁸_____. I'm not very good at math or chemistry, so I wouldn't want to be a ⁹_____. I do like telling stories and reading books, so maybe I could be a ¹⁰_____. I could work for a sports magazine!

22 | Unit 4

GRAMMAR Simple past statements review and *ago*

1 Complete the chart with verbs in the simple past.

Affirmative statements	Negative statements
She _____ a millionaire at age 21.	She *wasn't* a millionaire at age 20.
I *was* in a play a month *ago*.	I _____ in a movie last month.
He _____ in a restaurant.	He *didn't work* as a lawyer.
They *tried* to play tennis a week *ago*.	They _____ to play last month.
She _____ a race in 2010.	She *didn't run* any races in 2014.
We *won* the match a year _____.	We _____ the match.

2 Write the correct forms of the verbs.

1. I _*lived*_ in São Paulo when I was five. (live)
2. His father _____ in Hong Kong five years ago. (work)
3. They _____ for running shoes last weekend. (shop)
4. We _____ surfing when we were at the beach. (try)
5. She _____ a job with the New York City Ballet. (not get)
6. The band _____ their first video in 2011. (not make)
7. I _____ a job as a singer three months ago. (not have)
8. She _____ a popular book in 2007. (not write)

3 Write statements about Daniella using the simple past. Use information from the chart.

	Affirmative	Negative
1. live	Mexico City	Paris
2. want to be	painter	doctor
3. has	friends	brothers or sisters
4. work	in a library	in a café
5. win	awards	medals

1. *Daniella lived in Mexico City. She didn't live in Paris.*
2. _____
3. _____
4. _____
5. _____

4 Complete the sentences with the simple past and your own ideas. Write affirmative or negative statements.

1. I _*was in sixth grade*_ two years ago. (be)
2. I _____ five years ago. (live)
3. My friends and I _____ last year. (like)
4. I _____ last month. (play)
5. My parents _____ for three years before I was born. (be)
6. I _____ when I was five. (want to be)

Unit 4 | 23

VOCABULARY Adjectives of personality

1 Put the letters in the correct order to make personality words.

1. MALC _____calm_____
2. DIKN _____
3. NUFYN _____
4. EVBAR _____
5. EITUQ _____
6. ROSESIU _____
7. BRSTNUOB _____
8. LEFUCERH _____
9. DREFYLIN _____

2 Match the definitions with the correct words from Exercise 1. Write the number for each.

___5___ doesn't talk a lot

_____ makes you laugh a lot

_____ doesn't get excited

_____ isn't scared of things

_____ is always happy and smiling

_____ likes to meet new people

_____ studies all the time

_____ won't listen to others

_____ helps others and is nice

3 Complete the paragraph with the personality words from Exercise 1. Then write the name of each girl beside the picture.

| brave | ✓cheerful | funny | kind | serious |

My name is Stella. I want to tell you about my friends. First, there's Emily. She is very ¹ _cheerful_ . If you want to have a party, she will make it fun. My friend Tina is very ² _____ . She makes me laugh. My friend Mala is the ³ _____ one. She's not scared of anything. Jane is my nicest friend. She is very ⁴ _____ . Then there's Anna. She studies a lot, so my friends say that she's ⁵ _____ .

_____

_____

___Emily___

_____

_____

4 Use the adjectives of personality to write sentences about yourself, your friends, and your family.

1. _My brother is funny._
2. _____
3. _____
4. _____
5. _____

24 | Unit 4

GRAMMAR Simple past questions review and *ago*

1 Match the questions with the correct answers.

1. How was she few minutes ago?
2. Where was she?
3. Did you see the shark?
4. How long ago did it start following her?
5. Who did you call?
6. What did they say?
7. Was she scared then?

a. It started five minutes ago.
b. Yes, I did.
c. I called the beach patrol.
d. She was happy and having fun.
e. She was far from the beach.
f. Yes, she was!
g. They said to wave at her and point to the shark.

2 Complete the questions.

1. What ___did___ you ___do___ yesterday? (do)
   We went camping.
2. _____ you _____ the fire? (see)
   Yes, we did.
3. Where _____ you when it started? (be)
   We were in the tent.
4. How long ago _____ it _____? (start)
   It started two hours ago.
5. Where _____ you _____? (run)
   We ran up that hill.
6. Where _____ they _____ the campers? (put)
   They put them on the fire truck.

3 Write questions in the simple past.

1. how / he / a few hours / ago
   How was he a few hours ago?
2. it / start / a few minutes / ago
3. what / they / talk about
4. he / study / last night
5. they / at the library
6. why / you / think / that
7. we / sad / last year

4 Answer these questions with your own information.

1. How did you feel a few minutes ago?
   I was calm a few minutes ago.
2. Did you study English last night?
3. Where did you go last week?
4. Who did you text yesterday?
5. Did you see a movie last weekend?

Unit 4 | 25

CONVERSATION Everyday heroes

1 Put the words in the correct order to make sentences to complete the conversation.

1. **A:** Who's / hero / your / ?
   Who's your hero?

2. **B:** think / I / are / athletes / heroes / .
   _____

3. **A:** mean / you / do / What / ?
   _____

4. **B:** mean / athletes / I / hard / train / .
   _____
   at / are / the / They / their / best / sport / .
   _____

5. **A:** that / winners / heroes / Are / you / are / saying / ?
   _____
   _____

6. **B:** Not exactly. / make / that / What / to / say / heroes / is / us / try / I'm / harder / trying / .
   _____
   _____

2 Circle the phrases in Exercise 1 that ask for and give clarification.

3 Use the phrases to complete the conversations. There is more than one way to complete them.

> Are you saying that
> I mean
> ✓ What do you mean?
> What I'm trying to say is that

1. **A:** My heroes have always been cowboys.
   B: _What do you mean?_

2. **A:** I don't think business people are heroes.
   B: _____ they can't be heroes?

3. **A:** _____ superheroes are like real people.
   B: Oh, I see.

4. **A:** You think celebrities don't want to help others?
   B: _____ celebrities want to be _famous_ for helping others.

26 | Unit 4

READING TO WRITE

1 Read about a hero. Then fill out the chart about her.

My hero is Serena Williams. She is famous *because* she is a great tennis player. In 2002, she became number one in the world for the first time. From 2002 to 2003, she held all four Grand Slam titles at the same time. She also won four Olympic medals.

I admire Serena Williams because she is a great tennis player. I also admire her because she is very strong and can come back to win after almost losing. Since she was brave enough to overcome her injuries, she can still play. She's also very kind and built a school in Kenya, Africa. Due to these reasons, she's my hero.

Who	Serena Williams
Her job	
Her personality	_____, _____, _____
Heroic things she has done	
Why I admire her	

2 Circle the connector words (*because, due to, since*) in Exercise 1. Then rewrite the sentences using different connector words.

1. *Since she is a great tennis player, she is famous.*
2. _____
3. _____
4. _____
5. _____

3 Choose the correct connector words.

1. I admire Jane Goodall **since** / **due to** her work with chimpanzees.
2. Rick helps ocean animals **due to** / **because** he used to train them.
3. Erika has raced motorcycles **because** / **since** 2011.
4. **Due to** / **Since** his last movie, he's no longer popular.
5. **Since** / **Because** she works very hard, she is my role model.

4 Write sentences about your role model. Use connector words.

| because | due to | since |

1. *The Dalai Lama is my role model because he is so calm.*
2. _____
3. _____
4. _____
5. _____

Unit 4 | 27

REVIEW UNITS 3–4

1 Match the descriptions with the correct pictures. Then write the names of the places.

1. a place to buy shoes ____ _____

2. a place to get something to eat ____ _____

3. a place to deposit money ____ _____

4. a place to get medicine ____ _____

5. a place to buy many different things ____ _____

a.

b.

c.

d.

e.

2 Look at the pictures. Circle the correct answers.

Jeff: Since I like to study wildlife, I want to be a ¹**lawyer / runner / scientist**. Because I'm ²**brave / funny / cheerful**, I can work with dangerous animals like snakes. And I'm ³**quiet / stubborn / serious**, so I can get close to them.

Nina: I love music. Ever since I was little, I've wanted to be a ⁴**singer / actor / painter**. I'm a good performer because I can be ⁵**kind / calm / stubborn** on stage. But I also need to be ⁶**quiet / serious / friendly** so I can talk to the audience between songs.

Alex: I love reading stories. Some people say I'm ⁷**cheerful / funny / kind** because I tell jokes. Other people say I'm ⁸**cheerful / serious / friendly** because I read a lot. I think I'd like to be a ⁹**soccer player / dancer / writer**. Then I could write funny stories.

3 Complete the sentences with the present continuous or simple present forms of the verbs.

1. I _____ (not watch) a movie right now.

2. She _____ (earn) money at her weekend job.

3. We usually _____ (spend) money on video games.

4. They _____ (deposit) the money into my account right now.

5. She _____ (lend) her cousins money every month.

4 Circle the correct answers.

1. **A:** How _____ money do you have?
   a. many   b. much   c. enough
   B: I have _____ money.
   a. any   b. enough   c. don't

2. **A:** Are there _____ shoes in your closet?
   a. many   b. how much   c. much
   B: Yes, _____.
   a. there is   b. there are   c. there aren't
   B: No, _____.
   a. there is   b. there isn't   c. there aren't

3. **A:** How _____ books do you have?
   a. much   b. any   c. many
   B: I don't have _____ books.
   a. many   b. much   c. some

4. **A:** _____ did you ride your bike last weekend?
   a. Where   b. When   c. Why
   B: I _____ to the beach.
   a. biking   b. am going   c. biked to bike

28 | Review 2

5. **A:** Where is Tim _____ on his vacation?
   a. go   b. going to go   c. went

   B: He _____ to the mountains.
   a. 's going to go   b. are going   c. goes

5 Circle the correct words. Then match the questions with the correct answers.

1. When **was / were / did** she go to China? _____
2. **Was / Were / Did** Lara play soccer last summer? _____
3. **Was / Were / Did** your friends visit last night? _____
4. Where **was / were / did** your cousins last weekend? _____
5. Where **was / were / did** Jason study last night? _____

a. No, she didn't.
b. They were at the pool.
c. She went in June.
d. He studied at the library.
e. Yes, they did.

6 Complete the sentences with the simple past.

Arline	Seth	Kyla
– study English on Wednesday	– play soccer Monday	– act in a movie in April
– go to Canada in June	– join soccer team in February	

1. Seth _____ soccer on Monday.
2. Arline _____ English on Wednesday.
3. Kyla _____ in a movie in April.
4. Arline _____ to Canada in June.
5. Seth _____ a soccer team in February.

7 Complete the conversations.

a lot of	lend
Are you saying that	much
borrow	started
enough	

Arthur: I really want to buy this hoodie!

Brittany: What do you like about it?

Arthur: It's made by a company that Bono ¹_____ in 2005. He's my hero.

Brittany: ²_____ you'd buy that just because of Bono?

Arthur: Well, it looks cool, too.

Clerk: May I help you?

Arthur: I'd like to buy this hoodie.

Clerk: Here you are. That'll be $79.

Brittany: That's ³_____ money!

Arthur: Oh no! I don't have ⁴_____ money! Can I ⁵_____ some?

Brittany: I don't have that ⁶_____ money either. Maybe your hero Bono can ⁷_____ it to you!

8 Answer the questions about your hero or role model. Write complete sentences.

1. Who is your hero or role model?
   _____

2. What is his or her job?
   _____

3. What heroic things does he or she do?
   _____

4. What is his or her personality like?
   _____

5. Why do you admire him or her?
   _____

6. When were you brave or heroic?
   _____

Review 2 | **29**

5 It's a Mystery!

VOCABULARY Action verbs

1 Label the pictures with the words.

caught	fell	ran
chased	hid	stole
✓climbed	jumped	threw

1. _climbed_

2. _____

3. _____

4. _____

5. _____

6. _____

7. _____

8. _____

9. _____

2 Complete the story. Use the action verbs from Exercise 1.

The squirrel saw a nut up high in the tree. He ¹ _climbed_ the tree. The squirrel got the nut, but then a bird flew by, and the squirrel ² _____ out of the tree. But the squirrel still had the nut!

But the bird wanted the nut. The bird ³ _____ the squirrel. The squirrel ⁴ _____ behind the tree. He ⁵ _____ the nut under a leaf. Then the bird ⁶ _____ the nut.

As the bird flew away, the squirrel ⁷ _____ up on a log. He ⁸ _____ the bird by the leg.

But the bird ⁹ _____ the nut into the pond. The squirrel let go of the bird's leg. This time, no one got the nut!

3 Correct the sentences. Use the simple past.
                  climbed
1. I ~~climb~~ trees a lot when I was young.
2. She said she never steal anything.
3. They hides the key under a rock.
4. She throw the ball really fast.
5. I catched the ball in my glove.
6. Did you see where she run?
7. The apple fells off the tree.
8. They jumpeds over the hole.
9. The dog chase his tail for an hour.

4 Write sentences using the action verbs from Exercise 1. Think of sports you play or activities you do. Use your own information.

1. _I climbed a tree last weekend._
2. _____
3. _____
4. _____
5. _____

GRAMMAR Past continuous; adverbs of time

1 Match the questions with the answers.

1. What were you doing?
2. What was your friend Kevin doing?
3. What was the thief doing?
4. Was the police officer chasing her?
5. What was the thief wearing?
6. Was Kevin taking a picture with his phone?

a. He was using his phone.
b. Yes, he was.
c. No! He was texting and didn't see it.
d. I was buying a hat.
e. She was wearing a baseball cap.
f. She was stealing a hoodie.

2 Read the blog entry. Then answer the questions. Use the past continuous.

My Exciting Day by Ken

Yesterday was an interesting day. I was skateboarding to school at 8:00 a.m. At about 8:05 a.m., I was passing the bank, and a man ran by me. He was carrying a bag, but he didn't look like he was exercising. He wasn't wearing running shoes. Next, a police officer ran up to me and asked if he could use my skateboard. I let him, of course. Then the police officer was skateboarding down the street! He was chasing the man with the bag. The police officer skated in front of the thief, and the thief fell. The police officer caught him!

1. What was Ken doing at 8:00 a.m.?

   He was skateboarding to school at 8:00 a.m.

2. What did Ken notice about the man's shoes?

   _____

3. What was the man carrying?

   _____

4. How was the police officer chasing the thief?

   _____

3 Unscramble the questions. Then answer the questions with information from the chart.

Last weekend	Last night	At 10:00 p.m.	This morning	At 9:00 a.m.
climbing a mountain	playing video games	sleeping	running a race	chasing a thief

1. night / doing / What / last / she / was / ?

   What was she doing last night?

   She was playing video games.

2. last / she / What / doing / weekend / was / ?

   _____

   _____

3. this / What / she / was / morning / doing / ?

   _____

   _____

4. she / homework / doing / 9:00 a.m. / at / Was / ?

   _____

   _____

5. 10:00 p.m. / at / doing / she / was / What / ?

   _____

   _____

4 Write questions in the past continuous. Answer the questions with your own information.

1. Where / you / live / last year?

   Where were you living last year?

   I was living in Brazil.

2. What / your friend / do / last weekend?

   _____

   _____

3. What / you / wear / yesterday afternoon?

   _____

   _____

4. What / you / do / this morning / at 8:00 a.m.?

   _____

   _____

5. What / you / watch / last night?

   _____

   _____

Unit 5 | 31

VOCABULARY Adverbs of manner

1 Find eight more adverbs of manner.

✓badly	happily	loudly	quietly	terribly
carefully	hard	quickly	slowly	well

W	E	H	A	P	P	I	L	Y
E	Q	U	I	E	T	L	Y	A
L	H	A	R	D	W	E	L	L
L	T	E	R	R	I	B	L	Y
Q	U	I	C	K	L	Y	A	R
C	A	R	E	F	U	L	L	Y
E	L	O	U	D	L	Y	Y	I
E	E	A	S	L	O	W	L	Y
E	K	E	(B	A	D	L	Y)	R

2 Match each word with its opposite.

1. sadly — b. happily
2. loudly — a. slowly
3. well — c. badly
4. quickly — d. quietly

3 Complete the paragraph with the correct words.

| carefully | ✓ happily | hard | quickly | terribly |

I was ¹ ___happily___ playing my video game last night. It was a difficult game. I didn't want to make any mistakes, so I was playing ² _____. I was trying really ³ _____, and maybe that's why I didn't hear the noise at first. But then it got louder. And then there was a bright light outside the window. I paused the game and went to the window. As I opened the curtain to look, an orange light ⁴ _____ flew by. And then it was gone. I don't know what it was! I was a little scared. After that, I went back to my game, and I played ⁵ _____.

4 Correct the incorrect sentences. Write *correct* if no changes are needed.

1. They did badly on the test. ___correct___
2. He played the piano ~~terrible~~. ___terribly___
3. The thief ran quickly. _____
4. I tried hardly to win the tennis match. _____
5. The turtle was walking slow. _____
6. We happily sang the birthday song. _____
7. The truck drove by loud. _____
8. We spoke quiet during the movie. _____
9. She was making the model careful. _____

5 Use adverbs of manner to answer the questions with your own information.

1. How do you read?
   I read slowly so I can enjoy the story.

2. How do you spend your money?
   _____
   _____

3. Do you walk slowly or quickly?
   _____
   _____

4. Do you play tennis well or badly?
   _____
   _____

GRAMMAR Simple past vs. past continuous; *when* and *while*

1 Underline the past continuous.

> While my sister and I <u>were watching</u> a movie, our dog came into the living room with us. When we were watching the exciting part, the dog started barking. My sister didn't notice the noise. But I did. So I put the dog out in the yard when my sister wasn't looking. Then I was getting snacks for us while my sister watched the movie. The phone was ringing while I was in the kitchen. I told my sister to answer it. She didn't, so I did. It was our neighbor. He saw our dog two blocks away! I gave my sister the snacks. Then I went out to look for the dog. She was watching another movie when I came home with the dog.

2 Match the phrases to make sentences.

1. I was playing soccer well
2. Helen saw the thief grab a hat
3. I heard the fire alarm
4. When we were hiking,
5. While it was raining,

a. while I was cooking dinner.
b. we stayed dry inside.
c. when I scored a goal.
d. we saw a deer with its baby.
e. while we were shopping.

3 Complete the sentences with *when* or *while*. Sometimes both answers are possible.

1. The picture fell loudly ___when / while___ my brothers were playing.
2. I was using the computer _____ I heard the news.
3. _____ the team won, he was cheering loudly.
4. _____ she was surfing, she saw a shark.
5. I was hiking _____ I heard someone singing.
6. _____ he was playing the piano, we were listening happily.

4 Complete the conversation with the simple past or past continuous forms of the verbs.

Mark: Hey, I called you last night at 9:00.

Steve: I know. Sorry. I was watching the game when you [1] ___called___ (call).

Mark: Yeah, well, while I [2] _____ (watch) the game, our TV broke!

Steve: No! You missed the game! What [3] _____ (happen) when it broke?

Mark: Spain was playing well when their center [4] _____ (fall). The TV broke after that.

Steve: Well, you didn't miss much. After that, Spain was losing badly. I [5] _____ (turn) the TV off when the game was almost over.

Mark: You didn't watch the ending! Do you know who won?

Steve: Yeah, I [6] _____ (see) the headline when I was checking my email. Spain lost.

5 Use the verbs to write five sentences about events that were interrupted. Use your own information or write about someone you know.

| cooking | reading | ✓sleeping |
| playing | running | walking |

1. *I was sleeping when the storm began.*
2. _____
3. _____
4. _____
5. _____

Unit 5 | 33

CONVERSATION An unusual dream

1 Complete the conversation. Put the words in the correct order to make sentences. More than one answer may be possible.

1. **Mei:** I / you / the / about / Did / movie / tell / ?
   <u>Did I tell you about the movie?</u> The one about a guy named Jeff who has these weird neighbors?

2. **Carlos:** No. / me / Tell / it / about / .

3. **Mei:** Jeff / the / was / sleeping / beginning, / In / .

4. Then / while / looked / talking / on / the / out of / the / was / window / Jeff / phone / he / .

5. his / watching / neighbors / was / He / .

6. **Carlos:** they / were / What / doing / ?

7. **Mei:** was / while / man / A / woman / in / her / bedroom / a letter / hid / reading / a / .

8. went / bedroom / there / man / the / the / and / was / screaming / into / Then / .

9. **Carlos:** weird / That's / .

10. happened / what / Then / ?

2 Choose the correct phrase to tell or react to a story.

Frank: ¹That's weird / (Did I tell you about) the play?

Olga: ²No, what happened? / Then what happened?

Frank: Well, ³did I tell you / in the beginning, the actor was saying his lines when the power went out.

Olga: ⁴In the beginning. / That's weird.

Frank: Yeah, it was. Then there was a scream in the audience. We thought it was part of the play.

Olga: ⁵Then what happened? / Did I tell you?

3 Complete the sentences.

| ✓Did I tell you about | In the beginning |
| That's weird | Then what happened |

Sally: ¹ <u>Did I tell you about</u> my ski trip?

Jack: No. What happened?

Sally: ² _____ I was skiing very carefully, and then I got tired. I started skiing badly.

Jack: Oh, oh. ³_____?

Sally: Well, I jumped over a log and I landed badly. I fell into the deep snow. I heard a noise and thought my leg was broken. But my leg was fine.

Jack: ⁴_____.

Sally: Yeah, it was strange. I really thought I broke my leg. But it was the sound of my ski breaking!

Jack: That's funny.

READING TO WRITE

1 **Put the parts of the story in order.**

___ But when I got there, the door was locked.
I didn't have a key. At first, I was surprised because I didn't lock the door. So who did?

___ Then I heard barking. My dog was inside.
A few minutes later, he came to the door. Then he jumped on the door.

_1_ It was a dark and stormy night. I was feeding the animals in the barn when I heard the rain.
I closed the barn and ran to the house.

___ In the end, I climbed in through a window.

___ Then I thought maybe his foot locked the door on accident. After that, I was less scared. But I was wet from all the rain!

___ Next, I was scared. What if someone was in the house?

2 **Look at Exercise 1. Draw a square around the beginning and draw an X through the end. Then circle the sequencing words.**

3 **Rewrite the story above. Try to use only one sentence for each part.**

| At first | Later | ✓One night |
| Finally | Next | Then |

1. *One night, it started to rain.*
2. _____ I was surprised that _____.
3. _____ I was afraid that _____.
4. _____ my dog _____.
5. _____ I was less _____.
6. _____ I _____.

Unit 5 | 35

Home, Sweet Home

VOCABULARY Furniture and other household items

1 Put the letters in the correct order to make furniture and household words.

1. DEB _____bed_____
2. SEDK _____
3. OHREWS _____
4. LOTEIT _____
5. SEBAKOCO _____
6. REDSRES _____
7. FOAS _____
8. MARACHRI _____
9. RACIH _____
10. RORMRI _____
11. LETBA _____
12. BISTNACE _____

2 Label the pictures with the words from Exercise 1.

1. _sofa_

2. _____

3. _____

4. _____

5. _____

6. _____

7. _____

8. _____

9. _____

10. _____

11. _____

12. _____

3 Write the names of the furniture and household items from Exercise 1 in the correct columns.

Kitchen	Living room
chair	

Bathroom	Bedroom

4 Complete the sentences.

| bed | cabinets | desk | mirror | ✓sofa |

1. I sit on a ____sofa____ when I watch TV.
2. We keep cups and glasses in _____.
3. I sleep in a _____.
4. He does his homework at a _____.
5. Who do you see in the _____?

5 Answer the questions with your own information.

1. What's in your kitchen?
   There's a table and chairs.
2. What's your favorite thing to sit on?
   _____
3. What color is your bed?
   _____
4. What's in your dresser?
   _____
5. What's your favorite piece of furniture? Why?
   _____
   _____

GRAMMAR Comparative and superlative adjectives and adverbs

1 Complete the rules and write the comparative and superlative forms of the adjectives.

1. For most comparative adjectives and adverbs with one syllable, add ____-er____.

    warm → ____warmer____

    long → _____

2. For most superlative adjectives and adverbs with one syllable, add _____.

    warm → the _____

    long → the _____

3. For most comparative adjectives and adverbs with two or more syllables, add _____.

    exciting → _____

    slowly → _____

4. For most superlatives adjectives and adverbs with two or more syllables, add _____.

    exciting → the _____

    slowly → the _____

5. Some comparative adjectives are irregular:

    good → _____

    bad → _____

6. Some superlative adjectives are irregular:

    good → the _____

    bad → the _____

7. Some comparative adverbs are irregular:

    well → _____

    badly → _____

8. Some superlative adverbs are irregular:

    well → the _____

    badly → the _____

2 Write the comparative and superlative forms of the adjectives.

Adjective	Comparative	Superlative
big	bigger	the biggest
strange		
beautiful		
exciting		

3 Write the comparative and superlative forms of the adverbs.

Adverb	Comparative	Superlative
quickly	more quickly	the most quickly
slowly		
far		
hard		

4 Complete the sentences using the comparative and superlative adjectives and adverbs.

1. My parents' living room is ____nice____. But my grandparents' living room is ____nicer____. (nice)

2. My brother's bedroom is the _____ bedroom in our house. It is _____ than our parents'. (big)

3. My sister cooks _____. But I cook _____. (well)

4. She speaks Spanish _____. But she speaks Chinese _____ Spanish. (quick)

5. In our house, the living room is _____ the dining room. But the kitchen is the _____. (popular)

6. Our bookcase is _____. But the dresser is _____. (dark)

VOCABULARY Household appliances

1 Complete the crossword puzzle with the names of household appliances.

ACROSS

2.
3.
4.
5.
9.
10.
11.
12.

DOWN

1.
6.
7.
8.

2 Write the names of the household appliances.

1. This keeps your food cold. __refrigerator__
2. You use these to cook food. _____, _____, _____, _____
3. You put your dishes in this to wash them. _____
4. You clean your clothes in this. _____
5. You may need to use this on your shirt. _____
6. This is probably the first thing you hear in the morning. _____
7. You might use this after your shower. _____
8. When it's dark, you turn this on. _____
9. You clean the carpet with this. _____

3 What time of day do you use these appliances? Write the name of the appliance in the appropriate place in the word web. Add your own ideas. Some words can go in more than one circle.

| alarm clock | ✓dishwasher | hairdryer | lamp |
| microwave | refrigerator | stove | toaster |

Evening/Night
dishwasher
_____

Morning
_____
_____

Afternoon
_____

Day
_____

4 Write sentences about these household appliances. Use your own information.

| ✓alarm clock | dishwasher | hairdryer |
| iron | oven | vacuum cleaner |

1. I have a black __alarm clock__ in my bedroom.
2. I rarely use the _____.
3. My favorite appliance is the _____.
4. I use the _____ in the _____.
5. _____.

38 | Unit 6

GRAMMAR should (not), (not) have to, must (not)

1 Circle the correct verbs to complete the rules in the chart.

should (not), (not) have to, must (not)
1. Use **should not** / **not have to** for advice and recommendations.
2. Use **must** / **have to** for responsibilities.
3. Use **not have to** / **must not** for things that are not required.
4. Use **must** / **have to** for an obligation.
5. Use **should not** / **must not** for a prohibition.

(**should not** is circled in item 1)

2 Correct the sentences with the affirmative or negative.

shouldn't
1. You ~~should~~ keep bananas in the refrigerator.
2. You must not set your alarm clock if you want to wake up on time.
3. You don't have to follow the directions when you wash clothes.
4. You must look at your friend's test paper.
5. You don't have to keep your room clean to earn your allowance.
6. You have to do the dishes after dinner. Your brother is going to do them.

3 Write the correct answers.

1. (recommendation) You ____should____ cook the vegetables on the stove and not in the microwave.
2. (prohibition) You _____ use the hairdryer while you're in the bathtub.
3. (responsibility) When his mother cooks, he _____ load the dishwasher after dinner.
4. (things not required) But he _____ do the dishes if he cooks dinner.
5. (obligation) Read the label. It says you _____ wash that shirt in cold water. Don't use hot water.
6. (things not required) We _____ bring a hairdryer. The hotel will have one.

4 Answer the questions. Use your own information and *should* (*not*), (*not*) *have to*, or *must* (*not*) to answer the questions.

1. What advice can you give someone about how to dress today?
   You should wear a T-shirt. It's hot outside.
2. What do you recommend NOT to do in school?
   _____
   _____
3. What do you have to do every night?
   _____
   _____
4. What don't you have to do on weekends?
   _____
   _____
5. What must you NOT eat?
   _____
   _____

Unit 6 | 39

CONVERSATION I have to clean the house.

1 Put the words in the correct order.

1. like / some / you / Would / help / ?
   Would you like some help?

2. Can / ask / you / a favor / I / ?
   _____

3. out / help / me / Could / you / ?
   _____

4. you / hand / a / give / I'll / .
   _____

2 Complete the conversation with the questions and statements from Exercise 1.

Tim: Are you going to the park?

Iris: Well, I want to, but you look too busy to come with me. [1] *Would you like some help*?

Tim: Yes, I would!

Iris: OK. What can I do?

Tim: I should move the sofa to clean behind it.
[2] _____?

Iris: Sure. [3] _____.

Tim: Thanks. OK. And [4] _____?

Iris: Of course. What is it?

Tim: Can you put those dishes in the dishwasher?

Iris: No problem.

3 Complete the conversations with the phrases from Exercise 1. More than one answer may be possible.

1. **A:** I need a hand in the garden.
   _____
   _____?
   B: Sorry, but I'm busy right now.

2. **A:** These boxes are heavy!
   B: _____
   _____?
   A: Thanks.

3. **A:** _____
   _____?
   I need a ride to school.
   B: I can drive you.

4. **A:** I need to vacuum and put the dishes in the dishwasher.
   B: _____
   _____.
   A: Thank you!

40 | Unit 6

READING TO WRITE

1 Write the words in the correct places in the chart.

apartment	chairs	modern
armchair	desk	new
bathroom	dishwasher	old
bed	dresser	small
bedroom	house	sofa
✓big	kitchen	table
bookcase	living room	washing machine

Size, age, kind	_big_ , _____ , _____ , _____ , _____ , _____ , _____
Rooms	_____ , _____ , _____ , _____
Furniture	_____ , _____ , _____ , _____ , _____ , _____ , _____ , _____
Appliances	_____ , _____

2 Correct the comma errors in the sentences. Some sentences may not need correction.

1. There are three armchairs, and one sofa in the living room.
2. I have to turn on the dishwasher brush my hair and set the alarm clock before bed.
3. We have a dog, a cat, and a bird.
4. He washes his bike and car every weekend.
5. Please put the cups glasses and dishes in the cabinets.
6. We cleaned the bathroom bedroom living room and kitchen this morning.

3 Answer the questions about you. Use the words from Exercise 1 and your own information.

1. What kind of home do you (or your friends) live in?

   I live in an apartment. But it's in London, so we call it a "flat."

2. What is your home like?

   _____
   _____

3. What is in your bedroom?

   _____
   _____

4. Where in your house do you spend the most time?

   _____
   _____

5. What is your favorite piece of furniture in your home?

   _____
   _____

REVIEW UNITS 5–6

1 Match the descriptions with the correct furniture and household items. Then write the names of the items.

1. This cooks food quickly. ____
   _____
2. This helps you see when a room is dark. ____
   _____
3. This is where you wash your whole body. ____
   _____
4. You keep clothing in this. ____
   _____
5. You put bread in this. ____
   _____
6. You can sit at this to eat a meal. ____
   _____
7. You use this in the bathroom every day. ____
   _____
8. This makes washing dishes easy. ____
   _____
9. You keep things to read here. ____
   _____
10. You get into this to sleep. ____
    _____

a.
b.
c.
d.
e.
f.
g.
h.
i.
j.

2 Complete the sentences with adverbs of manner.

1. She was talking _____ on her cell phone. (loud)
2. John usually does his homework _____. (careful)
3. Ella _____ cooked dinner for her parents. (happy)
4. They were singing _____ because they were nervous. (terrible)
5. She didn't practice, so the performance went _____. (bad)
6. I studied a lot, so I did _____ on my test. (good)

3 Complete the paragraph with action verbs.

| caught | chased | fell | jumped | stole |
| caught | climbed | hid | ran | threw |

The movie started as the thief [1]_____ in the bathroom at a bank. After everyone left in the evening, he [2]_____ a lot of money and put it into a bag. He left through the back door. Then he [3]_____ up the back of the next building. From there, he [4]_____ onto the next roof. You could hear sirens. The thief's buddy was waiting for him on the ground. The thief [5]_____ the bag down to his buddy. The buddy [6]_____ it and then [7]_____ away! The police saw him and [8]_____ him. The buddy [9]_____, and the police [10]_____ him! Meanwhile, the thief was holding another bag as he watched this from the roof!

4 Circle the correct answers.

1. I can bike _____ than I can run.
   a. more quickly b. most quickly

2. He ran _____ today than ever before.
   a. farther b. the farthest

3. She practiced a lot, and her playing got _____.
   a. better b. the best

4. At night, it's _____ on the farm than it is in the city.
   a. darker b. the darkest

5. I like movies more than TV, but I like books _____.
   a. better b. the best

5 Complete the sentences with the correct forms of the verbs. Then write *past continuous* or *simple past*.

| jump | run | sing | talk |

1. I _____ while I was in the shower. _____

2. I _____ over the log when I fell. _____

3. _____ you _____ to Jillian on the phone last night when her sister sent you a text? _____

4. _____ Alan _____ in the race yesterday? _____

6 Complete the conversation.

Can I ask you for a favor?	not have to
Could you help me out?	should not
have to	Would you like some help?
I'll give you a hand.	
must not	

Manny: Want to go to the park now?

Claire: I'd love to! But I ¹_____ do all this laundry.

Manny: ²_____

Claire: You ³_____.

Manny: I know, but I want to.

Claire: Great! I need to put all this laundry in the washing machine. ⁴_____

Manny: Sure. But wait a minute! You ⁵_____ wash light and dark colors together. You must look at the labels first!

Claire: Oh! I never do that.

Manny: ⁶_____ I'll separate the colors into light and dark.

Claire: Great. You do that. I'll get the laundry soap. Oops. ⁷_____

Manny: Sure, what is it?

Claire: Can you reach the soap?

Manny: OK. Next time you ⁸_____ put it up so high.

Claire: I didn't put it up there. I never do the laundry!

Review 3 | 43

7 Visions of the Future

VOCABULARY Computers and communication

1 Find eight more computer words.

O	V	G	K	E	Y	B	O	A	R	D	F
L	Q	T	E	H	K	F	Y	P	A	O	L
T	O	U	C	H	S	C	R	E	E	N	A
L	P	T	O	U	C	H	P	A	D	E	S
Q	X	F	L	A	S	H	D	R	I	V	E
E	H	C	Y	F	T	A	B	L	E	T	D
I	M	I	T	Z	G	C	J	N	Q	Y	R
S	M	A	R	T	P	H	O	N	E	S	I
E	D	I	R	D	H	R	A	L	F	L	V
M	P	R	I	N	T	E	R	C	W	X	E
B	P	V	S	O	P	N	W	I	F	I	A
L	G	M	O	U	S	E	J	P	P	I	F

2 Complete the sentences. Use the computer words from Exercise 1.

1. You don't need a mouse for your laptop because you can use the ___touch pad___.
2. Save your work on a _____ so you can use it with another computer.
3. The _____ wasn't working, so we couldn't get on the Internet.
4. My mom prefers typing on the _____ to using the touch pad.
5. I prefer using a _____ to using a laptop.
6. I don't use my _____ very often. I email most of my assignments to my teacher.

3 Use the phrases and the computer words from Exercise 1 to write sentences.

communicate with friends	do homework
✓computing power	save information

1. _A smartphone today has more computing power than the first computers._
2. _____
3. _____
4. _____

4 Complete the sentences with your own information. Use the computer words from Exercise 1.

1. I have a ___tablet and a smartphone___.
2. I use a _____ to _____.
3. I never use a _____.
4. My parents _____.
5. My best friend _____.

44 | Unit 7

GRAMMAR will and won't for predictions

1 Rewrite the underlined phrases as contractions.

1. <u>Computers will</u> be smarter in the future.
   They'll
2. <u>This tablet will</u> get smaller in the future.
3. <u>My family will not</u> use a mouse in the future.
4. <u>You will not</u> cook your own meals.
5. <u>He will</u> use his smartphone to buy everything.

GRAMMAR Adverbs of possibility

2 Complete the chart using the adverbs of possibility.

certainly	maybe	probably
✓definitely	perhaps	

Sure	*definitely*
Pretty sure	
Not as sure	

3 Put the words in the correct order to make sentences.

1. will / planes / fly / Robots / probably / .
   Robots will probably fly planes.
2. future / we / use / Perhaps / in / won't / the / paper / .

3. our / Robots / houses / certainly / will / clean / .

4. have / our / clothes / them / will / touch screens / Maybe / in / .

5. company / I'll / for / software / work / a / definitely / .

4 Answer the questions using *will* and *won't* to predict the future. Use adverbs of possibility.

1. What will cars do in the future?
   They'll definitely drive themselves.
2. How will we use robots in the future?

3. Will bikes fly in the future?

4. Will we have cameras in our jewelry in the future?

5. How will you be different in the future?

Unit 7 | 45

VOCABULARY Technology verbs

1 Complete the technology verbs.

down	down	down	in	in
✓on	on	out	up	up

1. turn ___on___
2. zoom _____
3. click _____
4. zoom _____
5. back _____
6. sign _____
7. scroll _____
8. sign _____
9. scroll _____
10. shut _____

2 Write the technology verbs from Exercise 1. Some will be pairs of verbs.

1. ___scroll up___
   ___scroll down___

2. _____
   _____

3. _____

4. _____
   _____

5. _____

6. _____

7. _____

3 Circle the correct technology verbs.

1. Can you **zoom in** / **sign out** so we can see it better?
2. Did you **turn on** / **back up** your homework on the flash drive?
3. Don't forget the password or you won't be able to **sign in** / **zoom out**.
4. **Back up** / **Click on** this link to read the blog.
5. **Shut down** / **Scroll up** to look at the picture again.

4 Write sentences. Use technology verbs and your own information.

1. my email
   I never sign out of my email.

2. my school's website
   _____
   _____

3. my computer
   _____
   _____

4. my picture
   _____
   _____

5. my favorite website
   _____
   _____

46 | Unit 7

GRAMMAR First conditional with *will (not)*, *may (not)*, and *might (not)*

1 Circle the correct words.

1. If her laptop **breaks** / **might break**, her parents **buys** / **might buy** her a new one.
2. You **won't win** / **won't** the game if you **choose** / **won't choose** that character.
3. If you **get** / **will get** some money, what **you buy** / **will you buy**?
4. You **see** / **will see** it better if you **zoom in** / **might zoom in**.
5. **Will study** / **Will she study** science when she **goes** / **may goes** to college?
6. They **not get** / **may not get** good grades if they **study** / **don't study** harder.

2 Put the words in the correct order to make sentences.

1. of / yours / kind / will / stops / working / you / if / What / phone / get / ?

   What kind of phone will you get if yours

   stops working?

2. not / don't / get / a / money / tablet / I / I may / save / if / .

   _____

   _____

3. the fastest / you / play / new / a / computer / want to / video games, / you / might / need / If / .

   _____

   _____

4. back up / may / lose / them / If / our / photos, / we / we / don't / .

   _____

   _____

5. video game / make / learns to / kind of / will / he / if he / code / What / write / ?

   _____

   _____

3 Correct the sentences.

1. If you click on this link͵ you ˄see the video.   *, will*

2. Will you sign into my account if I may give you my password?

3. He may not see the text message if his phone might be off.

4. We not have Wi-Fi if we sit in the library.

5. If you will play the game, first you may not like the movie.

6. How you buy a tablet if you don't save your money?

4 Change the affirmative sentences to negative sentences and the negative sentences to affirmative sentences.

1. You'll answer your smartphone if you go to the movies.   *won't*

2. If there are girl characters, I won't play that video game.

3. We'll back up our files if we get a flash drive.

4. If Helen decides to watch a video, she'll choose a comedy.

5. If I post videos, they won't be cat videos.

5 Complete the questions and sentences with *will (not)*, *may (not)*, or *might (not)* and your own ideas.

1. If I don't do well in computer class,
   I might not get a computer job.

2. What kind of video will you post _____
   _____?

3. If I have a blog in the future, _____
   _____.

4. Will you buy a _____ if you _____
   _____?

Unit 7 | 47

CONVERSATION Using your cell phone

1 Put the words in order to make questions and answers.

1. do / upload / I / How / a / photo / ?
   How do I upload a photo?

2. need / You / click / to / picture / the / icon / on / .
   _____

3. How / does / touch pad / work / this / ?
   _____

4. you / to / All / do / have / touch / the / is / screen / .
   _____
   _____

2 Complete the sentences.

| All you have to | ✓ How does it work? |
| how do I | you need to |

Grandmother: Let's take a photo with your smartphone. ¹ *How does it work?*

Boy: First, ² _____ press the round button to turn it on.

Grandmother: Oh, look! There we are. Now, ³ _____ take the picture?

Boy: ⁴ _____ do is press this big button.

Grandmother: And there's our picture. That was easy!

3 Write the questions or answers. Use the phrases and your own ideas.

| All you have to | ✓ How do I | How do I |
| How does _____ work? | | You need to |

1. Ask someone for instructions to send a text.
   How do I send a text?

2. Ask someone how to use a GPS watch.
   _____
   _____

3. Tell someone how to turn on a digital camera.
   _____
   _____

4. Tell someone how to listen to music.
   _____
   _____

5. Ask someone how to watch a video.
   _____
   _____

48 | Unit 7

READING TO WRITE

1 Read the opinion paragraph. Then label the parts: underline the introduction and conclusion. Put a box around the reasons. Circle any facts or examples.

Future Robot Doctors
by Bill Lee

<u>I believe that in the future, when you go to see a doctor, you will see a robot, not a human doctor.</u> One reason I think that is because more and more doctors are using computers to help their patients. The last time I went to a doctor, she used her smartphone to look up what medicine to give me. Another reason I think we will see robots for a cough or cold is that they will give human doctors more time to spend with really sick people. This will save time and money. And another reason is that unlike human doctors, robots don't get sick! If you sneeze on the robot, it won't catch your cold. This way, doctors won't get sick. <u>In conclusion, I think in the future, we will see robot doctors for colds and simple illnesses.</u>

2 Complete the sentences with the opinion and reason phrases. Then number the sentences in order. More than one answer may be possible.

> Another reason is (that)
> For these reasons,
> I think (that)
> In conclusion
> ✓ In my opinion,
> One reason is (that)

_____ _____ people will be able to help each other directly.

_____ _____ people won't need to use money.

_____ _____ we are already doing this, for example with computer code that people share.

_____ _____ we won't need to use money because we will trade everything.

_____ _____ people can easily connect with other people over the Internet. This lets them trade services with each other.

__1__ __In my opinion,__ I believe that in the future, we won't use money.

3 Complete number 1 with an opinion. Complete numbers 2–4 with reasons for that opinion. Complete number 5 with a conclusion. Use your own ideas.

1. In my opinion, _____

2. I think (that) _____.

3. One reason is (that) _____.

4. Another reason is (that) _____.

5. For these reasons, _____.

Unit 7 | 49

8 The Choices We Make

VOCABULARY Life events

1 Put the letters in the correct order to make life events.

1. OG OT LEGLOCE
_____

2. TEAK A REYA FOF
_____

3. GTE ROUY VIRRED'S SINELCE
_____

4. REETIR
___*retire*___

5. OG OT CLOSOH
_____

6. EB NOBR
_____

7. TEG A OJB
_____

8. NIFHIS OLOHCS
_____

9. EHVA DHINCELR
_____

10. ETG ERIDMRA
_____

2 What are these things? Write the life events from Exercise 1.

1. Before you buy a car, you need to pass a test to do this.
   ___*get your driver's license*___

2. This is something you do after you've worked for a very long time.
   _____

3. People do this when they are in love and want to be together forever.
   _____

4. You will have teachers when you do this.
   _____
   And you will have professors when you do this.
   _____

5. You will make money when you do this.
   _____

6. This is the first thing you ever do.
   _____

3 Complete the sentences. Use forms of the words from Exercise 1.

1. Julian's grandfather ___*retired*___ from his job. He worked at the school for 30 years.

2. Tim's little brother is excited because he's finally old enough to _____.

3. First, you _____, and every year after that, you celebrate your birthday.

4. If my mom _____ at the mall, she'll need to _____ and buy a car because it's too far to walk.

5. After she _____ in June, she wants to _____ and travel before she _____.

50 | Unit 8

GRAMMAR be going to and will

1 Choose the correct words.

1. Use **be going to** / **will** to talk about plans in the future.
2. Use **be going to** / **will** to talk about predictions and unplanned decisions.
3. What is he **to do** / **going to do**?
   He is going **to play** / **play** basketball.
   He isn't going **do** / **to do** his homework.
4. Where will she travel first?
   She'll travel / **She travel** to China first.
   She not travel / **She won't travel** to China first.
5. Is he going **study** / **to study** biology?
   Yes, he is. / **Yes, he study.**
   No, he's not going. / **No, he isn't.**
6. **Going to** / **Will** they get married?
   Yes, they **will** / **going to**.
   No, they **aren't going to** / **won't**.

2 Complete the conversation with be going to or will.

Jody: Hi, Scott. Congratulations on finishing school!

Scott: Thanks! You, too. What ¹___are___ you ___going to___ do now?

Jody: I ²_____ go to college in the fall. I got into the Art Academy.

Scott: ³_____ you _____ study art?

Jody: Not exactly. I ⁴_____ study animation.

Scott: That's great.

Jody: What about you? What ⁵_____ you _____ do?

Scott: I'm not sure yet. Maybe I ⁶_____ take a year off and travel.

Jody: That sounds exciting.

Scott: Yeah, but my dad wants me to get a job at his company. I ⁷_____ probably travel in the summer and work in the fall.

3 Unscramble the sentences and questions.

1. probably / you / won't / He / listen / to / .
   He probably won't listen to you.

2. won't / thinks / after-school / get / she / job / She / an / .
   _____
   _____

3. year / off / they'll / take / Maybe / a / .
   _____

4. Australia / will / to / When / travel / Jack / ?
   _____

4 Complete the questions with be going to or will. Then answer the questions with your own information.

1. When ___will___ you finish school?
   _____

2. When _____ you get your driver's license?
   _____

3. Where _____ you live in 10 years?
   _____

4. Is your friend _____ go to college with you?
   _____

5. Are you _____ get married soon?
   _____

Unit 8 | 51

VOCABULARY Containers and materials

1 What materials are they made of? Write the container words in the chart.

1. Plastic
   bottle
   _____

2. Paper and cardboard
   _____
   _____

3. Glass
   _____
   _____

4. Cloth
   _____

5. Metal
   _____

2 Circle the correct words.

1. We bring our groceries home in a **(cloth bag)** / **metal can**.

2. At the supermarket, we put the apples in a **glass jar** / **paper bag**.

3. Shampoo comes in a **plastic bottle** / **cardboard box**.

4. My mother bought a **plastic carton** / **cloth bag** of orange juice.

5. I recycled the **glass jar** / **cardboard box** that my new shoes came in.

6. If you wash the **glass jar** / **metal can** the peanut butter came in, you can use it again.

7. I prefer to drink soda from a **cloth bag** / **glass bottle**, not a **cloth bag** / **metal can**.

3 Use container words and your own information to write sentences.

1. (recycle / cardboard box)
   We recycle cardboard boxes at my house.

2. (reuse / cloth bag)
   _____
   _____

3. (not / paper bag)
   _____
   _____

4. (metal can)
   _____
   _____

5. (plastic carton)
   _____
   _____

GRAMMAR Present continuous and simple present for future

1 Put the words in the correct order to ask questions. Use contractions if possible. Then match the questions with the answers.

1. helping / the / they / dolphins / Are / ?

   Are they helping the dolphins? __b__

2. hour / the / Does / leave / bus / in / an / ?

   _____

3. Ben / is / Why / making / video / a / ?

   _____

4. they / have / the / When / meeting / do / ?

   _____

5. plastic / are / collecting / How / they / the / ?

   _____

6. to / do / go / you / When / Japan / ?

   _____

a. They're using a bucket.
b. Yes, they are.
c. I go next month.
d. No, it doesn't.
e. He's teaching people about dolphins.
f. They have the meeting next Saturday.

2 Complete the sentences with the present continuous or simple present.

1. I _'m buying_ shoes made from recycled plastic bottles. (buy)
2. The plastic bag recycling drive _____ on June 3. (end)
3. Our town _____ a recycling program. (start)
4. At what time on Tuesday _____ he _____ for Costa Rica? (leave)
5. They _____ to school. (not drive)

3 Use the information in the invitation to complete the questions and answers with the present continuous or simple present.

Who?	You are invited to Kim's birthday party!
What?	Celebrate Kim's birthday. No need to buy gifts. We'll make them!
How?	Collect plastic bags, paper bags, and cardboard from your home and bring them to the party. We'll learn how to recycle them into fun gifts.
Where?	The Art of Recycling Center
When?	Saturday, October 12, at noon

Be green!
Ride your bike or take the bus.

1. _Does_ the party _start_ at noon? (start)

   Yes, it does.

2. Where _____ you _____ on Saturday? (go)

   _____

3. _____ you _____ gifts? (buy)

   _____

4. What _____ you _____ from home? (bring)

   _____

5. What _____ you _____ at The Art of Recycling Center? (learn to do)

   _____

4 Answer the questions with the simple present or present continuous and your own information.

1. Are you going to recycle anything next week?

   Yes, I am.

2. When does your family recycle things?

   _____

3. What things are you going to reuse?

   _____

4. What does your family *not* recycle?

   _____

Unit 8 | 53

CONVERSATION I'm going to get a degree.

1 Complete the conversation.

> Absolutely! ✓ I think
> I disagree. Maybe, but I think
> I suppose you're right.

Ingrid: Well, that was an interesting assignment!

Ted: A paper about "What I plan to do after I finish school"? That's easy!

Ingrid: You think so? What *are* you going to do after you finish school?

Ted: I want to study marine biology and the environment. Then I'm going to get a job that helps the ocean. [1] ___I think___ it's the most important part of the planet.

Ingrid: [2] _____ people are the most important part of the planet.

Ted: People? [3] _____ People cause the pollution!

Ingrid: [4] _____ That's why the most important thing we can do is change how people do things.

Ted: Hmm. I hadn't thought of it that way. [5] _____ So what are you going to after you finish school?

Ingrid: I'm going to study environmental law!

Ted: Cool! Maybe we can work together.

2 Write a response that agrees or disagrees with each statement. Use the words in the box and your own ideas.

> Absolutely!
> I disagree.
> I suppose you're right.
> Maybe, but I think

1. Everyone should study a foreign language.
   _____
   _____

2. I don't think people should eat meat.
   _____
   _____

3. I think everyone should get married.
   _____
   _____

4. I think everyone should have 10 children.
   _____
   _____

5. I think it might be fun to be the leader of a country.
   _____
   _____

READING TO WRITE

To: Ashley Morrison
From: Ben Smith
Subject: Summer Volunteer Opportunity

Dear Ms. Morrison,

I am interested in volunteering at the Senior Center this summer.

I 'd like to be a scientist and work with animals someday. I train dogs to be "service dogs." Service dogs help people who can't see or hear well. I train the dogs to visit with people. I think service dogs help people to feel better.

I want to help older people. My grandfather is sick, and I help him. I bring my service dog when I visit my grandfather. It really cheers him up. He is doing much better now.

I have a very well-trained dog named Max, and I'd like to bring him to the Senior Center to visit the older people. I'd volunteer by myself, but I'd rather bring Max with me. Thank you for considering us for the volunteer position.

Sincerely,

Ben (and Max the dog)

1 Read Ben's email. Complete the word web.

2 Circle examples of *want*, *would like* (*to*), and *would rather* (*'d rather*) in Ben's email.

3 Complete the sentences using *want*, *would like* (*to*), and *would rather* (*'d rather*). Use contractions. More than one answer may be possible.

1. She wants to be a doctor. She *'d like to* _____ work with children.

2. He _____ volunteer at the recycling center. He'd like to help people learn about recycling.

3. Ken wants to work outdoors. He _____ work in a park than an office.

4. Jillian and Bob _____ help people to lose weight.

5. Paula _____ help sea turtles. She _____ start a volunteer program at the beach than join one online.

Unit 8 | 55

REVIEW UNITS 7–8

1 Label each object. Then underline the materials words, circle the container words, and draw a box around the computer words.

a cardboard box	a metal can
a cloth bag	a paper bag
a glass bottle	a plastic carton
a keyboard	a touch pad
a flash drive	Wi-Fi

1. _____
2. _____
3. _____
4. _____
5. _____
6. _____
7. _____
8. _____
9. _____
10. _____

2 Complete the conversation with the words in the box.

Click on	sign in
finished school	smartphone
going to college	tablet
How do I	take a year off
printer	You need to

Hannah: My sister just ¹_____.
We had a big party. Want to see some photos? I have them on my ²_____.

Stella: Sure. But let's use my ³_____. The screen is bigger.

Hannah: Good idea. Where do I ⁴_____ to the website?

Stella: ⁵_____ this button.

Hannah: OK. Here they are.

Stella: Nice. She got a lot of gifts! Why is she holding that T-shirt?

Hannah: It's where she's ⁶_____ next year.

Stella: Isn't she going this fall?

Hannah: No, she isn't. She's going to ⁷_____. She wants to volunteer in the rainforest in Costa Rica.

Stella: Wow. That's far away.

Hannah: I can show you where she will be on this map. ⁸_____ zoom in?

Stella: ⁹_____ move your fingers like this.

Hannah: Thanks. Here's the website.

3 Write sentences in the future tense with *will* or *won't*.

1. We don't need a keyboard or mouse. (probably)
   _____

2. Computers think like humans. (perhaps)
   _____

3. Clothing and jewelry have touchscreen technology in them. (maybe)
   _____

4. My sister doesn't turn in printed papers for school. (definitely)
   _____

5. I don't go anywhere without my smartphone. (certainly)
   _____

4 Match the phrases to make sentences and questions.

1. If I make a video in the future, ____
2. What will he do ____
3. My friends may not be happy ____
4. If you buy a new smartphone, ____
5. He won't lose his files ____

a. if he backs them up regularly.
b. if I write about them on my blog.
c. which one will you buy?
d. if his smartphone breaks?
e. it won't be a cat video.

5 Answer the questions about Danielle's email (on the right) using *be going to* and *will*.

1. What's Danielle going to do after finishing school?
   _____
   _____
2. Who might she live with?
   _____
   _____
3. Where will she go first?
   _____
   _____
4. How will she get money to travel?
   _____
   _____
5. What is she going to study in college?
   _____
   _____

To: carla_g
From: danigarcia
Subject: I miss you!

Dear Aunt Carla,

How are things in Argentina? I miss you! I'm going to take a year off when I finish school. I'm not going to start college right away. I think it's important to travel and see the world. Mom disagrees with me, though. She wants me to start college right away. But I'd rather travel and learn languages and meet new people. If I save money from my after-school job, I might be able to travel for a year.

If your invitation is still open, would you like a visitor? I'd like to visit you in Argentina to start my year off. I won't stay too long. Mom said that maybe I can help in your restaurant. I'd really like that because I want to study hospitality. What do you think of my plan?

Love,
Daniela

6 Agree or disagree with the following statements. Use your own ideas. Give reasons for your opinions.

| Absolutely! | I disagree. | I suppose you're right. |

1. In the future, you'll probably have a flying car.
   _____
   _____
2. In the future, you'll definitely be rich and famous.
   _____
   _____
3. In the future, you're probably going to live in your hometown.
   _____
   _____
4. In the future, you're going to retire at age 30.
   _____
   _____

Review 4 | **57**

9 Watch Out!

VOCABULARY Accident and injury verbs

1 Find nine more words for accidents and injuries.

✓ bang	burn	cut	hurt	sprain
break	crash	fall off	slip	trip

O	Q	F	A	L	L	O	F	F
J	Y	Z	B	A	N	G	D	N
U	H	U	R	T	T	R	I	P
I	U	S	L	I	P	P	Y	M
S	P	R	A	I	N	S	E	Q
K	G	P	W	W	J	N	Y	M
H	Y	J	E	B	U	R	N	H
V	C	U	T	B	R	E	A	K
Q	G	Y	Z	C	R	A	S	H

2 Label the pictures with the words from Exercise 1.

1. _fall off_

2. _____

3. _____

4. _____

5. _____

6. _____

7. _____   8. _____

9. _____   10. _____

3 Complete the article with the accidents and injuries words from Exercise 1.

It's difficult being a teen. Teens often [1] _crash_ their bikes and get injured playing sports. But did you know that injuries happen to people over age 65, too? The number one injury might surprise you:

Falling down

Older people often [2] _____ down in the kitchen or on the stairs. They might [3] _____ on the stairs or [4] _____ on a wet kitchen floor. Twisting an ankle when falling down is one way people can [5] _____ an ankle. Falling down can [6] _____ the back and cause back pain. For older people, falling down can be very serious. Their bones can [7] _____ easily, especially their hips.

A fall can create other injuries, too. A person might [8] _____ his or her head on something, or even [9] _____ it on something sharp. Older people can avoid falling by wearing good shoes and keeping the floor clear of items they can trip over.

58 | Unit 9

GRAMMAR Present perfect statements with regular and irregular verbs

1 Write the past participle of the verbs. Then underline the verbs that are irregular.

Verb	Past participle
1. burn	*burned*
2. live	
3. slip	
4. study	
5. do	
6. fly	
7. lose	
8. take	

2 Complete the chart. Use *has/have* and the past participle of the words to form the present perfect. More than one answer may be possible.

| been | burned | hurt | ✓ sprained |
| broken | happened | seen | tripped |

	Affirmative
Regular	Ken ¹ *has sprained* his finger playing basketball many times. More falling accidents ² _____ to older people.
	Negative
	Tessa ³ _____ on the stairs before. We ⁴ _____ never _____ any food in the oven before.

Irregular	**Affirmative**
	Ella ⁵ _____ to Bogota twice. More older people ⁶ _____ a hip than younger people.
	Negative
	Mark ⁷ _____ his back before. We ⁸ _____ our team win before.

3 Write the present perfect affirmative (✓) and negative (✗) statements using the verbs from Exercise 1.

1. I *haven't burned* my fingers on a hot stove in months. (✗)
2. My team _____ more games than we have won. (✓)
3. Elizabeth _____ for the test. (✓)
4. We _____ dangerous things like this before. (✗)
5. Jack _____ in a helicopter before. (✗)
6. I _____ in this town for a long time. (✓)
7. They _____ the same bus to school for years. (✓)
8. Pete _____ on the ice during a hockey game before. (✗)

4 Use these phrases to write affirmative and negative present perfect sentences with your own information.

1. broke my arm

   I've never broken my arm before.

2. fly to Alaska

   _____

3. fall off a bike

   _____

4. sprain an ankle

   _____

5. sing on stage

   _____

Unit 9 | 59

VOCABULARY Parts of the body

1 Unscramble the words.

1. OFOT ___foot___
2. EKEN _____
3. STEO _____
4. RSWIT _____
5. DRSLOHUE _____
6. KELNA _____
7. COHMAST _____
8. KECN _____
9. BOLEW _____

2 Label the pictures with the words from Exercise 1.

1. ___toes___   2. _____
3. _____ 4. _____

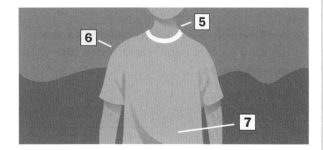

5. _____ 6. _____
7. _____

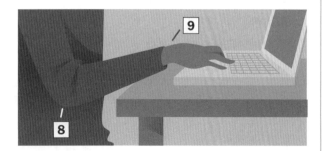

8. _____ 9. _____

3 Complete the sentences with the words from Exercise 1.

1. This is at the top of your arm. ___shoulder___
2. Your head sits on top of this. _____
3. You wear shoes on these. _____
4. You use this to move your foot. _____
5. You can wear a watch or a bracelet on this. _____
6. This is where food goes. _____
7. This is where the leg bends. _____
8. This is where the arm bends. _____
9. You have 10 of these on your foot. _____

4 Complete the conversation.

| ankle | knee | wrist |
| ✓ elbow | shoulder | |

Phillip: Hi, Rita! Hey, what happened to your wrist?

Rita: I was playing volleyball with Olivia last weekend. The ball came over the net, so I jumped up to hit it. But Olivia jumped up at the same time. I bent my arm, and my ¹ ___elbow___ hit her on the ² _____. I'm glad I didn't hit her head. But she fell and twisted her ³ _____ when she landed.

Phillip: Ouch!

Rita: Well, it gets worse. Olivia couldn't stand up at all! I went over to help her, but I slipped and fell. And I bent my ⁴ _____ too far when I landed on my hand. I think it's sprained. We're going to miss several volleyball games.

Phillip: I know how you feel. I was running during soccer practice and fell. I landed on my ⁵ _____. It really hurts to bend my leg now.

Rita: I guess we'll just have to *watch* our games for now!

60 | Unit 9

GRAMMAR Present perfect questions; present perfect vs. simple past

1 Match the questions with the correct answers.

1. Why has he had so many accidents?
2. Has she ever fallen down the stairs?
3. What happened on your vacation?
4. What bones have you broken?
5. Have you ever banged your head?
6. Have you ever sprained your ankle?

a. No, she hasn't.
b. Yes, I have.
c. Because he's clumsy.
d. I tripped and fell. I hurt my wrist.
e. Yes, I have. I sprained it yesterday.
f. My arm and my finger.

2 Complete the questions in the present perfect.

1. A: ___Have___ you ___ever gone___ windsurfing? (ever, go)
   B: No, we haven't.
2. A: _____ you _____ in a helicopter? (ever, ride)
   B: Yes, I have. I rode in one last week.
3. A: _____ they _____ Portuguese? (ever, study)
   B: Yes, they have.
4. A: Where _____ you _____? (live)
   B: In Guadalajara and New York.
5. A: Why _____ he _____ the bus every day this week? (take)
   B: Because his bike is broken.
6. A: _____ she _____ a video? (ever, make)
   B: No, she hasn't.

3 Use the chart to write the questions and answers.

Who?	Doing what?	How?	What injury?	When?
Kate	dancing	trip	sprain ankle	in the past
George	biking	fall	none	never
Stacey	hockey	slip	broken wrist	last winter
Brian	car accident	crash	hurt neck	last May
Maria	surfing	fall off	hurt shoulder	on vacation

1. ___Has___ Kate ___ever sprained___ her ankle?
   Yes, she ___has___.
2. _____ George _____ off his bike?
   No, he _____.
3. Stacey, _____ you _____ playing hockey?
   Yes, I _____.
   When?
   _____.
4. Brian, what _____ last May?
   _____.
5. Maria, _____ you _____ off your surfboard?
   _____
   What _____?
   _____

4 Answer the questions with your own information. Write complete sentences.

1. Have you ever lost your backpack?
   Yes, I have. I lost it last week.
2. Have you ever broken any bones?
   _____
   _____
3. Have you ever tried to surf?
   _____
   _____
4. Have you ever traveled to another country?
   _____
   _____
5. What good books have you read?
   _____
   _____

Unit 9 | 61

CONVERSATION Good news, bad news

1 Complete the conversation with the words to react to good news and bad news.

✓ I'm sorry to hear that.	That's cool!
That sounds like fun.	that's too bad

Emily: Hi, Zack. How was your camping trip?

Zack: It was good and bad, I guess. First, the bad news – Jim climbed a tree, fell out of the tree, and landed in the fire!

Emily: Oh no! [1] _I'm sorry to hear that._ Is he OK?

Zack: He's fine, but he burned part of his shoe.

Emily: Oh, [2] _____ about the shoe.

Zack: I know. But it gets better . . . I took a video of him falling out of the tree and put it on my website. It's gotten more than 10,000 views so far.

Emily: [3] _____

Zack: Yeah! It is! And the local news heard about it. So we are going to be on TV.

Emily: Wow! [4] _____

2 Correct the reactions. Mark (✓) if the reaction is correct. Use the expressions from Exercise 1.

1. **A:** I'm going to Hawaii for vacation!
   B: ~~I'm sorry to hear that~~.
   That sounds like fun.

2. **A:** I'm sorry I can't come to your party on Saturday.
   B: That's cool.
   _____

3. **A:** My bike was stolen yesterday.
   B: That's too bad.
   _____

4. **A:** I made a new friend in guitar class.
   B: I'm sorry to hear that.
   _____

5. **A:** She broke her arm skateboarding.
   B: That's cool.
   _____

3 Write a reaction to each sentence. Use the phrases from Exercise 1.

1. **A:** My pet turtle died.
   B: _____

2. **A:** I won the skateboard competition!
   B: _____

3. **A:** We are going to the swimming pool this weekend.
   B: _____

4. **A:** I can't go to the movie tonight because I have to do homework.
   B: _____

READING TO WRITE

1 Number the paragraphs to put the parts of the email in the correct order.

To: Adriana S.
From: Laurel M.
Subject: Party invitation

Hi Adriana,

_____ We're going to take her to Donner Lake. She used to sail there when she was a girl. So, my Dad rented a sailboat to take her out. She doesn't know about it yet. It's a surprise!

_____ Again, I'm really sorry. Have a great time! Text me some pictures. Maybe we can go to a concert together next month.

_____ I'd love to come, but I can't go with you.

_1_ Thanks for inviting me to the concert on Saturday.

_____ It's my grandmother's birthday. She's going to be 70. We're spending the weekend with her.

Your friend,

Laurel

2 Read the email again. Answer the questions. Write complete sentences.

1. What phrase does Laurel use to thank Adriana for the invitation?
   Thanks for inviting me

2. What phrases does Laurel use to apologize?

3. What is Laurel's reason for not going?

4. What suggestion does Laurel make at the end?

5. What two places does Laurel apologize in?

3 Write sentences to refuse an invitation to go to the beach. Use phrases from Exercises 1 and 2.

A: Can you come to the beach on Saturday?

1. Thank the person for the invitation:
   B: _____

2. Apologize and refuse:
   B: _____

3. Explain why you can't go:
   B: _____

4. Suggest another time:
   B: _____

Unit 9 | 63

10 Have Fun!

VOCABULARY Free-time activities

1 Complete the free-time activity phrases.

celebrate	✓play
go	play
hang out	read
have	spend
listen	take

1. _play_ video games
2. _____ photos
3. _____ a party
4. _____ your birthday
5. _____ books
6. _____ with friends
7. _____ time with your family
8. _____ an instrument
9. _____ to music
10. _____ to a dance

2 Complete the paragraphs. Use the verbs from Exercise 1.

1. When you _celebrate_ your birthday, you _____ with your family, like your grandparents and cousins. You eat cake and open presents. Your parents always _____ photos when you blow out the candles on the cake.

2. My favorite things to do when I _____ with friends? That's easy. We like to _____ video games. We can play them for hours. And we often _____ to music, too.

3. My brother is very friendly. He doesn't like to spend time alone. His favorite thing to do is _____ to a dance at school. If my parents would let him, he'd _____ a dance party at our house!

4. My friend Carol is very quiet and spends a lot of time alone. She likes to _____ books. She also likes to _____ instruments. She is learning to play the drums. Maybe she won't be quiet any more!

3 Complete the chart with the activities from Exercise 1 and your own information. Then write sentences.

Activity	When?	Where?	Who?
1. hang out with friends	last weekend	sports park	Bill, Lisa
2. spend time with family			
3. celebrate birthday			
4. _____			
5. _____			

1. _I hung out with my friends Bill and Lisa last weekend. We went to the sports park._
2. _____
3. _____
4. _____
5. _____

GRAMMAR Indefinite pronouns

1 Label the graphs with indefinite pronouns.

anyone	no one
anything	nothing
anywhere	nowhere
✓everyone	someone
everything	something
everywhere	somewhere

PEOPLE

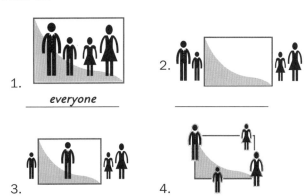

1. everyone
2. _____
3. _____
4. _____

PLACES

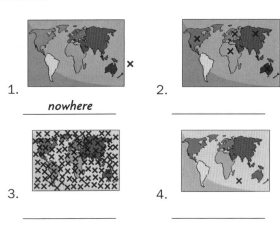

1. nowhere
2. _____
3. _____
4. _____

THINGS

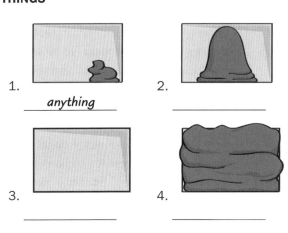

1. anything
2. _____
3. _____
4. _____

2 Complete the sentences with indefinite pronouns.

anyone	everywhere
anything	No one
✓everything	something

1. The food was delicious. He's eaten ___everything___ on his plate.

2. It's polite to bring _____ when you are invited to dinner.

3. Don't speak if you don't have _____ nice to say.

4. He can't remember _____'s name.

5. His passport is full of stamps because he's traveled _____.

6. _____ answered the last question correctly.

3 Correct the negative sentences. Mark ✓ if the sentence is correct.

1. I didn't go ~~nowhere~~ *anywhere* fun on my birthday. ____

2. He didn't know no one at the party. ____

3. I don't know someone who loves football more than me. ____

4. Julie didn't do everything exciting on vacation. ____

5. Everyone goes to the free concerts in the park. ____

6. There is always anything to do at the city center. ____

Unit 10 | 65

VOCABULARY Adjectives of feeling

1 Use the pictures to complete the crossword.

ACROSS

2. _____

3. _____

5. _____

9. _____

10. _____

DOWN

1. *embarrassed*

2. _____

4. _____

6. _____

7. _____

8. _____

2 Choose the correct words.

Scott: Hi, Ernie! Tell me about your camping trip with your brother.

Ernie: It was my first time camping. So I was ¹**embarrassed / excited**. I guess I was also a little ²**nervous / upset** because anything could be out there in the woods, you know?

Scott: You're ³**scared / tired** of bears, aren't you?

Ernie: Yes! I am very ⁴**afraid / bored** of them. So, anyway, I was in my tent about to fall asleep, and I heard a noise outside. It was coming closer. My heart started beating very fast. I felt ⁵**embarrassed / stressed**. After a minute, I peeked out of the tent.

Scott: What was there?

Ernie: Something furry landed in front of my tent! I screamed. Then I heard my brother laughing. He threw his furry hat in front of the tent to scare me!

Scott: You must have really been ⁶**excited / surprised**.

Ernie: For a moment I was. Then my brother said he was ⁷**bored / nervous**, so he thought it would be fun to scare me. That made me ⁸**afraid / angry**. Then I was ⁹**embarrassed / surprised** that I screamed because the people in the next campsite heard me. And then I was ¹⁰**nervous / upset** with my brother for teasing me. I couldn't sleep all night. Now, I'm just ¹¹**scared / tired**.

Scott: That's kind of a funny story, you know.

Ernie: *Now* it is!

GRAMMAR too and enough

1 Circle the correct words to complete the rules.

1. Use **enough** / **too + adjective** / **infinitive + infinitive** to show something is more than what we want or need.

2. Use **adjective + enough + infinitive** / **infinitive + enough** / **too + infinitive** to show something is what we want or need.

3. **Not + adjective** / **Not enough** / **Too + adjective** shows something is less than or more than what we want or need.

2 Complete the chart with too and enough.

	More than	What we want	Less than
tall	too tall	tall enough	not tall enough
warm			
brave			
nervous			
young			

3 Put the words in the correct order to make sentences.

1. ending / The / enough / wasn't / movie's / surprising / .

   The movie's ending wasn't surprising enough.

2. to / race / the / Bill / enough / wasn't / win / fast / .

   _____

   _____

3. home / was / sick / stay / Becky / enough / to / .

   _____

   _____

4. wasn't / He / nervous / too / to / remember / the / answer / .

   _____

   _____

5. it / They / talk / too / were / to / upset / about / .

   _____

   _____

6. spider / too / speak / was / when / he / Bob / saw / to / the / scared / .

   _____

   _____

4 Circle the correct words.

1. The boy is **too short** / **n't short enough** to ride the bike.

2. He was **too afraid** / **n't afraid enough** to answer the door.

3. The team was **too strong** / **n't strong enough** to win the game.

4. She was **too tired** / **n't tired enough** to finish her homework.

5. The tea is **too hot** / **n't hot enough** to drink. You might burn your mouth.

5 Complete the sentences with your own information.

1. I'm (not) old enough to _____*drive a car*_____.

2. I'm (not) too scared to _____.

3. I'm (not) brave enough to _____.

4. I'm (not) interested enough to _____.

5. Climbing a mountain is (not) something I'm _____.

6. Acting in a movie is (not) something I'm _____.

Unit 10 | 67

CONVERSATION Birthday plans

1 Match the suggestions with the responses.

1. Why don't we try surfing?
2. I want to see the new zombie movie.
3. Why don't we go shopping?
4. How about watching the skateboarders?
5. Why don't we go swimming?
6. How about calling our friends to join us?

a. That's a great idea! Luckily, I brought my bathing suit.
b. I'd rather watch the surfers. They're more exciting.
c. I'm too scared to try that. I'd rather go swimming.
d. That's a great idea! I heard it's really good.
e. That's a great idea! You call Jorge, and I'll call Kaitlin.
f. I'd rather be outside than in a mall. Maybe we can do that tonight.

2 Choose the correct suggestion or response.

1. **A:** Why don't we go see that new horror movie?
   B: I don't like horror movies. **That's a great idea! / I'd rather see the new action movie.**

2. **A:** It's a nice day. How about we go for a walk?
   B: I'd rather go for a walk. / That's a great idea!

3. **A:** We haven't seen our cousins in a while. **How about we stay home? / Why don't we visit them?**
   B: That's a great idea!

3 Complete the conversations with your own ideas. Use the phrases in the box.

| How about | That's a great idea |
| I'd rather | Why don't we |

1. **A:** Let's go skiing.
   B: It's too cold. _Why don't we go to the movies?_

2. **A:** _____ go skiing?
   B: There's not enough snow.
   _____
   _____

3. **A:** _____ playing video games?
   B: It's too nice outside.
   _____
   _____

4. **A:** _____ studying for the test this afternoon?
   B: _____
   _____

5. **A:** _____ go to the museum?
   B: _____
   _____
   _____

READING TO WRITE

1 Read the email and complete the chart.

```
To: Raquel
From: Paul
Subject: Let's go power-kiting!
```

Hey Raquel,

How are you? I saw your windsurfing photos online. There were some good <u>ones</u>!

I'm having a party this weekend, and you're invited. It's a party to introduce my friends to the sport of power-kiting. It's like skateboarding with a kite. We're going to try it at the park. I don't know if you've tried power-kiting before, but I think you'll like it because you like wind sports. I tried it last weekend, and it is easier than it looks.

We'll meet at the skate park at noon on Saturday. Then after we power-kite for a couple hours, we'll go to Rocky's for pizza. If you can't join us for power-kiting, you can meet us there.

Let me know by Thursday if you can join us. I need to let the park know by then how many people are coming.

Your friend,

Paul

Paul's Party	
1. What is the event?	*power-kiting party*
2. What is the reason for the event?	
3. When is the event?	
4. Where is the event?	
5. What are the activities?	
6. What response does Paul ask for?	

2 Read the email again. Underline the referencing words *ones*, *it*, *there*, and *then*. Then draw a line from the referencing word to the noun it refers to.

3 Complete the sentences with the correct reference words.

1. I have a lot of good friends. I have a lot of fun with _____*them*_____.

2. Why don't we go downtown on Saturday afternoon? Are you free _____?

3. How about coming to the concert with me tonight? I think you'll really like _____.

4. Are you learning to play the guitar? How is _____ going?

5. Why don't we spend some time with your cousins? I really like hanging out with _____.

6. I would like to go to the movie with you tomorrow, but I'm busy _____.

Unit 10 | 69

REVIEW UNITS 9–10

1 Look at the pictures. Circle the correct answers.

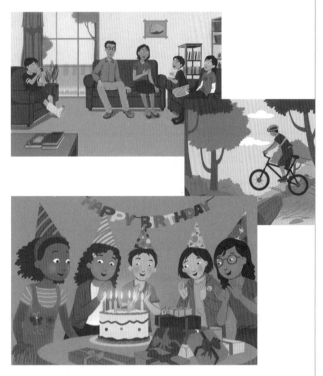

Ken: I fell playing ice hockey last winter, and I ¹**broke / fell off** my ²**ankle / shoulder**. Then I couldn't walk. While it was healing, I sat on the sofa a lot and ³**went dancing / spent time with my family**. They gave me a camera so I wouldn't be ⁴**bored / nervous**. That's when I started to ⁵**play an instrument / take photos**. I was ⁶**stressed / surprised** how much I liked it.

Emma: I love to ⁷**celebrate my birthday / read books**. This year, we had a big party at my house. There were candles on the cake, and they ⁸**burned / sprained** the paper on one of my gifts! I ate too much cake, and my ⁹**elbow broke / stomach hurt**. It was fun to ¹⁰**have a party / play video games**, but I was ¹¹**stressed / tired** afterwards.

Roger: Last summer, I was mountain biking, and I ¹²**crashed / sprained**. I ¹³**fell off / hurt** and ¹⁴**banged / slipped** my knee. I couldn't walk for a while. I thought I would play video games, but my mom said I should ¹⁵**have a party / play an instrument**. That's why I started to learn the guitar.

2 Match the actions with the feelings.

1. Jackie slipped on the floor in the cafeteria.
2. Bill fell asleep in school.
3. Pam didn't like playing video games.
4. Alex played the violin in his first concert.
5. Anna had to read a lot of books for her test.

a. He was nervous.
b. She was bored.
c. She was embarrassed.
d. She was stressed.
e. He was tired.

3 Circle the correct answers.

1. Have you ever broken a toe?
   a. Yes, she has.
   b. No, I haven't.
2. What bones have you broken?
   a. Yes, I have.
   b. My arm and a finger.
3. Has he ever gone power-kiting?
   a. Yes, he has.
   b. He slipped yesterday.
4. What happened when Mike fell off his bike?
   a. He sprained his arm.
   b. No, he hasn't.
5. Have they ever lost a game?
   a. Yes. They lost one last week.
   b. Yes, I have.

4 Circle the correct answers.

1. I don't see any_____ to buy in this store.
   a. -one   b. -thing   c. -where
2. I've looked every_____ for the cat.
   a. -one   b. -thing   c. -where
3. I don't think any_____ could surf those waves.
   a. -one   b. -thing   c. -where
4. There's _____ who can come on Saturday.
   a. anyone   b. everyone   c. no one

70 | Review 5

5 Write questions and answers with the present perfect or the simple past.

1. Millie / crash her bike / ever (yes, last month)

   Q: _____
   A: _____

2. Paula / go kite-surfing / before (no, power-kiting)

   Q: _____
   A: _____

3. Stefan / live Madrid / ever (no, Buenos Aires, last year)

   Q: _____
   A: _____

4. You / study English / ever (yes, two years ago)

   Q: _____
   A: _____

6 Rewrite the sentences to make them correct.

1. Tom didn't tell no one about the surprise party.

   _____

2. Why have he be late for school every day this week?

   _____
   _____

3. Cara hasn't broke any bones before.

   _____

4. Sam slip at the pool yesterday.

   _____

7 Complete the emails with the correct phrases.

haven't been	sounded like fun
How about	That's a great idea!
I'd rather	Too bad
I'm too scared	Why don't you

To: Dylan
From: Lena
Subject: RE: Invitation

Hi Dylan,

How are you? Thanks for the invitation to go swimming last weekend. I was out of town. We went surfing in Sayulita. Sorry I missed it. It ¹_____.

I'm taking a group of friends sky-diving next weekend. ²_____ coming along? It's not real sky-diving, like jumping out of a plane. It's indoors! You float in the air in a big wind tunnel. It looks cool. I ³_____ sky-diving before. Have you? ⁴_____ join us?

Let me know by Friday if you can make it.

Talk to you later,

Lena

To: Lena
From: Dylan
Subject: RE: RE: Invitation

Hey Lena,

Indoor sky-diving? ⁵_____
⁶_____ it's the same day as my cousin's birthday party. We're going to a car race. ⁷_____ try sky-diving than go to the race, but only because it's indoors. ⁸_____ to jump out of a plane. But thanks for inviting me.

Maybe we can go skateboarding on Sunday.

See ya!

Dylan

Review 5 | 71

Carpets of DAGESTAN

Unit 1 Video 1.1

BEFORE YOU WATCH

1 Look at the pictures from the video. Complete the sentences with the correct words.

| business | carpets | colors | wool |

It takes months to make these beautiful _____. These men work for a carpet _____ in Russia. They buy the _____ from sheep farmers and dye it different _____.

WHILE YOU WATCH

2 Watch the video. Are the sentences true (*T*) or false (*F*)? Correct the false sentences.

1. Dagestan is in southern Russia. _____
2. Khan has a car business. _____
3. He buys wool from his wife's sister. _____
4. Khan's business makes 250 carpets a year. _____
5. It takes four months to make a carpet. _____

3 Watch the video again. Circle the words you hear.

1. People here speak over **30 / 40** languages.
2. He gives work to many **villages / villagers.**
3. The water can't be too hot or too **cool / cold**.
4. Only **men / women** make Khan's carpets.
5. In the evening, many women work on their **homes / farms**.

AFTER YOU WATCH

4 Work with a partner. Take turns saying what you have in your backpack. Where do the items come from?

> I have a water bottle. It comes from China.

A Very INDIAN WEDDING

Unit 1 Video 1.3

BEFORE YOU WATCH

1 Look at the pictures from the video and read the sentences. Match the words with the definitions.

Traditional Indian weddings are often big and beautiful.

Women paint the bride's hands with henna before the wedding.

The bride gives the groom rice during the wedding.

1. wedding _____
2. bride _____
3. henna _____
4. groom _____

a. a woman who is going to be married
b. a special paint
c. a marriage ceremony
d. a man who is going to be married

WHILE YOU WATCH

2 Watch the video. Number the sentences 1–5 in the order you see them.

1. The groom rides a white horse. _____
2. The bride's family dances for her. _____
3. Fifty people work on the flowers. _____
4. The women draw henna on the bride's hands. _____
5. The bride gives the groom rice. _____

3 Watch the video again. Check (✓) the sentences you hear.

1. ❑ Some traditions are hundreds of years old.
2. ❑ People say red henna is a good sign.
3. ❑ They all prepare for the big day.
4. ❑ The groom is waiting.
5. ❑ They walk together today and for life.

AFTER YOU WATCH

4 Work with a partner. Make a list of wedding traditions in your country.

> 1. bride: white dress
> 2. groom: dark suit
> 3. wedding rings
> 4. music
> 5. flowers

Unit 1 | 73

A Life on BROADWAY

Unit 2 Video 2.1

BEFORE YOU WATCH

1 Look at the pictures from the video. Do you think the sentences are true (*T*) or false (*F*)?

1. In a musical, the actors sing and dance. _____
2. In most musicals, dogs sing. _____
3. There are many different kinds of jobs in the theater. _____

WHILE YOU WATCH

2 Watch the video. Circle the correct answers.

1. The star of the play is _____ years old.
   a. 10   b. 11   c. 12
2. The director tells the actresses _____ to move.
   a. where   b. who   c. what
3. The set designer creates the _____.
   a. play   b. lights   c. place
4. People prepare for _____ to put on a play.
   a. weeks   b. months   c. years

3 Watch the video again. Match the adjectives with the nouns you hear.

1. theater _____   a. effects
2. popular _____   b. designer
3. lighting _____   c. musical
4. special _____   d. capital

AFTER YOU WATCH

4 Work with a small group. Complete the chart below. Then discuss: What are some of your favorite plays or movies? Who were the actors? What parts did they play?

Movie / Play	Actor	Part	Actor	Part
X-Men	Hugh Jackman	Wolverine	Jennifer Lawrence	Mystique

> I really liked the new *X-Men* movie. Hugh Jackman was in it. He played Wolverine. Jennifer Lawrence played Mystique.

74 | Unit 2

MUMBAI: *From* COMPUTERS *to* FILM

Unit 2 Video 2.3

BEFORE YOU WATCH

1 Look at the pictures from the video. Circle the correct answers.

1. These people work **on farms / in offices** in Mumbai, India.
2. People make thousands of **films / computers** in Mumbai.

WHILE YOU WATCH

2 Watch the video. Number the places and things 1–5 in the order you see them.

1. a festival _____
2. a bus _____
3. a park _____
4. Mumbai at night _____
5. a train _____

3 Watch the video again. Are the sentences true (*T*) or false (*F*)? Correct the false sentences.

1. Mumbai is a rich city. _____
2. Ten years ago, the population of Mumbai was 20 million. _____
3. Many people work in modern offices. _____
4. Traditions are not important here. _____
5. Some traditional festivals are part of India's film industry. _____

AFTER YOU WATCH

4 Work with a partner. Discuss: What TV shows or movies take place in a big city? What do you learn about the city?

> *Spiderman* takes place in New York City. There are a lot of really big buildings . . . and a lot of people and cars.

Unit 2 | 75

Unusual FUN

BEFORE YOU WATCH | Unit 3 Video 3.1

1 Look at the picture from the video. Check (✔) the sentences you think are probably true.

Mall of the Emirates

1. ❏ The mall has over 1,000 shops.
2. ❏ There are about 50 cinemas here.
3. ❏ You can ride bikes through the mall.
4. ❏ You can go skiing here.

WHILE YOU WATCH

2 Watch the video. What are people doing in the mall? Write short answers to the questions.

1. Are some people ice skating? _No, they aren't._
2. Are some people snowboarding? _____
3. Is a little girl holding a balloon? _____
4. Are the boys looking at skis in the store? _____
5. Do the boys buy sunglasses? _____

3 Watch the video again. Circle the correct answers.

1. Dubai is in the United Arab **States / Emirates**.
2. It's often about **40 / 45** degrees Celsius here.
3. The mall has **120 / 125** restaurants.
4. The mall is in the middle of the **Arabian / Sahara** Desert.
5. A lot of kids come here to **eat / have fun** with their friends.

AFTER YOU WATCH

4 Work in small groups. Discuss the question at the end of the video: Is there a mall near you? What fun things can you do there? Where do you like to shop?

> Yes, there is. I like going to movies there . . . and I like visiting the electronics store.

76 | Unit 3

ZERO: PAST and PRESENT

Unit 3 Video 3.3

BEFORE YOU WATCH

1 Look at the pictures from the video. Complete the sentences with the correct numbers.

| 0 | 2 | 10 |

1. We use the ancient Indian system of _____ digits: 0–9.
2. The number _____ represents nothing, or no quantity.
3. In ancient India, people used the same word for *arms* and for the number _____.

WHILE YOU WATCH

2 Watch the video. Check (✓) the sentences you hear.

1. ❏ From nothing – or zero – came everything.
2. ❏ These ancients used numbers, not words, for quantities.
3. ❏ So, around 11 B.C.E., they invented symbols.
4. ❏ We use numbers with zero and nine.
5. ❏ Think about zero the next time you go shopping.

3 Watch the video again. Complete the sentences with the correct words.

1. The word *digit* comes from the Latin word for _____.
2. We have _____ numbers in our system.
3. Can you imagine life without _____?
4. In computing, there are _____ digits.
5. Prices usually contain _____.

AFTER YOU WATCH

4 Work with a partner. Complete the chart with your information. Then read it to your partner, who will write the information using words, not numbers.

Time	I slept for _____ hours and _____ minutes last night.
Weight	My backpack weighs about _____ kilos.
Price	A new laptop costs about _____ pesos.
Speed	An airplane flies at about _____ kilometers an hour.

Unit 3 | 77

Wildlife HERO

Unit 4 Video 4.1

BEFORE YOU WATCH

1 **Look at the pictures from the video. Complete the sentences with the correct words.**

| in danger | rhino | wildlife | vet |

1. Animals that live in nature are called _____.

2. A _____ is a doctor who takes care of animals.

3. A _____ is a large animal with thick skin.

4. Some animals are not safe. There are only a few of them in the world. They are _____.

WHILE YOU WATCH

2 **Watch the video. Number the animals 1–5 in the order you see them.**

1. A giraffe in a truck   _____
2. Two zebras drinking water   _____
3. A rhino running in a field   _____
4. A lion opening its mouth   _____
5. Two elephants playing   _____

3 **Watch the video again. Match the phrases to make true sentences.**

1. Yanna wants the animals to _____
2. Yanna's job is dangerous because _____
3. Yanna is going to _____
4. At first, the sedative _____
5. Yanna does this job because _____

a. the black rhino is in danger.
b. take the rhino to a new home.
c. the animals are wild.
d. be safe from hunters.
e. makes the rhino fall asleep.

AFTER YOU WATCH

4 **Work in a small group. Discuss: Have you, or has someone you know, ever saved an animal? What happened?**

> My brother and I once found a kitten. We took it home. We gave it food and water.

78 | Unit 4

The Chilean MINE RESCUE

Unit 4 Video 4.3

BEFORE YOU WATCH

1 Look at the picture from the video. Match the words from the video with the definitions.

1. drill _____
2. miner _____
3. refuge _____
4. rescue _____

a. to save someone from danger
b. a safe place
c. a machine that makes holes
d. a person who works in a mine, deep underground

WHILE YOU WATCH

2 Watch the video. Are the sentences true (*T*) or false (*F*)? Correct the false sentences.

1. In 2010, there was a terrible accident in Chile. _____
2. There were 32 men in the mine. _____
3. The rescue workers found the miners seven days after the accident. _____
4. The miners wrote a note to the rescuers. _____

3 Watch the video again. Circle the correct answers.

1. What happened when the giant rock fell?
   a. It killed many miners.   b. It closed the exit to the mine.   c. It made a deep hole.
2. The rescuers gave the miners a _____.
   a. drill   b. TV   c. phone
3. The men were in the mine for more than _____ months.
   a. two   b. three   c. four
4. How many people watched the final rescue of the miners?
   a. two billion   b. one million   c. one billion

AFTER YOU WATCH

4 Work with a partner. Discuss: Imagine you are trapped inside a mine. What do you feel? Say? How do you keep calm?

> I feel afraid. I'm really worried. I tell my friends that people will save us. I try to breathe deeply.

Unit 4 | 79

Mysteries in the MOUNTAINS

Unit 5 Video 5.1

BEFORE YOU WATCH

1 Look at the picture from the video and read the story. Then match the words and the definitions.

Archaeologists study ancient civilizations. They ask questions: Who were these people? How did they live? Some archaeologists were working in Bolivia when they found bones. They looked at the bones with a microscope. They were the bones of a young woman . . .

1. archaeologist _____
2. civilization _____
3. bones _____
4. microscope _____

a. the hard, white pieces that form the frame of a human or animal body
b. a tool that makes small things look bigger
c. a scientist who studies ancient cultures
d. a culture; a society

WHILE YOU WATCH

2 Watch the video. Are the sentences (*T*) or false (*F*)? Correct the false sentences.

1. Last year, Scotty went to Tiwanaku. _____
2. He was studying an ancient culture. _____
3. The archaeologists found bones and hair. _____
4. They found corn next to the bones. _____
5. The Tiwanaku people grew lots of corn. _____

3 Watch the video again. Circle the words you hear.

1. They look for clues and **answer / answers** to questions.
2. They lived here in the mountains about **a thousand / two thousand** years ago.
3. The bones were strong and the teeth were **heavy / healthy**.
4. He wanted to look at it **closely / carefully** under a microscope.
5. So, this woman wasn't **from / of** here!

AFTER YOU WATCH

4 Work in a small group. Discuss: Do you like reading about mysteries or watching mysteries on TV? What are some of your favorites?

> I like *Paper Towns* by John Green . . . and *Buzz Kill* was a great book.
> I always watch *Pretty Little Liars* – it's amazing!

80 | Unit 5

The Case of the MISSING WOMAN

BEFORE YOU WATCH

Unit 5 Video 5.3

1. Use the clues and the words to complete the crossword puzzle.

| disappear | interview | missing | remember | search | worry |

ACROSS

2. not there, absent

3. to look for

5. to think of someone or something from the past

6. to feel nervous or anxious

DOWN

1. to leave; to go out of sight

4. to ask someone questions, get information

WHILE YOU WATCH

2. Watch the video. Number the sentences 1–5 in the order you see them.

1. The police found Amber's car. _____
2. A video camera showed Amber in a shop. _____
3. The police interviewed Amber's family and friends. _____
4. The police found a woman in a park. _____
5. Amber's car keys were missing. _____

3. Watch the video again. Match the sequencing words you hear with the events.

1. One day, _____
2. Soon _____
3. Two days ago, _____
4. Then _____
5. Finally, _____

a. Amber was safe.
b. police found a woman in a park.
c. Amber disappeared from her hometown.
d. the police found the next clue.
e. Amber was inside the shop alone.

AFTER YOU WATCH

4. Work with a partner. Think of a mystery (a book, a TV show, or a movie) you both know. Take turns describing what happened.

> **A:** In *Veronica Mars*, Veronica has an interview in New York City.
> **B:** Then her boyfriend calls her.
> **A:** Right. So she returns to Neptune . . .

A Cool LIFE

Unit 6 Video 6.1

BEFORE YOU WATCH

1 Look at the picture from the video. Circle the correct words to complete the sentences.

1. This house in Coober Pedy, Australia, is **underground / above ground**.
2. When it is very hot outside, it is **cooler / warmer** in this house.
3. This house needs a lot of **lamps / bedrooms**.

WHILE YOU WATCH

2 Watch the video. Number the sentences 1–5 in the order you see them.

1. Two people walk into a mine. _____
2. People play golf outside at night. _____
3. A woman cooks in her kitchen. _____
4. A woman finds an opal in a mine. _____
5. A man cleans his living room. _____

3 Watch the video again. Look carefully at the rooms in the underground house. Check (✔) what you see, and where.

Object	Living room	Dining room / Kitchen	Bedroom
lamps			
pictures			
beds			
table			
chairs			

AFTER YOU WATCH

4 Work with a partner. What do you do when it is really hot or cold outside – during the day or at night?

> When it's really hot, I swim during the day. At night I read. When it's very cold, I go ice skating during the day. At night, I watch TV.

82 | Unit 6

Moving HOUSE

Unit 6 Video 6.3

BEFORE YOU WATCH

1 Look at the picture from the video and read the text. Then match the words with the definitions.

Joey was looking for a new house. He found a cabin he liked. He put the cabin on logs. He used a bulldozer to pull the cabin to a new place.

1. cabin _____
2. log _____
3. bulldozer _____

a. a big machine that can move things
b. a small wooden house
c. a thick piece of a tree

WHILE YOU WATCH

2 Watch the video. Circle the correct answers.

1. Joey lives in the _____ of Tanana, Alaska.
   a. city   b. town   c. state
2. He lived with his father until _____ ago.
   a. a month   b. a year   c. two years
3. He doesn't have _____ money.
   a. much   b. more   c. some
4. He wanted to live _____ his family and friends.
   a. with   b. next to   c. closer to
5. Joey's _____ move the logs.
   a. brothers   b. cousins   c. friends

3 Watch the video again. Check (✔) the sentences you hear.

1. ❑ Can he buy the house and move?
2. ❑ So first, they must get some logs.
3. ❑ It's really hard work.
4. ❑ I'm very excited!
5. ❑ It's perfect!

AFTER YOU WATCH

4 Work with a partner. Take turns describing your favorite room at home. What does it look like? What do you like to do in it?

> My bedroom is my favorite room. There's a bed and two windows . . . and my computer. I like listening to music in my bedroom.

Unit 6 | 83

A Pizza ROBOT

Unit 7 Video 7.1

BEFORE YOU WATCH

1 Look at the picture from the video. Find the words in the puzzle.

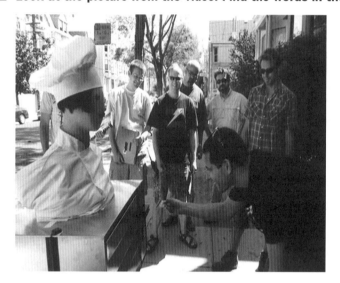

| customer | deliver | order | pizza | robot |

B	O	R	L	C	N	F	R	A	Z
P	I	C	U	S	T	O	M	E	R
A	E	Q	Z	S	P	I	Z	Z	A
R	O	B	O	T	O	T	A	C	I
A	F	R	D	O	X	Z	F	U	B
S	D	H	V	M	K	Z	X	A	O
P	E	J	D	E	L	I	V	E	R
O	R	D	E	R	A	P	B	R	O

WHILE YOU WATCH

2 Watch the video. Circle the correct answers.

1. The men work on _____ in the US.
   a. a lake   b. a river   c. an island
2. The pizza from the blimp is _____.
   a. cold   b. hot   c. delicious
3. One of the men in the robot car is _____.
   a. driving the car b. watching a video c. using a computer
4. The men put _____ on the smaller robot.
   a. glasses   b. clothes   c. a sign
5. One man opens Luigi's _____ with a credit card.
   a. oven   b. box   c. window

3 Watch the video again. Complete the sentences with the correct words.

| itself | map | problems | ready | without |

1. A robot car drives _____.
2. The car has _____ at first.
3. In the future, robots will use a city _____.
4. Luigi goes around the car _____ a problem.
5. They get a hot pizza _____ to eat.

AFTER YOU WATCH

4 Work with a partner. Discuss: What do you think robots will do for people in the future? Make a list, and then share it with another pair.

> **A:** I think robots will clean houses in the future.
> **B:** I think they'll cook dinner.

84 | Unit 7

Music SHARING

Unit 7 Video 7.3

BEFORE YOU WATCH

1 Look at the picture from the video. Complete the paragraph with the correct words.

| download | industry | sharing | store |

Twenty years ago, people had to buy music from a music ¹_____. Then it became possible to ²_____ music files on a computer. This changed the music ³_____. Will file ⁴_____ be illegal in the future?

WHILE YOU WATCH

2 Watch the video. Are the sentences true (*T*) or false (*F*)? Correct the false sentences.

1. In 1999, it wasn't easy to get music. _____
2. Shawn Fanning created a computer to download songs. _____
3. Soon Napster became a big business. _____
4. Bands got money from Napster for their music. _____
5. Record companies stopped file sharing. _____

3 Watch the video again. Complete the sentences with the words you hear.

1. What part will music _____?
2. In one _____, more than 10,000 people had it.
3. Soon a million _____ had it.
4. So they closed Napster _____.
5. Maybe you will have the _____ big idea!

AFTER YOU WATCH

4 Work in small groups. Discuss: What do people buy online, and what do they buy in a store?

> My parents buy books and DVDs online. They buy food at a store.

A School at HOME

Unit 8 Video 8.1

BEFORE YOU WATCH

1. Look at the pictures from the video. Read the definition. Do you think the sentences are true (*T*) or false (*F*)?

homeschool (verb) to teach your children at home

1. Children in many countries are homeschooled. _____
2. Very few homeschooled students attend a college or university. _____
3. Many homeschooled students are active in their communities. _____
4. Homeschooled students usually learn about only one subject. _____

WHILE YOU WATCH

2. Watch the video. Circle the correct answers.
   1. Maggy's **mother / father** helps her on the computer.
   2. Her **mother / father** teaches classes at home.
   3. The Botros children study science, English, and **math / history**.
   4. Maggy **would / wouldn't** like to go to a large school.
   5. Maggy wants to be a **teacher / scientist** in the future.

3. Watch the video again. Match the phrases to make true sentences.

   1. My oldest son has _____   a. work out for him.
   2. School just didn't _____   b. away from home.
   3. Maggy is really _____   c. some special needs.
   4. Sometimes Maggy studies _____   d. close to her brothers and sisters.

AFTER YOU WATCH

4. Work with a partner. Compare your school to the school in the video. What do you like best about each type of school?

   > My class is bigger than the class in the video. I like the small classes in the video. I really like playing soccer at my school.

86 | Unit 8

Time for an ADVENTURE!

BEFORE YOU WATCH

Unit 8 Video 8.3

1 Look at the pictures from the video. Match the words with the correct defnitions.

1. chef _____
2. archaeologist _____
3. dinosaur _____
4. volunteer _____

a. an animal that lived on Earth millions of years ago
b. a professional cook
c. someone who chooses to help or do work without getting paid
d. a scientist who studies ancient cultures

WHILE YOU WATCH

2 Watch the video. Check (✔) the sentences you hear.

1. ❑ So I'm taking a year on after high school.
2. ❑ Perhaps I'll go to Siena and work as a volunteer.
3. ❑ It has wide, open spaces and green forests.
4. ❑ Or I'll visit a village and see people my age.
5. ❑ Maybe I'll help an archaeologist look for a T-Rex!

3 Watch the video again. Match the adventures with the places.

1. Rome _____
2. Siena _____
3. South Africa _____
4. Madagascar _____

a. repair old buildings
b. look for dinosaur bones
c. learn to cook
d. help animals

AFTER YOU WATCH

4 Work in small groups. Discuss: What adventures are you going to have when you finish school?

> I'm going to go hiking in the mountains for a week . . . and I'm going to college in a big city. That will be an adventure.

Unit 8 | 87

DANGER *in our* FOOD

Unit 9 Video 9.1

BEFORE YOU WATCH

1 Look at the pictures from the video. Do you think the sentences are true (*T*) or false (*F*)?

1. Many people become sick every year from eating bad food. _____
2. Food that will make you sick usually looks delicious. _____
3. Water in public places is always safe to drink. _____
4. Fruits and vegetables are safer to eat than cookies. _____

WHILE YOU WATCH

2 Watch the video. Complete the sentences with the correct words.

1. Madison was like many _____.
2. Sometimes there is E. coli in food and _____.
3. The _____ are worried.
4. The E. coli was in the _____ dough.
5. _____ was very lucky.

3 Watch the video again. Check (✓) the sentences you hear.

1. ❑ She enjoyed dancing and singing with her friends.
2. ❑ E. coli 0157 is a kind of bacteria.
3. ❑ How did Madison get E. coli?
4. ❑ The doctors taste many different kinds of food.
5. ❑ Soon over 70 people are ill with E. coli.

AFTER YOU WATCH

4 Work in small groups. Discuss: Have you or a family member ever eaten something that made you really sick? What did you eat? What did you feel like?

> I ate some fish a year ago and got really sick. I felt sick to my stomach. I didn't want to eat anything for days.

A DEADLY Job

Unit 9 Video 9.3

BEFORE YOU WATCH

1 Look at the pictures from the video. Label the pictures with the correct words. Then answer the questions.

crocodile   kangaroo   snake   spider

1. _____   2. _____   3. _____   4. _____

5. Which of these animals are dangerous? _____

6. Which of these animals sometimes live in people's homes? _____

WHILE YOU WATCH

2 Watch the video. Number the snakes 1–5 in the order you see them.

1. a snake in a pantry   _____
2. a snake on a rock   _____
3. a snake in a bag   _____
4. a snake in a box   _____
5. a snake on the floor of a room _____

3 Watch the video again. Circle the correct answers.

1. Adelaide is on the **south / north** coast of Australia.
2. The brown snake is the **most / second most** dangerous snake in the world.
3. Snake-Away takes snakes **to / from** people's homes.
4. The man must hold the snake by its **head / tail**.

AFTER YOU WATCH

4 Work with a partner. What animals or insects live in people's houses? Which are dangerous? Complete the chart.

Animal	Dangerous?
Cat	No
Dog	Sometimes
Ant	

Unit 9 | 89

A New York City FOOD TOUR

Unit 10 Video 10.1

BEFORE YOU WATCH

1 Look at the pictures from the video. Complete the sentences with the correct words.

| delicatessen | desserts | hot dogs |

1. New York City has food from all over the world. You can get a delicious lunch in a _____ like this one.

2. People sell _____ and sandwiches on the streets of New York.

3. Some places only serve _____, like this ice cream sundae.

WHILE YOU WATCH

2 Watch the video. Circle the correct answers.

1. Katz's Delicatessen is the ____ in New York.
   a. largest   b. oldest   c. busiest
2. Sylvia's Restaurant opened in ____.
   a. 1888   b. 1952   c. 1962
3. People go to Serendipity to eat ____.
   a. desserts   b. hot dogs   c. pizza
4. The fudge that people eat at Serendipity is made of ____.
   a. ice   b. cream   c. chocolate

3 Watch the video again. Number the sentences 1–4 in the order you see them.

1. A man in a red T-shirt dancing   ____
2. A woman with big earrings eating a sandwich ____
3. A man in a black T-shirt cutting meat   ____
4. A group of horses crossing a street   ____

AFTER YOU WATCH

4 Where can you go to get great food where you live? Complete the chart below. Share your list with a partner.

For . . .	Place	Great food
Lunch	Rosetta	seafood tacos
Dinner		
Dessert		

90 | Unit 10

Punkin CHUNKIN!

Unit 10 Video 10.3

BEFORE YOU WATCH

1 Read the definitions of the words from the video. Then find the words in the puzzle.

pumpkin (noun) a large, round, orange vegetable

chuck (verb) to throw

launch (verb) to send something into the air

shoot (verb) to cause something to fly or move quickly; to use a gun

U	M	P	O	P	R	L	C
I	A	L	A	U	N	C	H
X	H	W	P	M	Q	Z	S
T	S	H	Z	P	R	E	T
C	H	U	C	K	F	D	O
B	O	A	V	I	H	V	M
H	O	I	N	N	J	O	E
E	T	H	O	T	R	R	R

WHILE YOU WATCH

2 Watch the video. Are the sentences true (*T*) or false (*F*)? Correct the false sentences.

1. Everyone calls this sport a mess. _____
2. People build machines to chuck the pumpkins. _____
3. People come here every two years for this festival. _____
4. Jake works so hard because of his family. _____
5. Jake's father was the world champion. _____

3 Watch the video again. Check (✓) the sentences you hear.

1. ❑ Have you heard about the Punkin Chunkin contest?
2. ❑ Some people say it's a sport.
3. ❑ So why do people do this?
4. ❑ Now the whole family helps shoot pumpkins!
5. ❑ To chuck pumpkins, why else?

AFTER YOU WATCH

4 Work in small groups. Discuss: What are some unusual traditions in your town or country? Does your family have any unusual traditions?

> My family has an unusual tradition for New Year's Eve. At midnight, we break dishes in the kitchen. Then we go outside to plant a tree!

Notes

Notes

Credits

The authors and publishers acknowledge the following sources of copyright material and are grateful for the permissions granted. While every effort has been made, it has not always been possible to identify the sources of all the material used, or to trace all copyright holders. If any omissions are brought to our notice, we will be happy to include the appropriate acknowledgements on reprinting.

p.3 (TL): Shutterstock Images/Sergiyn; p.5 (TR): Alamy/©The Photolibrary Wales/Steve Benbow; p. 10 (1): Getty Images/Steve Granitz/WireImage; p. 10 (2): Getty Images/Sonja Flemming/CBS; p. 10 (3): Alamy/©ZUMA Press; p. 10 (4): Getty Images/Steve MORT/AFP; p. 10 (5): Getty Images/Jasin Boland/NBC/NBCU Photo Bank; p. 10 (6): Getty Images/Alexander Tamargo; p. 10 (7): Alamy/©Jochen Tack; p. 10 (8): Alamy/©Pictorial Press Ltd; p. 10 (9): Alamy/©AF archive; p. 11 (TL): Alamy/©Blend Images/Jeff Greenough; p. 14 (CL): Shutterstock Images/FXQuadro; p. 18 (CL): Alamy/©Daniel Dempster Photography; p. 27 (TL): Alamy/©Everett Collection Inc; p. 33 (TR): Alamy/©Megapress; p. 37 (CR): Alamy/©Andreas Von Einsiedel; p. 39 (TL): Shutterstock Images/Julian Rovagnati; p. 47 (TL): Shutterstock Images/Ermolaev Alexander; p. 50 (1): Alamy/©MBI; p. 50 (2): Getty Images/Jupiterimages; p. 50 (3): Shutterstock Images/Michaeljung; p. 50 (4): Shutterstock Images/Pierdelune; p. 50 (5): Getty Images/MachineHeadz; p. 50 (6): Shutterstock Images/Denis Kukareko; p. 50 (7): Alamy/©Jim West; p. 50 (8): Shutterstock Images/oliveromg; p. 50 (9): Alamy/©age fotostock Spain, S.L.; p. 50 (10): Shutterstock Images/Sofia Andreevna; p. 51 (BL): Alamy/©Andres Rodriguez; p.53 (BL): Shutterstock Images/Mariyana M; p.53 (BC): Alamy/©Oote Boe 3; p. 56 (1): Shutterstock Images/Africa Studio; p. 56 (2): Shutterstock Images/Roadk; p. 56 (3): Shutterstock Images/Photosync; p. 56 (4): Shutterstock Images/Veronchick84; p. 56 (5): Shutterstock Images/Stephen Mcsweeny; p. 56 (6): Shutterstock Images/Africa Studio; p. 56 (7): Shutterstock Images/R.Legosyn; p. 56 (8): Shutterstock Images/Kellie L.Folkerts; p. 56 (9): Shutterstock Images/Liu Anlin; p. 56 (10): Shutterstock Images/MichaelJay Berlin; p. 56 (11): Getty Images/Wavebreak Media; p. 59 (CL): Shutterstock Images/PhotoSky; p. 63 (TR): Alamy/©Purcell Team; p. 64 (BL): Getty Images/Tim Hall; Back cover: Shutterstock Images/Vibrant Image Studio.

Front cover photograph by Alamy/©Marc Hill.

The publishers are grateful to the following illustrators:

Janet Allinger p. 6, 32, 54; Galia Bernstein p. 19, 25, 26, 31, 40, 41, 45, 55, 66 (TR), 67, 70; Anni Betts p. 2, 21, 28, 30, 60, 61, 68; Alberto de Hoyos p. 22 (1-5, 7, 9, 10), 58 (1-10); Nigel Dobbyn p. 4, 8, 48, 52 (TR), 62; Mark Duffin p. 44 (1-3, 5-7); Simon Ecob p. 9, 14, 15, 17, 24, 35; Q2A Media Services, Inc. p. 7, 19, 25, 26, 31, 40, 41, 44 (4), 45, 46, 52 (TL), 55, 65, 66, 67, 70; Jose Rubio p. 12, 13, 20, 22 (6, CR), 34, 42, 43, 58 (C); David Shephard p. 36; Norbert Sipos p. 38, 49.

All video stills by kind permission of Discovery Communications, LLC 2015.